DATE DUE			

COLUMBIA UNIVERSITY
STUDIES IN THE
SOCIAL SCIENCES

405

The series was formerly known as
Studies in History, Economics and Public Law

WOMEN IN EIGHTEENTH-CENTURY AMERICA

AMS PRESS
NEW YORK

WOMEN IN EIGHTEENTH-CENTURY AMERICA

A STUDY OF OPINION AND SOCIAL USAGE

BY

MARY SUMNER BENSON, Ph.D.

NEW YORK
COLUMBIA UNIVERSITY PRESS
LONDON: P. S. KING & SON, LTD.
1935

Library of Congress Cataloging in Publication Data

Benson, Mary Sumner, 1903-
  Women in eighteenth-century America.

    Reprint of the 1935 ed. published by Columbia
University Press, New York, which was issued as
no. 405 of Studies in history, economics, and public
law.
    Originally presented as author's thesis, Columbia
University, 1935.
    Bibliography: p.
    Includes index.
    1. Women—United States. 2. Women—History
and condition of women. 3. Women in literature.
4. Literature, Modern—18th century—History and
criticism. I. Title. II. Series: Columbia studies in
the social sciences; no. 405.
HQ1416.B4 1976   301.41'2'0973   75-41025
ISBN 0-404-51405-7

Reprinted from the edition of 1935, New York
First AMS edition published in 1976
Manufactured in the United States of America

Library of Congress Catalog Card Number: 75-41025
International Standard Book Number:
    Complete Set: 0-404-51000-0
    Number 405: 0-404-51405-7

AMS PRESS INC.
NEW YORK, N.Y.

803234

PREFACE

The purpose of this study is to show certain aspects of the position of women in eighteenth-century America—in theory and in fact. Such a treatment of theoretical material is almost of necessity confined to women of the upper and middle classes. Advice offered women presupposed at least a bare competence and the opportunity for a conventional education however meagre that might be. Few writers, if any, concerned themselves with the appropriate accomplishments or peculiar moral duties of women of laboring families or on the frontier. Letters and journals written by women themselves usually represent educated and leisure classes; hence our knowledge of women in the lower ranks of society is relatively incomplete and offers a wide field for further investigation.

The first six chapters of the essay deal primarily with the theoretical aspects of women's position. When education attained any considerable proportions it was inextricably bound up with theory. For this reason it has seemed best to treat most phases of feminine education in the section on theory though individual schools often represented actual attainments as well as ambitious plans. The material selected for the study of the European background represents only a portion of the literature on the subject in England and France, but it is that part known to have been available in eighteenth-century America through reprints and importations, or to have been read and discussed by Americans. Comparatively little attention is given to the European background of the ideas of the Mathers and their contemporaries. There was such influence through books and through direct contact, but the books which they read had little bearing on American developments after 1730, and it has seemed best to emphasize the material which influenced writers who like Franklin and Rush had lasting effect in shaping feminine education in America.

This essay was begun as a treatment of opinion on women's position as set forth by contemporary theorists, but since their ideas alone gave an inaccurate picture it seemed wise to include the later chapters which deal with women's life as reflected in legislation, in the activities of women themselves, and in the comments of prominent Americans and travellers. Such personal narratives are sometimes colored by the peculiar ideas of the writers but taken collectively they show how far the views of the theorists were carried out in everyday life. This part of the study, touching on a variety of topics, is of necessity somewhat general but it is hoped may pave the way for more specialized work on particular phases of feminine activity.

For the use of rare material the writer is indebted to the officials of the New York Historical Society, the Library of Congress and the Massachusetts Historical Society. Mr. V. H. Paltsits of the New York Public Library was most kind in permitting the examination of the Hawley manuscripts. The resources of the New York Public Library, especially in early newspapers, periodicals and Americana generally, have been invaluable. Much interesting material is in the library of Union Theological Seminary and in the educational collections of Teachers College. The author is most grateful to the officials of the rare book room at Yale University for permission to examine the manuscript diary of Esther Burr.

This study is the outgrowth of a seminar paper undertaken at the suggestion of Professor Dixon Ryan Fox of

Columbia University, who read the manuscript at an early stage and has been most helpful with advice and criticism throughout the work. Professor Allan Nevins of Columbia University kindly read the completed manuscript. To Professor Evarts B. Greene of Columbia University, whose suggestions, criticisms and encouragement have been most generously and constantly given, the writer offers her deepest gratitude and thanks. The work could never have been undertaken without this assistance and advice but for any errors and inaccuracies the writer alone is responsible.

NEW YORK, AUGUST, 1934.

TABLE OF CONTENTS

CHAPTER I

EARLY EUROPEAN SOURCES OF AMERICAN OPINION

AMERICAN culture, in the years immediately preceding the Revolution, was still largely that of the old world. Not merely fashions and luxuries but thoughts and standards made the slow and hazardous Atlantic passage, and were amalgamated into the life of our higher classes. The educated American saw most philosophical and literary matters through European eyes. In this the status of women was no exception. It was a problem on which there were few American works before the Revolution, and when, at the close of the war, distinct American opinions arose they had doubtful claims to independence. The eighteenth century was one of marked literary interest in women's careers; for more than a hundred years before 1776, British and French authors had discussed in detail, women—their capacities, training and duties. Such works found their way into colonial bookstores and private libraries, and by means of excerpts, into American periodicals. As a result the more serious of these European authors became guides for the upbringing of American daughters. The more one studies these trans-Atlantic writings, comparing with them not only American discussions of women's intellectual and social activities but the actual usage of the colonies in such matters, the more clearly does one realize our cultural dependence on the upper and middle classes of the old world. The truly American woman, uninfluenced by European ideas, if she existed at all, was to be found on the frontier, not in the comfortable homes of the Atlantic seaboard.

For the intellectual background of educated American women and of those who wrote concerning their place and training, one must turn first to English and French books. The origins of the ideas prevalent in 1760 were to be found in the seventeenth century and earlier. Some books which furnished these ideas were reprinted in the colonies; but more, one learns from booksellers' advertisements and from letters, were imported for the American reader. One must however distinguish between material familiar only to cultivated circles in Great Britain and that which actually reached and influenced America.[1] It was the widely read book, the commonly accepted idea, and not the particular views of an individual which set American standards. In England there was definite progress, in opinion about women between the Restoration and the middle of the eighteenth century, toward the idea of individual development; but one does not find European publications reaching America in any corresponding order. Thus *The Ladies' Library* with its quotations from Lord Halifax, Archbishop Fénelon, and other seventeenth-century writers, was offered for sale in Philadelphia at the same time as the newly published *Pamela* of Richardson and the works of Mrs. Haywood. This condition changed with the development of printing and bookselling in this country, and later books like those of James Fordyce and Dr. Gregory were available here within a year of their appearance in England.[2]

Among early American references to works dealing with women is one in a letter written by Cotton Mather in

[1] For an excellent account of works by women and concerning women in England at this time see Myra Reynolds, *The Learned Lady in England 1650-1760* (Boston and New York, 1920). Of the works which she discusses only a comparatively small proportion seems to have reached the colonies.

[2] For the work of Gregory and Fordyce see pp. 58-76 *infra*. A typical list of imported books may be found in *The Journals of Hugh Gaine Printer*, P. L. Ford editor (2 vols., New York, 1902).

1715/16.[3] Oddly enough the essay to which he alludes is far more liberal than most of the books which were to define the scope of women's activities for the next half century. One cannot be quite sure from Mather's letter whether he himself was familiar with the work of Mademoiselle de Gournay or knew it only by reputation, but he used his knowledge to turn a pretty compliment to his sister-in-law in England, saying:

I have thought that Mademoiselle de *Gournay*, the Lady, who a while since wrote an Essay to demonstrate, the *Equality of Women to men* might victoriously enough defend her problem, (tho' that learned and famous and wondrous Lady A. Maria Schurman, had the modesty to disallow it) while she had such as you, as friend, who help so notably to render your Husbands useful and considerable.[4]

This essay was written in 1622 by Marie de Gournay who was something of a scholar and had been a protégée of Montaigne. She was much distressed by the failure of the Parisian literary circles in which she moved to take her work seriously; doubtless this feeling led to her writing on the equality of the sexes. She began her essay by setting aside the work of those who wished to place women above men —she was content to be ranked as their equal. She sought a true equality, having scathing words for those who believed women's greatest heights attained if they reached the achievements of common men. Men, who held these views, Mademoiselle de Gournay thought braver than Hercules for he had merely slain twelve monsters in twelve combats, whereas they wished to glorify themselves by destroying half the world at a single blow. Her arguments for the equality of the sexes were developed along two lines, the historical and

[3] For Mather's other reading about women see pp. 107-08.

[4] Cotton Mather, *Diary* (Mass. Hist. Soc., *Colls.*, ser. 7, vii-viii, 1911-1912), ii, 325.

the religious—both much used by later writers. Socrates, Plato, Plutarch and Castiglione were among the authorities she cited as believing in the equal ability of women. The place given women in Plato's Republic was, she thought, especially significant. She explained the Salic law as due to special circumstances and referred triumphantly to the position of the Spartan women. Logically enough she pointed out the injustice of comparing the attainments of the sexes without allowing for the difference in their educational opportunities.

There were many ramifications of Mademoiselle de Gournay's treatment of the religious argument. The Scriptures in recording that man was created male and female did not place one sex above the other. Virtue was the same in men and women. If therefore their natures were the same, the esteem in which they were held and their actions should be equal. In support of this she cited the writings of St. Jerome and St. Basil and St. John's epistle to the Elect Lady. St. Paul's attitude towards the sex had, of course, to be explained. She attributed it either to chance or to the fear that women in ministering publicly might show themselves in so favorable a light that they would place men under too strong a temptation. The only Gentiles among the Ancients who had been permitted to foretell the coming of Christ were the Sybils, another sign of the honorable position of women. The Church permitted women to baptize on occasion. This, to be sure, was only in case of necessity but it did not invalidate the sacrament—and if this were true of one sacrament, why not of the others? Obviously women were barred from the ministry in order to maintain the position of men. Mademoiselle de Gournay closed this portion of her essay with the statement that a sex made in the image of the Creator, and enjoying the benefits of the Eucharist, Redemption and Paradise could not be inferior. She afterward wrote another essay *Grief des dames* (1626), which attacked even more bitterly the attitude of men toward women.[5] Her essay may have influenced Mather who gave his own daughters a comparatively high degree of education for the time and place in which they lived; but it is clear from his *Ornaments for the Daughters of Zion* that he believed in the proper submission of women.

Pilgrim's Progress, read by women as well as men on both sides of the Atlantic, offered spiritual advantages without distinction of sex. In the second half of the book Christiana made the pilgrimage as her husband had done before her, encountering the same difficulties, though in some instances she and her companion received special guidance because of their sex. Bunyan justified this equality by the New Testament argument, also used by Sewall and the Mathers, that though one woman had brought death into the world by sin, another had brought life and health in the birth of Christ. Since women had ministered to Christ, had wept as he went to the cross, and had been first with him at the resurrection, it was plain that they were " sharers with us in the grace of life." [6]

It is probable that few books written before 1660, except possibly those read by Mather, exercised appreciable influence on feminine training in the Colonies. In England, even after this date, in spite of many statements regarding women's intellectual equality with men and pleas for more opportunities for the sex, the popular view of women's place was not high. This was shown by the attitude of men like Addison and Steele who were earnestly trying to improve

[5] Mario Schiff, *La fille d'alliance de Montaigne Marie de Gournay* (Paris, 1910) gives an account of her life. See pp. 55-77 for the text of *Egalité des hommes et des femmes* and pp. 87-97 for *Grief des dames.*

[6] John Bunyan, *The Pilgrim's Progress* (Bradford ed., London, 1792), pp. 364-65. Part II deals with Christiana's experiences.

women's condition, whose comments revealed all too clearly the shallow social and intellectual life of most women of their time. In the latter part of the seventeenth century there appeared three serious books, two of which were addressed directly to women. All three were concerned with the improvement of feminine life and all were conservative in the fields of action which they assigned to women. Through the medium of *The Ladies' Library* and in more direct ways these works exercised a decided influence in America. They were *The Ladies Calling* (1673), *The Lady's New Year's Gift: or, Advice to a Daughter* (1688), by the Marquis of Halifax, and Fénelon's *L'Éducation des filles* (1687), known in England through the translation by George Hickes. *The Ladies Calling,* whose authorship has remained in some doubt down to the present, bore on its title page the inscription "By the Author of the Whole Duty of Man" who was probably Richard Allestree, noted royalist preacher and provost of Eton College. It was primarily a religious work.[7] George Savile, first Marquis of Halifax (1633-1695), offered advice more immediately applicable to domestic duties and the responsibilities of a wife than that of Allestree. Halifax, a statesman of much influence during the reigns of Charles II and William of Orange, found time to write his views of woman's place for his daughter Elizabeth, a lady who was reputed to have inherited no inconsiderable portion of her father's ability and who was also the mother of the celebrated Earl of Chesterfield.[8] The third author, Fénelon, Archbishop of Cambrai, outlined a comprehensive scheme of education maintaining a nice balance between the ideas of the *précieuses,* already making themselves felt in the French

---

[7] Reynolds, *Learned Lady,* p. 316 discusses authorship. See also P. C. Yorke, "Richard Allestree," *Encyclopedia Britannica,* 11th ed.

[8] P. C. Yorke, "George Savile, first Marquis of Halifax," *Encyclopedia Britannica,* 11th ed.

salons, and those of the conservatives who believed in wholly domestic education for women.[9]

Unlike Mademoiselle de Gournay none of these writers was prepared to put women on a plane of equality with men. The author of *The Ladies Calling* thought women needed a sense of their own value in order to realize their capacity for higher spiritual development. He pointed out the difficulty of proving the natural inferiority of women to men in matters of understanding because of the difference in opportunities for learning given the two sexes. If women could be secured against the vanity of learning there was no reason why they should not be oftener entrusted with the privilege.[10] Whatever might be thought of their respective intellectual endowments the souls of the sexes were equal; since the development of the soul was the transcendent excellency in human nature it was safe for women to confine themselves to this end.[11] To the belief in the spiritual equality of women Archbishop Fénelon also committed himself, saying, " Women constitute half of the human race redeemed by the blood of Christ and destined to eternal life; "[12] immediately the spiritual plane was left behind, women became again subordinate.

The Ladies Calling dealt with the virtues to be cultivated by women in virginity, wifehood, and widowhood; certain virtues—modesty, meekness, compassion and piety—were peculiarly feminine. The entire book was an enlargement on the desirability of these qualities and a description of methods

[9] " Fénelon, François de Salignac de la Mothe," *Encylopedia Britannica,* 14th ed. Jules Lemaitre, *Fénelon* (Paris, 1910).

[10] *The Ladies Calling* (1677, 5th impression). Partly quoted in Reynolds, *Learned Lady,* p. 319.

[11] He quoted Gal. 3 : 28 in proof of this.

[12] References to Fénelon in this section are to Kate Lupton's translation, *The Education of Girls* (Boston, 1891), see p. 13. See also *Oeuvres de Fénelon* (3 vols., Paris, 1835), ii, 487-526.

of cultivating them. In considering both *The Ladies Calling* and the writing of Lord Halifax one must bear in mind the corruption of social life, following the Restoration, doubtless one reason for the great stress laid on moral qualities, as well as for opposition to the novel, the theatre and other forms of amusement. This reaction to current excesses of social life may be traced in varying degree through many subsequent writings on women, including those of Addison.[13]

Lord Halifax's advice to his daughter dealt with the marital state of women rather than with their education though he devoted much space to religion. Nowhere in his book was there any discussion of intellectual training, of reading as a diversion, or even as a means to piety for women. His primary interest was in their relationship to their husbands. Realizing that lack of freedom to choose their partners in marriage often involved women in unfortunate situations, Halifax devoted much of his book to explaining the method of treating any particular fault in a husband, such as drunkenness or penuriousness. He also indicated the consolations which might be found even in those unhappy states. There was, he thought, fundamental inequality between the sexes. Men as lawgivers had the larger share of reason. Nevertheless the wise use of a wife's influence often gave her control of the situation.[14] It is a bit amusing to note that not only Halifax but many authors who thought women mentally inferior, at the same time urged on them indirect methods of control in the family circle which demanded much adroitness and alertness.

Archbishop Fénelon, unlike Halifax, was much interested in the education of women, which he discussed in specific

[13] This Puritan reaction is discussed in Reynolds, *Learned Lady*, p. 317 and Florence Smith, *Mary Astell* (New York, 1916).

[14] Halifax, *op. cit.*, pp. 13-16, deals particularly with the inequality of the sexes. The viewpoint is evident throughout his book.

terms. He knew something of the practical aspects of the matter since he had been for a time " superior " of a " New Catholic " sisterhood in Paris devoted to the conversion of Huguenot ladies. His treatise on feminine education had much influence on French ideas throughout the succeeding century though his educational theories were not confined to this one volume. In the new world his work was important not merely for the number of its readers but for its influence on many later writers. *Télémaque* (1699), his best-known work on this side of the Atlantic, was not reprinted in America until 1784, though both French and English editions had been advertised for sale for many years.[15] It was among the works mentioned by Jonathan Edwards in his catalogue of important books.[16] Written for Fénelon's royal pupil, Louis Duke of Burgundy, grandson of Louis XIV, *Télémaque* was a study of education of interest to teachers of both men and women. Instructors often commended it to feminine readers hoping they would adopt as a model the heroine, Antiope, who was devoted to domestic pursuits in which she excelled because of her thorough knowledge of household affairs and other feminine accomplishments.[17] The outstanding traits of her character were her modesty, reserve, evenness of temper, and filial obedience. Because of the popularity of *Télémaque* in this country, Antiope probably served as an example to many girls who did not know *L'Éducation des filles*. This latter essay which em-

[15] For instance see notices in Parker's *New York Gazette*, May 7, 1750 and July 7, 1755. The latter notice advertised both French and English editions. For text see *Oeuvres de Fénelon*, iii, 1-154.

[16] Other books dealing with women on Edwards's list were Richardson's *Clarissa* and *Pamela*, and Fielding's *Amelia*. See F. B. Dexter, " The Manuscripts of Jonathan Edwards," Mass. Hist. Soc., *Procs.*, ser. 2, xv (1901), 15-16.

[17] Emily V. Mason, *Journal of a Young Lady of Virginia* (Baltimore, 1871), p. 45. Muilman, *Letter to the Earl of Chesterfield* (New York, 1751), p. 29.

bodied a moderately conservative and devoutly Roman Catholic attitude toward the upbringing of young girls was known in America to Dr. John Witherspoon, president of New Jersey College, who cited it in his writings on education,[18] and to Edward Shippen who wrote from Lancaster, Pennsylvania, about 1765 that he was extremely anxious to obtain a copy of it either in French or in English. Shippen thought its suggestions might also be valuable for sons.[19] *L'Éducation* was first published in France about the year 1687, but was not separately reprinted in America until the nineteenth century.[20] George Hickes made a translation which went through several English editions; and certain parts of the book were in *The Ladies' Library,* one of the important channels through which Fénelon's ideas reached America. Fénelon did not adopt the extreme views of intellectual pursuits for women held by some contemporary ladies of the French salons. He thought women weaker than men in both mind and body, and therefore unfitted for the pursuit of the mechanical arts. Politics, war, jurisprudence, philosophy, and theology were also fields in which women were forbidden to meddle; they should rather cultivate industry, neatness and thrift, qualities peculiarly adapted for use in the home.

Fénelon went into much detail on education, selecting what seemed to him the most conspicuous evils of the time and endeavoring through his book to counteract them. His emphasis on the importance of modesty in learning, which prevented women from carrying their studies too far,

[18] *Works of John Witherspoon* (2nd ed., Philadelphia, 1802), iv, 149. From "Letters on Education."

[19] Thomas Balch, *Letters and Papers relating to Pennsylvania* (Philadelphia, 1855), p. 215.

[20] Charles Evans, *American Bibliography,* lists François Fénelon, *A Patern of Christian Education* (Christopher Sower, Germantown, 1756). This may have included part of his work on feminine education.

limited his conception of feminine education. He did not wish girls to become pedants nor to engage in studies which might turn their heads, but certain instruction was necessary.[21] Mature women, he believed, should undertake the training of all their children in early years and that of daughters until they married or entered a convent. They should also take charge of the servants, of family expenditures, and, at times, should manage estates and incomes.[22] These activities must be taken into account in planning feminine education. Girls should be taught to read and write correctly and be familiar with the four rules of arithmetic. They should be instructed in religion, but in such a manner as would avoid raising abstract philosophical and theological questions.[23] With an eye to their possible responsibilities in managing affairs, young women should know something of the principles of law, understanding the difference between a will and a deed of gift, the nature of a contract and an entail, and the distinction between real and personal estate.[24] Fénelon, believing the method of teaching important, gave much advice on what is today known as the psychology of instruction. Training along these lines would, he believed, result in forming capable religious women, free from foolish affectations and courageous when unusual problems arose.

Fénelon permitted the reading of secular literature which contained nothing dangerous to the passions, such as Greek and Roman histories, the history of France and neighboring countries. The study of Italian and Spanish he discouraged

---

[21] Fénelon, *L'Éducation*, Lupton trans., p. 12.

[22] *Ibid.*, p. 96.   [23] *Ibid.*, pp. 61-65.

[24] *Ibid.*, pp. 104-106. Many later writers apparently borrowed this idea from Fénelon. See H. G. Good, *Benjamin Rush and his Services to American Education* (Berne, Ind., 1918), pp. 226-34. The plan was included in *The Ladies' Library*. For actual use of legal information by a woman in colonial America see H. H. Ravenel, *Eliza Pinckney* (New York, 1896), pp. 51-52.

save for the few who were likely to need the languages for court attendance on some princess. Knowledge of these languages led as a rule to the reading of dangerous books. Latin was a more reasonable pursuit if studied by girls of sound judgment and modest behavior. Works of poetry and eloquence, Fénelon recommended to those with a taste for much reading.[25]

Before leaving these three authors something should be said of a later book, *The Ladies' Library* (1714), in which much of their work was incorporated. It was published by Richard Steele and probably compiled by him.[26] According to his preface it was the result of the papers on a lady's library in the *Spectator*.[27] He called it a collection of writings from the greatest divines, " disposed under heads to fix in the mind general rules for conduct in all the circumstances of the life of woman." [28] At least three-fourths of the book was taken from well-known authors though some of their material was slightly rearranged. Besides the writers already mentioned there were selections from Jeremy Taylor, Mary Astell, John Locke, and several others.[29] The compilation undoubtedly served to give certain views a much wider currency in America than they would otherwise have had.[30] The general tone of the three volumes was both pious

[25] Fénelon, *L'Éducation*, pp. 108-09.

[26] For the suggestion that Lady Mary Wray was the compiler see *Notes and Queries*, ser. 1, xii, 12. See reference to Aitken's article in note 29.

[27] *Spectator*, nos. 37, 92.   [28] *Ladies' Library*, Preface.

[29] George Aitken in the *Athenaeum*, July 5, 1884, p. 16, gave references showing the authorship of more than three-fourths of the book and reasons for believing Steele to be the compiler. There were many editions. (1st, 1714; 4th, 1732; 7th, 1772, etc.)

[30] Advertised in *Pennsylvania Gazette*, May 18-25, 1738, Feb. 7, 1739/40, Jan. 21, 1755; *New York Gazette*, May 7, 1750; *New York Gazette or Weekly Post Boy*, 1764 by Garrat Noel; *Connecticut Courant*, August, 19, 1767, etc.

and conservative. It was a book which Benjamin Franklin especially recommended to his daughter.[31]

From the standpoint of the ideas presented, the little book of the Marquise de Lambert (1647-1733), *A Mother's Advice to her Son and Daughter*, should be named here rather than with later works, since the author was a friend and contemporary of Fénelon. The precise date at which she wrote is not known, for her book was published subsequently without her knowledge or desire; but she belonged to the seventeenth and not to the eighteenth-century tradition.[32] The *Advice*, for the most part a recapitulation of generally accepted ideas, by some chance, became popular in America towards the end of the eighteenth century. A selection from it was reprinted in the *Royal American Magazine* in 1774.[33] The advice to her daughter was included in Mathew Carey's *Lady's Pocket Library* and in *The Young Lady's Parental Monitor*, both published in 1792. In the same year a book by the Marquise, *The Polite Lady; Or, a Course in . . . Education*, was printed at Salem, though the so-called " first American edition " of the *Advice* did not appear until 1814.[34] The Marquise's work though useful was not productive of many original ideas. Her list of suggested studies permitted Latin to the ambitious, but decried Italian and was in other ways reminiscent of Fénelon's outline. She complained of the great neglect of feminine education. Her sex, she felt, was treated as a race apart. People failed to realize that this

---

31 Franklin, *Works*, ed. Sparks (Boston, 1844), vii, 167.

32 The first edition was anonymous. Michaud's *Biographie Universelle* states that the 3rd edition was in 1727; the first date in the Catalogue of the Bibliothêque Nationale is 1728.

33 I (1774), 219-21.

34 See Evans, *American Bibliography* for the 1792 publications. Selections from her work may have been included in *Instructions for a Young Lady*, advertised by Garrat Noel in 1764 in the *New York Gazette or Weekly Post Boy*.

neglect of women reacted unfavorably upon men, through the loss of companionship, and upon the education of children. The Marquise discussed at some length the value of religion in filling the voids of women's later life and assuaging their inevitable sorrows. Modesty should be cultivated by all women but at the same time they should not neglect the " masculine virtues of friendship, probity, fidelity to duty." [35] Within the limits conventionally allotted to women the book placed much emphasis on character development.

Another book which indirectly affected the training of women was John Locke's *Some Thoughts Concerning Education* (1693). Many women who had not read it themselves knew something of it from the remarks in the later volumes of *Pamela*,[36] or from the pages of *The Ladies' Library*. The essay referred particularly to the upbringing of sons; the emphasis on physical care through what might be called the hardening process reflected Locke's early medical studies.[37] For daughters, Locke believed a private education the only type possible. Samuel Richardson was much interested in Locke's plan, by which a mother, though previously ignorant of the language herself, could teach her son the early stages of Latin; it is mentioned in *Pamela* and *Sir Charles Grandison*.[38] Locke did not offer any extended suggestions as to the position or training of women.

Certain sixteenth and seventeenth-century books on house-wifery, found in colonial libraries though they were not reprinted in America, revealed popular standards for women, displaying in everyday matters an ideal akin to that

[35] Lambert (ed. 1814), pp. 62, 73-75.

[36] *Cf. infra*, p. 49.

[37] Locke, *Some Thoughts concerning Education*, ed. Daniel (London, n. d. prob. 1880), p. 63 *et seq.*

[38] *Ibid.*, pp. 139, 317. Richardson, *Pamela* (ed. 1883), iii, 343. *Sir Charles Grandison* (ed. 1929), i, 84.

of Lord Halifax. Thomas Tusser in his *Points of Hus-wifery* (c. 1561) instructed wives first to serve God and second to live with their husbands as they should. He followed this advice with directions for management of household and servants in every phase from dairying to physic.[39] Gervase Markham who wrote in the next century prefaced his recipes for food and medicine with similar remarks but cautioned women that setting a religious example to their families did not mean " usurping to themselves a power of preaching and interpreting the Holy Word." The wife should instead devote her time to the " worthy knowledges which do belong unto her vocation." [40]

Aside from formal works dealing with women, another aspect of the subject may be found in books on marriage. Such writings, which were not uncommon, discussed marriage either in a religious or a semi-humorous fashion.[41] As an example of the former treatment one may take John Wing's *The Crown Coniugall or, The Spouse Royall,* two sermons on the text, " A vertuous Woman is the Crowne of her Husband." [42] Wing was pastor of the English congregation at Flushing in Zeeland, to which these sermons, published in English at Middleburgh, Holland in 1620, were perhaps delivered.[43] The husband's authority, Wing upheld by scriptural quotations. When the husband was obliged to

[39] Thomas Tusser, *The Points of Huswifery united to the Comfort of Husbandry,* in *Five Hundred Points of Husbandry,* William Mavor ed. (London, 1812).

[40] Gervase Markham, *The English House-Wife* (9th ed., London, 1683), pp. 2-4. Most of Markham's material was in his *Way to Get Wealth.* For this and similar titles in America see *Writings of Col. William Byrd,* p. 425; *Journals of Hugh Gaine Printer,* i, 192, 198, 203.

[41] In the preface to Wing's sermons he mentions the abundance of material on the subject.

[42] Prov. 12: 4.

[43] The place and date of publication make it possible that this work was known to early settlers in New England.

chastise his wife, he was to do so only as he would discipline himself, in a negative manner and not by blows.[44]   The wife though inferior to her husband was still worthy of his honor, for this natural inferiority was not so great as " most men doe (customarily) conceive it to be." [45]   Pastor Wing highly praised the gracious wife, showing what a great blessing she might prove, and urging prospective husbands to look for moral and religious qualities in women.[46]   Of women's intellectual life either as companions to their husbands or for their own sakes Wing made no mention.   The whole tone of his writing was much like that of the funeral sermons for pious women, delivered by the New England divines a century later.

In 1673 appeared William Seymar's *Conjugum Conjurgium: or some Serious Considerations on Marriage*.   This author, of whose life no record appears to have survived, thought marriage desirable only as a lawful way of palliating lust.   In general the inconveniences of married life outweighed its gains.   Seymar was bitter against women and believed that most love came from the devil rather than from God.[47]   The duties which he assigned to the wife included reverencing her husband's person, regarding him as her superior in all respects, assisting him in every way, especially in the economical management of his affairs, keeping his secrets, and proving herself a complete helpmeet.[48]

There was also a satirical and much coarser type of work dealing with love, marriage and kindred topics which appealed to a less serious group of readers than did the books just mentioned.   Prominent among writers of such material was John Dunton, London publisher and bookseller,

[44] Wing, *op. cit.*, pp. 44-48.

[45] *Ibid.*, pp. 133-34.   [46] *Ibid.*, pp. 7, 21.

[47] References given here to Seymar's work are to 2nd ed., London, 1675.   See sec. iii for objections to marriage.

[48] Seymar, *Conjugum Conjurgium*, p. 10.

with his questions in the *Athenian Mercury* which discussed love and marriage, often in salacious fashion.[49] Somewhat similar was the *Athenian Spy,* published in London in 1704, purporting to be letters between men and women on Platonic and natural love in which the latter was made to triumph. Edward Ward, a humorist of this class who kept a punch shop and tavern in London, had considerable popularity in America. The title of one of his books, *Female Policy Detected: or the Arts of a Designing Woman Laid Open,* suggests the material it contained.[50] It dealt with little save women's malice, their desire for revenge in petty matters and other traits of a like nature which the author thought almost the exclusive property of the sex. His *Nuptial Dialogues* (1710), in the same vein, was also popular. In the latter part of the *Female Policy,* however, he described a good wife, one who followed closely the rules laid down in the New Testament and was a living example of the wise woman of the book of Proverbs. While works like Ward's were perhaps more read in England than in America they were certainly known here; their titles occur in booksellers' advertisements and in library lists. Both *The Athenian Oracle,* a selection of the questions and answers which formed the most dubious part of the *Athenian Mercury,* and Ward's *Nuptial Dialogues* were in the subscription library at Hatboro, Pennsylvania and their withdrawals were noted at intervals in the years 1762-1774, often in such respectable company as Hervey's *Meditations,* the *Province Laws* and Young's *Night Thoughts.* The records of this library, fortunately preserved, reveal the books read in a small agricultural community twenty miles from Philadelphia.[51]

---

[49] Dunton spent some time in Boston.

[50] First edition, London, 1695. American editions appeared in 1742, 1786, 1793, 1795 (2 eds.).

[51] "A Colonial Reading List," Chester T. Hallenbeck, ed., *Pennsylvania Magazine of History and Biography,* lvi, 289-340.

Students of ethics were also interested in women's position. In one of the most popular deistical works of the period, *The Religion of Nature Delineated*,[52] William Wollaston (1660-1724), treating marriage from what he considered a scientific and rational point of view, wrote that its objects were the propagation of mankind and the joint happiness of the couple intermarrying. The idea of the husband's authority had been carried too far; the persons concerned should be ruled by reason.[53] This book was the source of many ideas expressed in Franklin's *Reflections on Courtship and Marriage*,[54] which gives it peculiar interest as one of the influences which turned American thought from the older Puritan conception to more liberal views on women.

About 1700 there was a trend in the direction of increased education for women. Formal plans to this end were given in the writings of Mary Astell and of Daniel Defoe, and suggestions of a less formal type in the essays of Swift, Addison, and Steele. The opinions of the latter group probably bore more fruit in the colonies than did the former because of the general knowledge of the *Spectator* and the *Tatler*. The ideas of the other writers were not, however, entirely unknown; *The Ladies' Library* which was much read here contained selections from Mary Astell's *Serious Proposal*,[55] and Franklin had read Defoe's *Essay on Projects*.[56] Mary Astell's work was probably not recognized as hers since Steele did not give the authorship of his selections. Defoe's *Religious Courtship* and *The Family Instructor* were

[52] Privately printed 1722. Published 1724. References here are to 6th ed., London, 1738.

[53] Wollaston, *op. cit.*, p. 154.

[54] New York, 1796, pp. 43-46. First ed. 1746.

[55] For references to *The Ladies' Library* see note 29 *supra* and Franklin, *Works*, ed. Sparks, vii, 167.

[56] Franklin, *Writings*, ed. Smyth, i, 238.

also available in America but dealt more with piety and good works than with the position of women.[57]

Mary Astell (1666-1731), who attained some note as a writer of pamphlets, was a friend of many socially and intellectually prominent people in her day including Lady Elizabeth Hastings and Lady Mary Wortley Montagu to whose Turkish letters she wrote a preface containing some remarks on the ability of women.[58] Mary Astell engaged in political and religious controversy and her authorship was evidently known though she and most contemporary women writers published their works anonymously for fear of public prejudice. On this account opinion is still divided as to the authorship of the *Essay in Defence of the Female Sex* (1696) which was long attributed to Mary Astell. Since this essay represents a comparatively advanced set of ideas for the time it may be discussed with two which were certainly her work, *Reflections on Marriage* and *A Serious Proposal to the Ladies*.[59] The author did not agree with those who believed that there were definite sexual characteristics in the feminine mind. There was, she said, admittedly no distinction of sex in the soul, a point in which her views were shared by such conservative writers as Halifax and Fénelon; skilful anatomists found none in the brain structure. The life of primitive peoples showed no sexual differentiation on mental lines except that in the presence of strangers women were more polite and ready of

[57] Evans, *American Bibliography*, does not list any reprints of the *Essay on Projects* or Mary Astell's work. *The Family Instructor* was reprinted in America in 1740. Booksellers' advertisements of the *Spectator* and the *Tatler* were frequent.

[58] For her life see Florence M. Smith, *Mary Astell*. The preface to Lady Mary's *Letters*, written 1724, was published 1763. Lady Mary's letters were read and admired in America but she was regarded as a brilliant exception not as a pattern for other women.

[59] For a discussion of the authorship of the *Essay in Defence of the Female Sex*, see Smith, *Mary Astell*, pp. 173-82.

approach than men. None of these facts afforded an argument for the inferiority of women. Therefore men must be
keeping them in submission for fear they should come into
their own and threaten masculine dominion.[60] Since men
had imposed women's lower status upon them, no argument
based on custom or tradition could be used to prove its
validity.[61] Girls were not generally given the same education as their brothers but this was no proof of their inferiority, being merely another masculine device to confine
women to a narrow sphere.[62] Defoe also held this opinion;
it seemed to him barbarous that a civilized country should
deny learning to women and then reproach the sex with folly
and impertinence which the advantages of education could
have prevented. Ignorance was no ornament to women to
whom God surely would not have given the capacity for
learning had he not meant them to use it.[63]

The views of these two writers and of some others were
thus based on the theory that the sexes were approximately
equal in ability but that women had been hitherto unduly
repressed. Both Defoe and Mary Astell felt that this could
be remedied by appropriate training so that educated women
might prove agreeable and capable companions in married
life, in which of course they would be ruled by their husbands.
Illiberal as this seems today, it was comparatively advanced
at that time, for the equal ability of women was not widely
accepted in either England or America until the nineteenth
century. It was commonly thought that since women were
intellectually as well as physically weaker than men their only
goal in life was to be good wives and mothers. Defoe and

[60] *Essay in Defence of the Female Sex* (4th ed., London, 1731), p. 10
et seq.

[61] Astell, *Reflections on Marriage* (4th ed., London, 1730), pp. 136-39.

[62] Astell, *Reflections on Marriage*, p. 172.

[63] Daniel Defoe, *Essay on Projects*, in *The Earlier Life and Chief
Earlier Works of Daniel Defoe*, ed. Morley (London, 1889), pp. 144-45.

Mary Astell would have been far from denying that this last was women's destiny but their estimate of feminine ability left women, granted proper training, some scope for individual development. Even more advanced thinkers did not deny the husband's authority over his wife but rather upheld it, saying that once marriage had occurred the wife was to accept her husband's decisions entirely. The education of women would not interfere with obedience, for the more sense women had, the more readily would they submit to just authority. Proper education would not make women too good for any but foolish men since rightly trained wives would be real companions to their husbands.[64] Feminine competition might even prove beneficial to men by stimulating them to emulate women's achievements, provided of course they included something more than the desirability of getting a husband. Perhaps there was, in practice, little difference between this idea of marriage and the doctrine of obedience to men as superiors, but it contained at least a nucleus for future developments.

It would be tedious to recite in detail all the proposals for the education of women. Mary Astell's *Serious Proposal to the Ladies,* published in 1694, was perhaps the first real suggestion of a school for women on a scale at all comparable to the men's institutions of the time. She planned for a " religious retirement," in effect a sort of lay nunnery, where women might study and, if they wished, be free from the cares and importunities of the world. She appealed to Queen Anne and several persons of prominence to support such an establishment but Bishop Burnet and others, alarmed at any plan for an institution which resembled even remotely

[64] Astell, *Reflections on Marriage,* pp. 82-84, 118; Defoe, *Essay on Projects,* pp. 151-52; Wollaston, *The Religion of Nature Delineated,* p. 154.

a Roman Catholic convent, prevented the scheme from being carried out. Satirists found in any suggestion for the education of women matter for ridicule and made the most of this one. Consequently the plan was never tried.[65] Samuel Richardson, forty years later, in one of his novels made a similar suggestion, thinking of such a place as a refuge for respectable unmarried ladies of moderate incomes.[66] Defoe also had plans for an academy but one less sheltered than that proposed by Mary Astell.[67] He was familiar with her ideas, but though he respected her plan thought it impracticable. His ladies were to be given more freedom though men were forbidden to propose marriage to any woman while she was in residence at the school.[68] Since none of these plans was carried into effect in England their influence on this side of the Atlantic was obviously only remote. It is possible too that Bishop Burnet's imputation of Catholicism to Mary Astell's plan served to prevent Protestant readers from considering it seriously.

Defoe and Mary Astell both made suggestions regarding subject matter which may have had wider influence than their plans for academies. The usual feminine education, Mary Astell found, was not so defective as was commonly supposed. It included a knowledge of the vernacular and of French, which gave a good background for the subject matter of polite conversation, provided of course that one read widely and made judicious use of translations. Certainly the classical studies of men were no great preparation for polite society and improving conversation. Indeed better results

[65] For details of the plan and objections to it see Smith, *Mary Astell*, pp. 48-63. Reynolds, *Learned Lady*, pp. 301-07. Also a letter of Elizabeth Elstob from the Ballard Manuscripts, quoted in *Mary Astell*, p. 21.

[66] Richardson, *Sir Charles Grandison*, iii, 383-84, letter 32.

[67] Defoe, *Essay on Projects*, pp. 145-48.

[68] *Ibid.*, p. 146.

might be obtained from the lighter program of studies given to women which allowed them to enter earlier into society and to read books of a less serious nature. The earlier maturity of girls was probably due to their greater social opportunities.[69] Defoe thought Italian should be added to the list of feminine studies, as should accomplishments such as music, dancing, the graces of speech, and the wide reading of history.[70] He believed the aim of education should be the cultivation of women's understanding in order to minimize the difference between the sexes.[71]

Thus by the beginning of the eighteenth century two trends regarding women's sphere were clearly marked. On the one hand was the conservative writer who consigned women to a place of inferiority, from which they were not to stray, and invoked religious sanctions to keep them on this plane. The education of women was not essential in the minds of some of the conservatives, though others like Fénelon and the Marquise de Lambert found it helpful in meeting the sorrows and responsibilities of women's position. Preachers and, through the coarse tone they adopted, humorists were likely to share this narrow view. On the other hand, a few writers like Mary Astell and Daniel Defoe, who believed in individual development for women, were forerunners, though unconsciously, in a movement which led in the eighteenth century to widely increased educational opportunities for women and at the end of the century to pleas for feminine rights in other directions. This period had no exact counterpart in American literary development but the allusions to women in the writings of Samuel Sewall and Cotton Mather indicate that New England shared the ideas of Lord Halifax and Archbishop Fénelon, not those of Mary Astell and Daniel Defoe.

[69] *Essay in Defence of the Female Sex*, pp. 32-42, 50-51.
[70] Defoe, *Essay on Projects*, p. 148.
[71] *Ibid.*, pp. 149-52.

CHAPTER II

European Theory from 1700 to 1775

BETWEEN 1700 and the American Revolution European works about women were widely read in the colonies, so that the influence of individual authors on colonial literature and practice is easily traced. During the first part of this period the opinions of essayists and novelists were particularly influential; later more didactic works dealing with the behavior and education of women became popular.

I

The rise of the periodical essay early in the century had its importance in the position of women. Contributors to the *Tatler* and the *Spectator* were especially sensitive to women's intellectual and social needs and gave much space to topics of feminine interest. Their comments were instructive as well as amusing so that later writers highly recommended the essays in their reading lists for young ladies. They were popular in America, almost every bookseller's advertisement mentioning copies of one or both. The influence of the *Spectator* on Franklin's early work was marked. Since women were regular readers of his paper Addison, in particular, believed that he could do much for the sex by throwing out suggestions regarding conduct and by holding various foibles up to ridicule. Many minor matters of which he and his fellow essayists complained were transient affairs like the wearing of party patches, high headdresses, and masculine riding habits by women, so that the papers dealing with them are today of interest chiefly as they throw light on the customs of the early eighteenth century.   There was also much serious advice on the education and character of women and on marriage, in delivering which the *Spectator* had a more elevated tone than did the *Tatler*.[1] The idle social life of women of the better classes which these authors pictured was not altogether attractive. There was much criticism of the too frequent appearance of women in public and of the excessive amount of time given to amusements, often of a doubtful sort. These criticisms fitted British society much better than American though doubtless there were many American women who would gladly have imitated these customs had opportunity offered and some, in the cities, managed to do so. The continuous social activity of women was evidently viewed as a recent innovation, for the *Tatler* assured its readers that Shakespeare had not given women a large place in his dialogues because in his day they had been merely domestic characters and had not set themselves up as wits and literary critics. The writer went on to describe a woman of his own time with a wide range of interests who lived quietly and was a model worthy of imitation.[2] The essayists had little patience with ladies who, because of their interest in wit and reading, neglected their families or their appearance.[3] The pose of a learned lady was not the only dangerous one; the character of a " notable woman "—the current term for a bustling housewife, and that of an affected invalid were both extremes to be avoided. Women should try to keep mind and body in a state of perfection which could be done through proper reading and through amusements designed for them as rational beings, not simply as members of their own sex. It was natural when her serious occupations were embroidery and the mak-

[1] *Spectator*, ed. Chalmers (London, 1872), no. 4.

[2] *Tatler* (London, 1713), no. 42.

[3] *Tatler*, no. 75.

ing of sweetmeats that the conversation of the average woman should be superficial, dealing with dress, fashion, and similar matters.[4]

A few women possessed higher interests and knowledge; to increase their number and to provide entertainment for them was one of the purposes of the *Spectator*. This elevation was to be accomplished largely through directed reading. The necessary amount of domestic training was taken for granted; but the matter of books called for serious thought. The description in the *Spectator* of Leonora's library is perhaps too well known to call for repetition. It was a curious miscellany—a few classical titles, Lord Halifax's *Advice to a Daughter,* works of piety, and a number of popular plays and romances. The whole, though quite innocent, Addison thought, might have been much improved from the standpoint of real learning. These books had brought Leonora into a romantic frame of mind which was reflected in everything about her. It seemed a pity that a woman of her ability should not have had her reading guided into more intellectual channels. The question of books for women aroused so much interest that a later essay gave some of the titles sent by readers. These suggestions were colored by the occupation of the sender, those from ladies being nearly all romances or plays.[5] According to Steele it was this interest of the readers of the *Spectator* which afterwards culminated in his publication of *The Ladies' Library.*[6] Learning for ladies was not to go too far but no matter what the amount of education given it should be sufficient to enable them to judge a man according to his character and not merely by sex. This, according to the *Tatler,* would prevent women 'from falling in love with the butler.[7] Steele made

---

[4] *Tatler,* no. 248; *Spectator,* nos. 10, 15.

[5] *Spectator,* nos. 37, 92.

[6] See the Preface to that work.   [7] *Tatler,* no. 61.

fun of the female virtuoso who neglected ordinary duties for learning.[8] He had, however, some serious advice on feminine education. He praised Fénelon's writings on the subject, with their recommendation of arithmetic and accounts as practical subjects, and their warning against making women scholars.[9] The usual education of girls, Steele thought, cared for their bodies through the medium of social accomplishments but neglected their minds. The reverse was true in the education of boys. Feminine training was all directed to the making of an agreeable person for the benefit of the future husband with the unfortunate result of producing a race of coquettes.[10]

The essayists were far from confining their comments on women to specific customs and lists of studies but delighted to wander into abstract discussions of the sexes and their respective qualities. A comparison of men and women was believed to show that there were traces of sex in the soul, a term here applied to mental rather than to spiritual traits. Although men and women were very different this did not necessarily mean that one sex was superior to the other. It did mean that different qualities were to be emphasized in upbringing and that what was a minor fault in one might prove serious in the other. Party rage was given as an illustration of such a fault. Since women's virtues were domestic, if they must show zeal it should be against those who were not of their own religion and nation. There was a tendency to balance traits of character against one another. Thus wisdom was important for men but prudence for women; courage was rated high in the masculine code as chastity was in the feminine, perhaps because these qualities

---

[8] *Spectator*, nos. 242, 278.

[9] *Ibid.*, no. 95. Steele included selections from Fénelon in *The Ladies' Library*.

[10] *Spectator*, no. 66.

gave them the highest values in the eyes of the opposite sex.[11]
The essayists placed women's capacities far above their
actual attainments and offered suggestions for their larger
development.   As women were naturally gayer and more
vivacious than men they must guard against thoughtless gallantry and against becoming coquettes.   The two sexes were
designed to balance one another although women often
failed to realize this and devoted their time to coxcombs with
feminine characteristics rather than men of sense.[12]   The
opinion was sometimes hazarded that the faults of women
were due to false standards set up for them by men and that
the most serious errors committed by women came from the
social attitude which condoned in men what it did not in
women whom they had led astray.[13]

Advice on marriage varied from number to number according to the author's mood.   Some was given in jest, some
had a serious purpose behind it.   Addison advised men to
look for good nature, even temper, virtue, good sense, love,
and constancy in the women they were to marry.[14]   Steele
urged ladies to seek in a prospective husband a virtuous disposition, an agreeable person, and an easy future, but above
all a good understanding.[15]   The husband should counter-
balance and correct undesirable qualities in the wife.[16]   The
Tatler warned readers especially against great disparity in
age.[17]   Steele thought that much marital unhappiness resulted from men's lack of judgment, for men had romantic
sentiments and expected too much of human nature.   Thus

[11] *Spectator*, nos. 57, 81, 99; *Tatler*, nos. 52, 172.
[12] *Spectator*, nos. 128, 433.
[13] *Tatler*, nos. 33, 200.
[14] *Spectator*, no. 261.
[15] *Ibid.*, no. 522.
[16] *Tatler*, no. 75.
[17] *Ibid.*, nos. 20, 22.

love did not last beyond the first passion. To keep it alive demanded lasting effort on both sides.[18] Addison advised women on the management of jealous husbands, observing that this was one of the few problems of the sort not treated by Lord Halifax.[19] The sole concern of the wife should be to please her husband in every particular. She should dress to attract him, and read to obtain material for interesting conversation with him; her vivacity should serve to lighten his cares.[20] It is interesting to note that the wife's having her own pin money was strongly opposed in more than one paper. It seemed unwise, a sign of distrust of the man she had married. Separate purses for husband and wife were unnatural. If she could not trust to his generosity why should she marry him? The marriage would not prove happy unless there were common interests.[21]

Addison's real interest in women as moral and social beings was unquestioned and Steele's compilation of *The Ladies' Library* showed a sincere and serious treatment of women's problems. One brilliant writer, however, among the essayists who charged women with faults and foibles in a merciless way was perhaps influenced by his own experiences with the sex. This was Dean Swift, who, in addition to his contributions to periodicals, wrote one or two other essays on women and their place. In a discussion of Platonic love in the *Tatler* he bitterly attacked Mary Astell and her educational schemes, prompted perhaps more by personal feeling than by disapproval of her plans for women's education. Mrs. Astell had indeed accused Swift of irreligion in an essay attacking the Kit Kat Club, but this hardly justified a response which made unfounded insinuations as to her per-

18 *Spectator*, nos. 479, 506.
19 *Ibid.*, nos. 170, 171.
20 *Ibid.*, nos. 15, 128, 245.
21 *Spectator*, no. 295.

sonal character.[22] Some of Swift's verses dealing with
women were decidedly coarse, notably the " Lady's Dressing
Room." [23] His personal experiences with women were
hardly of a normal or happy nature. Some unknown ob-
stacle apparently prevented his marriage with Stella, the one
woman for whom he really cared; this may have resulted
in bitterness against other women which showed itself in
his writings.[24] In his " Letter to a Very Young Lady on
her Marriage " he gave his ideas on the training of women.
His advice, though probably well designed, treated the lady
to whom it was addressed with contempt. It was possible,
Swift wrote, that by following his directions she might in
time make herself worthy of her husband for whose companionship Swift's suggestions were intended to fit her.
There was no interest, even for a woman, in the society of
other women since their talk was of nothing but dress and
folly. Improvement was to be attained through reading but
no matter how much she read no woman would ever attain
to the perfection of a common school boy. [25] All of this was
harsh comment to a young woman of ability, the daughter
of an old friend.[26] This essay was known to Benjamin
Franklin who regarded it with approval although he thought
the Dean at times severe.[27] Swift's advice on literature and
studies made the letter well known and even popular in spite

[22] *Tatler*, no. 32; Smith, *Mary Astell*, pp. 25, 29.

[23] In *The Poetical Works of Jonathan Swift* (Aldine ed., London,
1833), i, 247-51.

[24] Carl Van Doren, *Swift* (New York, 1930), pp. 56-59, 148-49 discusses Swift's attitude towards women. This author thinks his failure
to marry may have been a matter of temperament.

[25] Swift, *Works*, ed. Sir Walter Scott, 2nd ed., ix, 208-220.

[26] The letter was addressed either to Lady Betty Moore, wife of George
Rochfort, or to Mrs. John Rochfort. Swift, *Works*, ed. Temple Scott,
xi, 114.

[27] Franklin, *Reflections on Courtship and Marriage*, pp. 57-58.

of its low estimate of women. Mathew Carey of Philadelphia included it in his *Lady's Pocket Library* in which most of the selections dealt more charitably with women. Swift showed the same harsh feeling in an unfinished sketch in which he advised men to choose as wives, women with good sense and some education, but observed that it was difficult to find such women, who were even rarer than the occasional man of genius.[28] While one can hardly regard Swift's views on women as typical of his era yet they did have some influence in America. Year after year the advertisements of Hugh Gaine, New York editor and printer, and of other booksellers announced a supply of Swift's works in fourteen volumes.[29]

Another writer, vastly inferior in literary ability to the essayists and to Richardson, must nevertheless be considered because of the widespread circulation of her ideas on women. Mrs. Eliza Haywood, a novelist and essayist of doubtful reputation, was at first known as a writer of romances of passion and novels of scandal, some of which were too libelous to bear her signature; but towards the latter part of her life, she changed her attitude, either from principle or from policy, and produced several works of pious and moral advice.[30] Of these her *Female Spectator* (1744-46) and to a lesser extent her *Epistles for the Ladies* (1749-1750) were sold and read in the colonies. The former was frequently advertised in New York, Philadelphia, Hartford and other papers after 1750. The *Female Spectator,* obviously an imitation of Addison's more polished work, dealt with a number of subjects though not in any original or striking manner.[31]

28 Swift, *Works,* ed. Sir Walter Scott, 2nd ed., ix, 267-71.

29 *The Journals of Hugh Gaine Printer,* i, list of books imported.

30 George Whicher, *The Life and Romances of Mrs. Eliza Haywood* (New York, 1915).

31 The *Female Spectator* was advertised in the *Pennsylvania Gazette,* Feb. 6, 1750; *New York Gazette,* 1764; *Connecticut Courant,* Aug. 10, 1767, etc.

In the opening numbers Mrs. Haywood attributed the work to a group of women whom she described in some detail but there is no internal evidence to show that this club of ladies ever existed; in all probability Mrs. Haywood was herself the author of the four volumes.[32]   Many of the ideas which she expressed bore a close resemblance to those of Addison in the *Spectator* and of Samuel Richardson in his novels.   It may be significant that the *Female Spectator* appeared only four years after the first edition of *Pamela,* but Richardson's ideas were not different enough from those of his time to warrant the charge that Mrs. Haywood borrowed directly from him.   Most of Mrs. Haywood's comments on feminine education and her suggestions for reading lists may be found better expressed elsewhere.

Mrs. Haywood was enough of a feminist to hold men largely responsible for women's faults because of the mistaken education they imposed on the sex.   Men need not fear that proper training would harm women; it would merely enable them to perform their duties more effectively. Women who were more than mere " notable housewives " would be agreeable companions because of their education.[33] The fact of women's unfitness for the pulpit or the bar should not keep them from receiving instruction, for the same argument could be used with equal effectiveness against the education of many men.[34]   Mrs. Haywood's goal in the training of women was a general understanding of worldly affairs rather than profound learning.[35]   One of her less hackneyed ideas was that of the value of natural philosophy, which was nothing more than nature study, based chiefly on observations made during country residence.   Her real

[32] Whicher, *op. cit.,* pp. 141-45.

[33] *Female Spectator* (3rd ed., Dublin, 1747), ii, 155-56.

[34] *Ibid.,* ii, 158.

[35] *Ibid.,* iii, 119.

motive in urging such study was the prevention of mischief in leisure time and the cultivation of a taste for a retired life.[36] She gave a reading list, including many histories and translations of classical authors, which was not likely to appeal to most of her readers.[37] She thought French social life most favorable to the education of young ladies, believing that Frenchmen were ready to converse with them at any moment on profound topics, thus rendering their auditors adepts in philosophy, geography, and other branches of learning. The possible superficiality of such knowledge troubled her not at all.[38]

Perhaps Mrs. Haywood's own experiences had deeply impressed upon her the unhappy side of married life, for she wrote much concerning it in her works; the moral tone of her later books was unexceptionable. Young women might be right in refusing suitors proposed by their parents; they could not be so in entering upon other marriages without parental permission. Those who could not obtain such consent ought to remain single, at least during the lifetime of their parents. Once a marriage was undertaken, though it should be rendered as easy as possible, it must be endured. The husband was the absolute head of the family; the wife his confidante and companion, exerting a refining influence on his activities. To do this well, she must have prudence, even temper, fortitude, wit, and gentle behavior, a list of desirable traits, strongly reminiscent of that in the *Spectator*.[39]

Mrs. Haywood's ideas on marriage, and on feminine conduct generally, were also set forth in *The History of Miss*

[36] *Female Spectator*, ii, 158-59; iii, 103, 218; iv, 26. *Epistles for the Ladies* (2 vols., London, 1749-50), i, 140.

[37] *Ibid.*, iii, 118-20.

[38] *Ibid.*, ii, 227-28.

[39] *Ibid.*, ii, 156; iii, 143; iv, 50-51, 216. *Epistles for the Ladies*, i, 61.

Betsy Thoughtless (1751), as completely as in her essays. The heroine of this novel was a young woman who, by carelessness and inattention to the proprieties, had involved herself and her friends in a great variety of difficulties. Repentant too late, she was unhappily married but performed her duties to the utmost of her ability, and was rewarded by the timely decease of her husband, followed, after a proper interval, by a happy second marriage. This book claimed also to illustrate the dangers and temptations of life in London. It was quite popular, perhaps not altogether for the moral lesson which it contained. In the Hatboro Library from 1762 to 1774 the *Female Spectator* actually surpassed Richardson's *Pamela* in circulation and *Betsy Thoughtless* was almost as popular.[40]

Mrs. Haywood, both as novelist and essayist, represented the two types of writing most influential in women's lives; for novels, whether with or without moral purpose, furnished a large share of the literary diet of the English woman and her American sister at this epoch. That they held their prominent place, in spite of the repeated warnings of moralists and didactic writers against this form of literature, can be seen from references in books and diaries and from the advertisements in newspapers. Novels had undoubtedly more influence over the standards held by women than did more formal works designed for that purpose. The great majority of them were highly romantic, with a superlatively beautiful heroine, " possessing all the graces of her sex," who suffered numerous escapes from seduction and other disasters, and became at length the bride of a wealthy and titled hero.[41] Coincidence was stretched beyond the limit of

[40] " A Colonial Reading List," in *Pennsylvania Mag. of Hist. and Biog.*, lvi, 289-340. *The Husband* and *The Wife* also by Mrs. Haywood were in this Hatboro collection but were less popular.

[41] Examples of these novels are T. Leland, *Earl of Salisbury*; Anonymous, *Cynthia* (6th ed., London, 1715) ; the later works of Mrs. Radcliffe, and many others.

probability to produce the desired results, the heroine showing as a rule no initiative but submitting tamely to circumstances. Whatever accomplishments she possessed were
usually superficial. Books of this type in spite of extravagant terminology in praise of ladies hardly served to improve
intellectual or social standards for women; but in some
measure justified writers who protested against much reading of novels. An occasional author saw the humor as well
as the danger of these romances, and one, Charlotte Ramsay
Lennox, furnished an amusing antidote in *The Female
Quixote*.[42] It treated of the imaginary vicissitudes of
Arabella, a young lady whose head had been turned by reading
too many romances. She saw a lover in every passer-by and
romantic plots in the most common occurrences. *The
Female Quixote* perhaps did some good in America, for a
letter of Eliza Huger to Mrs. Pinckney in 1774 referred to it
as a proper book to show young folks the consequences of
being overfond of romances.[43] An American imitation
many years later, entitled *Female Quixotism*, presented an
equally foolish heroine in a trans-Atlantic setting.

The eighteenth century fortunately produced a number of
novelists of a better sort, of whom the figure *par excellence* in
women's history was the London printer, Samuel Richardson.
His work was treated as worthy of attention even by the
strictest moralists, the chief objection to his detailed character studies of women being that his ladies were almost
paragons of virtue. His purpose was avowedly moral
though from a twentieth-century standpoint his code of
values appears false in many ways. In the preface to the 1740
edition of *Pamela* the author gave as his aim the easy incul-
cation of religion and morality. A letter published with this
edition suggested that the book might not only find friends

---

[42] 2nd ed. (London, 1752).

[43] Ravenel, *Eliza Pinckney*, p. 254.

in England but serve as an example to a neighboring nation.[44] *Pamela,* first of the three works which made so deep an impress on the times, was the story of a servant girl, educated somewhat beyond her station, with whom her master fell violently in love. She firmly rebuffed his overtures until finally his pride was conquered by her patience under all the trials to which she was exposed and he married her. The remainder of the book exhibited his virtuous traits and showed him supplementing his wife's education to fit her for her exalted station. Richardson who was strongly class-conscious treated Pamela's promotion as a signal honor. It seems a doubtful morality which depicts a woman as caring deeply for a man who had held her prisoner and threatened her honor but none the less the book became instantly popular in America as well as in England, being one of the five " best sellers " at a Boston auction in 1744.[45] The later and inferior volumes of the book, which were little more than a treatise on the duties of a wife and mother, though very dull, afford an excellent picture of middle class standards.

The ethics of Richardson's *Clarissa* (1747-1748), the second of his novels, were on a higher level than those of *Pamela.* Clarissa, the daughter of a prosperous country family, was portrayed as nearly perfect in her education, accomplishments, and character. From mercenary motives her family endeavored to force upon her the attentions of a gentleman whom she neither loved nor respected. She wished to be a dutiful daughter but drew the line at entering upon such a match. The family persisted in every form of persecution, at length driving Clarissa into the hands of another suitor and abandoned rake, Lovelace, who carried

[44] Reprinted in *Pamela* (Stratford-on-Avon, 1929), i, p. iv.

[45] Alexander Hamilton, *Itinerarium,* p. 137. *Pamela* was advertised in the *Pennsylvania Gazette,* Jan. 1, 1745. It was one of the most popular books in the Hatboro Library, 1762-1774. See *Pennsylvania Mag. of Hist. and Biog.,* lvi, 289 *et seq.*

her off to London. After many expedients and ruses he succeeded in his attempts on her honor. Touched by her sufferings he would later have married her but she refused any relationship with a man of his character and died a few months afterwards. There was not with her, as with Pamela, any question of respect or affection for the man who had mistreated her. Before her misfortunes she had been known as an ideal young lady and she maintained an exemplary and dignified conduct to the end. Thousands of readers wept over her pathetic tale.

Richardson's third novel, *Sir Charles Grandison* (1753), was written to portray a perfect gentleman, to do for the other sex what *Clarissa* had done for women. Richardson knew less of men in the higher social ranks than he did of women with the result that his hero was a bit of a prig. Harriet Byron, the young lady whom Sir Charles married, was another Clarissa without her tragic experiences but with her exemplary character and appropriate education. More interesting and vivacious, though not drawn as an example for readers, was Richardson's delineation of Charlotte Grandison, the younger sister of Sir Charles. All Richardson's novels were composed of letters exchanged between the characters, thus affording him an opportunity for the detailed analyses of character and motive in which he delighted. He knew much of women and of their interests; as he became famous, he was himself the center of an admiring group of feminine friends which included some names of distinction. If his heroines were a bit priggish at times they were nevertheless individuals who often manifested a remarkable degree of common sense quite unlike the ladies of the romances.

Richardson's widespread popularity rendered his theories on the training and education of women of great importance. It can be seen on every page of his works that he had a profound respect for women and the place which they occupied in society. He varied his statements on education a little according to the character by whom they were expressed, thus affording an interesting cross section of the ideas of contemporary society on the matter. He himself favored a considerable degree of education for women and thought them capable of even more advanced work than he suggested; but he was a little afraid that too much attention to learning was incompatible with other duties. Women must not leave their talents undeveloped, even though education was not their principal aim; such development ought not, however, to be at the expense of housewifely accomplishments.[46] These last should not be neglected by women of wealth and good family who should know as much of them as was needed for the proper supervision of their servants. Richardson made the careers of his heroines serve as practical illustrations of a combination of intellectual and domestic attainments, but the supreme importance of being a fit companion for one's husband was never forgotten.[47] At the same time he realized the embarrassments to which an educated woman might be subjected in a company which did not believe in feminine learning. He explained that it was policy, not justice, which had kept women from study and that many gentlemen, save for " a few accuracies of speech," had no more education than ladies of the same class. Want of opportunity alone made the difference between the sexes in this particular.[48] At the same time women were worthy of respect only when they kept to their own spheres, for nothing was more odious than a masculine woman.[49] There was

---

[46] *Clarissa*, Sotheran ed. (London, 1883), v, 465; *Pamela*, Sotheran ed. (London, 1883), i, 298; *Sir Charles Grandison*, Shakespeare Head ed. (Stratford-on-Avon, 1931), i, 52.

[47] *Sir Charles Grandison*, i, 4.

[48] *Pamela*, iii, 350, 419; *Clarissa*, v, 465. See latter part of *Sir Charles Grandison*, esp. v for discussions on the respective abilities of the sexes.

[49] *Sir Charles Grandison*, i, 57-58.

no question in Richardson's mind as to the superior authority of men. Much as he respected women, he regarded the husband as the head of the family whose orders were to be obeyed when any dispute arose although a wise man would do much to avoid such occasions. This rule applied in matters of conscience though in a few extreme cases a wife was justified in obeying the law of God rather than her husband's command. *Pamela* contained a long discussion on this point.[50]

According to Richardson, the mother was to begin the education of her children and often to carry it to a fairly advanced stage; her own training was therefore important. Pamela, at her husband's request, studied Locke's *Some Thoughts Concerning Education,* keeping a notebook with a long analysis of it which incidentally revealed the points wherein Richardson disagreed with Locke.[51] Only the early stages of education were the same for both boys and girls; Richardson believed in equipping women for the sphere which they were to occupy in later life. Girls should learn the use of the English language, spelling and good handwriting, partly to counteract the general neglect in such matters and partly to prepare for the writing which was an excellent amusement for women's leisure hours.[52] Women should read gracefully, be experts in music and drawing, and adepts at needlework though they should not waste long hours over samplers. They must know how to play cards in case of social necessity but should not otherwise waste time on them.[53] They should be well read in English, French, and Italian books, and perhaps in translations of Latin authors, Their English reading should include the Bible, Milton,

[50] *Pamela,* iii, 48-59.

[51] *Ibid.,* iii, 151, 292, 343.

[52] *Clarissa,* v, 463.

[53] *Ibid.,* v, 467; *Pamela,* iii, 348, 366, 412; *Sir Charles Grandison,* i, 10.

Addison, and works of history and geography. In the discussion of Harriet Byron's education Richardson described the learned languages as too apt to overload women's minds though he did not entirely ban their study. If the appropriate education of a woman had been neglected in early life the husband could do much to remedy it after marriage through directed reading, travel and intelligent conversation. The lowly social station of *Pamela* afforded an excellent illustration of these principles.[54]

All three novels dealt much with the question of marriage, its obligations and pleasures, for even Richardson scarcely conceived of feminine existence as interesting apart from marriage though it might be useful.   Sir Charles Grandison, that model of excellence, Richardson pictured as a matchmaker among his friends.   Fine points of honor and duty were the subject of long conversations in which it was concluded that the married life was much the happiest.   Richardson thought choice should be based on personal qualities since marriage should take place only with the consent of the persons concerned, though the advice of friends was not to be despised.   Property ought not to be disregarded but it was of less importance than compatibility.   Pamela, though her situation was pointed out as exceptional, showed that it was not always necessary for persons marrying to be of the same social class.   It was always better for women to remain single than to marry profligate men.   The husband from his superior position had the right to make many demands upon his wife if he chose to do so, but if he were a good man there would be no compulsion on his part, for he would ask nothing which was not reasonable or just. Hence his wife would cheerfully comply except in cases binding her conscience.   God's commands came first, the husband's second, and the lady's own ideas, should she have

[54] *Pamela*, iii, 349; *Sir Charles Grandison*, i, 69.

any, a poor third. She must bear with her husband's imperfections, watch and study his temper, carry her points by sweetness and complaisance since acquiescence in obedience was for the wife the lesser of two evils. The married state was generally one of subservience, " a kind of state of humiliation for a Lady," though Richardson maintained that there was equality in a real marriage.[55]

The sentimental and moral appeal in Richardson's books found favor for many years. Alexander Graydon in his *Memoirs* told how as a boy he had avoided them under the impression that they treated only of dull ceremonies relating to courtship and marriage but happening to open *Clarissa* at the account of the duel between Lovelace and Morden he became more interested in it than in any book he had ever read. He admired Clarissa but thought Lovelace's portrait dangerous, as it was not black enough to emphasize the evils of such a career.[56] A note in the *Ladies' Magazine* (1792) spoke of the universal admiration aroused by the character of Harriet Byron but pointed out to young readers that this admiration was of little value unless one had an imitative turn of mind.[57] Richardson's novels, however, did not receive unmixed approbation. In 1799 an essay in the *Weekly Magazine* of Philadelphia criticized them as unadapted to American customs, speaking of the lack of reality in both the heroines of *Sir Charles Grandison*.[58] Occasionally someone was astute enough to see the moral flaws in Pamela's situation. Esther Edwards Burr, daughter of Jonathan Edwards and wife of the second president of Princeton, after reading *Pamela* in her early married life,

[55] *Pamela*, i, 401; ii, 15, 94; iii, 5, 48, 52, 54, 59, 420; *Sir Charles Grandison*, i, 30-31.

[56] Graydon, *Memoirs of his own Time* (Philadelphia, 1846), pp. 94-5.

[57] *Ladies' Magazine*, i, 261.

[58] " The Ubiquitarian," No. 18 in *Weekly Magazine*, iii, 223.

wrote that although the book contained many excellent observations and rules the author [59] had degraded the female
sex horridly in representing the virtuous Pamela as falling
in love with Mr. B. during his abominable actions. In
occasional comments in her journal Mrs. Burr showed her
belief in the ability of women. Her final estimate of
Pamela was that it was of doubtful value for it made riches
and honor too important, and "besides Mr. B.'s being a
libertine he was a dreadfull high spirited man." [60]

Richardson's contemporaries did not devote the same
amount of attention that he did to women's place and development, but their feminine characters were much more real
than those of the earlier romances. Fielding poked much
fun at learned women and fashionable ladies of London.
One of his characters, Mrs. Western, he made a real "learned
lady" of the type often held up to ridicule on the stage. She
had read plays, operas, oratorios, poems, romances, histories,
and political pamphlets, and so felt herself immeasurably
superior to her country brother. She was represented as
masculine in appearance and was an object of ridicule
throughout the book. [61]   When Fielding was not making fun
of female pedants he inclined to question the utility of learning for women rather than their capacity for it, pointing out
that a husband who had a learned wife might become jealous.
Fielding's heroines, Amelia in the work of that name and
Sophia in *Tom Jones,* had all the domestic virtues and were
retiring individuals who exemplified his theory that a true
wife should bear everything patiently, even her husband's
infidelity. [62]   Fielding talked much of the unreasonableness

[59] She erroneously named Fielding as the author.

[60] Josephine Fisher, "The Diary of Esther Burr" in *New England
Quarterly*, iii, 301.

[61] *Tom Jones* (6th ed., 1900).

[62] *Amelia* (New York, 1911), iii, 79-83.

of allowing parents to choose arbitrarily for their children in marriage. He did not believe in marriage without parental consent but thought it both cruel and ridiculous to force a partner on any one.[63]

Goldsmith's *Vicar of Wakefield* (1766), though written a little later than these other novels, contained an excellent picture of the "notable housewife" in the person of the Vicar's wife, which soon became well known in the colonies,[64]

She was a good-natured notable woman; and as for breeding, there were few country ladies who could shew more. She could read any English book without much spelling; but for pickling, preserving, and cookery, none could excel her. She prided herself also upon being an excellent contriver in housekeeping; tho' I could never find that we grew richer with all her contrivances.[65]

Goldsmith believed that the two sexes had different sorts of abilities, those of the one supplementing the other.[66]

These novels, essays and books of advice were among the more important writings dealing with women down to the middle of the eighteenth century. They furnished the background of the first American publications on the subject and colored much colonial practice which did not find expression in books. It would be unwise to generalize overmuch from so varied an assortment of writers, but certain concepts stand out clearly. Woman's character was believed to be essentially domestic and, perhaps because of this, she was treated in theory and often in fact as subordinate to man. Only in the field of religion did the sexes stand on an equal plane— and even that was in the light of a future life rather than

[63] Fielding's *Amelia* was no doubt the "history of Amelia" which Peter Manigault sent to his mother in South Carolina while he was studying in London in 1752. See his letters in *South Carolina Historical and Genealogical Magazine*, xxxii, 59.

[64] *Belknap Papers* (Mass. Hist. Soc., *Colls.*, ser. 5, ii-iii), i, 233.

[65] *Vicar of Wakefield* (Scholartis Press, 1929), p. 1.

[66] *Ibid.*, pp. 46-47, 63.

the present one.   In the field of education the range of ideas was broader so that every sort of plan was suggested from mere training in housewifely arts to extensive reading. With few exceptions those advocating a more extended education designed it for the pleasure and service of men, to make women more agreeable companions for them, and better teachers for their children.   Only in the proposed retreats for unmarried women was there much suggestion of women's studying primarily for their own development and enjoyment.

II

After 1750 there was a change in the published material dealing with women.   The periodical essay declined somewhat as a medium for the presentation of social and moral standards, though the *Spectator* and other writings of that class were still recommended for perusal by the ladies.   Incidental material on women continued to have its place particularly in the increasing number of monthly magazines; the novel, with a greater variety in its heroines, was omnipresent.   Characteristic of the period were didactic works dealing with women which went into extended and often dreary detail on suitable reading for educational purposes. The volumes by Fordyce, Dr. Gregory, and Mrs. Chapone had a religious emphasis, provoked perhaps by fear of deism. Like Lord Halifax's work, these books were addressed directly to the ladies; but other studies like Thomas's essay on woman philosophized concerning feminine status with little thought of giving advice.   All these works were soon available in America where they furnished much material for books and addresses on women which appeared after the Revolution.[67]

[67] Gregory's book was published in England in 1774, in Philadelphia in 1775; Fordyce's in England in 1765 and advertised in Boston in 1767; Thomas's in Paris in 1772 and Philadelphia in 1774, etc.

Before discussing the more important books there are several minor works which may be briefly mentioned. One, interesting because it was one of the earliest books dealing with women to be reprinted in America, was the *Lady's Preceptor* by the Abbé d'Ancourt. Originally addressed to French young ladies of the upper classes, the book in translation had several English editions. It was reprinted in New York by Parker in 1759 and Woodbridge in 1762.[68] It was hardly more than a pamphlet, a sort of pious etiquette book, with minute directions for behavior not particularly well adapted to American conditions. The author regarded young ladies as decidedly subject to authority. For instance they were not to concern themselves about reasons for the rites and ceremonies of their church but simply conform to them. They should avoid all discussion of public affairs and signs of party spirit. The choice of rank and fortune in marriage should be left to relatives though a young lady might refuse a man who was personally disagreeable. The book contained a fairly complete but conventional and narrow outline of education.

There were two or three short works by English writers whose moral tone contrasted amusingly with the private lives of their authors. One, a pamphlet written by Mrs. Teresia Constantia Muilman (or Philips), the *Letter to the Earl of Chesterfield,* appeared in London in 1750 and was reprinted in New York in the following year. The author claimed it was an effort to set forth the whole duty of woman, inspired by a suggestion of Chesterfield's and by his authorship of the *Whole Duty of Man,*[69] but it was probably designed to blackmail the earl and other prominent men with whom her

[68] See Evans's *American Bibliography.* The first English edition recorded is that of 1743. The date of the original French edition is apparently unknown.

[69] Muilman, *Letter,* pp. 32-39. References are to the London edition.

association had been notorious. She was perhaps attempting to justify her own career when she complained of the custom which barred women from society for offenses condoned in men. Why the letter should have been reprinted in America unless Mrs. Muilman's reputation had crossed the Atlantic does not appear. In spite of her dubious character she wrote in a conservative and moral tone warning the reader against the dangers of prudery. She outlined briefly a scheme of education for her niece recommending Fénelon, Dr. Tillotson, La Bruyère and for the mature reader, the *Whole Duty of Man*.[70] The purpose of this education was to enable the girl to hold the interest of men, who never tired of " a well-taught honest mind." [71]

The *Whole Duty of Woman* by " A Lady," was in reality the work of William Kenrick and was evidently popular in America, for there were nine editions between 1761 and 1797, printed for the most part in Boston and Philadelphia.[72] Kenrick, a hack writer of London, notorious as a libeler and a drunkard, produced this slender volume of pious sentiments, a book probably chosen for young ladies by their older friends, and almost as probably neglected by the recipients. It was written in imitation of the *Economy of Human Life*,[73] more or less in the style of the book of Proverbs. Kenrick who dealt primarily with moral qualities also discussed marriage, advising a choice made for one's own happiness with parental approbation. The section on marriage ended by calling " subjection the portion of the daughters of Eve." [74] The work epitomized an extremely conservative point of view in regard to education. The author wrote:

[70] Muilman, *Letter*, pp. 29-30.
[71] *Ibid.*, p. 27.
[72] The first English edition was London, 1753.
[73] *Infra*, p. 58, note 79.
[74] Kenrick, *op. cit.*, p. 75.

Seek not to know what is improper for thee; thirst not after prohibited knowledge; for happier is she who knoweth a little, than she who is acquainted with too much. . . . It is not for thee, O woman, to undergo the perils of the deep, to dig in the hollow mines of the earth, to trace the dark springs of science, or to number the thick stars of the heavens. . . . Thy kingdom is thine own house and thy government the care of thy family.[75]

The writings of Lord Chesterfield, though read in colonial America, were hardly accepted as authoritative on women's position. His letters to his son were published in England in 1774, the first American edition five years later. In the correspondence of Abigail Adams occur several references to this book which her husband thought unworthy of a place in her library. She read it elsewhere and expressed herself most antagonistically towards the Earl whom she called " a Hypocritical polished Libertine, a mere Lovelace." [76] One American edition of the volume was bound with Dr. Gregory's *Father's Legacy to his Daughters,* an odd combination, but no doubt in the eyes of the bookseller a profitable one because of the great popularity of both works.[77] Chesterfield considered women as conveniences to men. Their society was useful to young men as a means of improving manners and acquiring polish; but though women were entertaining and sometimes even helpful in intrigue, they lacked the power of solid reasoning and the ability to act consistently. They had no passions save vanity and love and so could be easily moved through flattery of their persons. Men of sense, though pretending to take women seriously, would only trifle with them.[78] If Chesterfield was, as seems prob-

[75] Kenrick, pp. 5, 17.

[76] Adams, *Familiar Letters* (New York, 1876), pp. 143, 153; *Warren Adams Letters* (Mass. Hist. Soc., *Colls.*, 72-73), ii, 128-29.

[77] This joint edition was published in Boston, 1791.

[78] Chesterfield, *Letters* (New York, 1857), pp. 129, 137, 182, 233.

able, the author of the *Economy of Human Life* (1750), Mrs. Adams's adjective " Hypocritical " was well applied, for the *Economy* contained a collection of pious sentiments like those of Kenrick's book.[79] It was widely read; Peter Manigault of South Carolina, studying in England in 1751, sent his mother a copy calling it a book which had " made a great noise here," and the only one he had seen which he thought would please her.[80]

All these writers, whatever may have been their personal characters, stressed religion, modesty, affability, and patience as desirable qualities in women and adverted frequently to the teaching of St. Paul and St. Peter and to the description of the wise woman in the book of Proverbs. Masculine superiority they took for granted.[81]

There were five writers between 1760 and 1775 whose work on women had very definite and far-reaching American influence, and so merits detailed examination. Three were British authors, the Reverend James Fordyce, Dr. John Gregory, and Mrs. Hester Mulso Chapone. The others were Jean Jacques Rousseau and Antoine Leonard Thomas—the last known to English and American readers through the translation of his essay by William Russell.

James Fordyce, whose *Sermons to Young Women* were published in 1765, was a popular London preacher of Scottish origin, noted for his polish and pomp of style. He used as texts the description of the wise woman in the book of Proverbs, and I Timothy 2 : 9-10.[82] The English edition

[79] The *Economy* is often ascribed to Dodsley but on its authorship consult *Notes and Queries* (ser. 1), x, 8, 74, 318. For an instance of its being read by American women see *Colden Papers* (New York Historical Society, *Collections*, 1917-1923), iv, 302, letter of Elizabeth DeLancey.

[80] " Peter Manigault's Letters," Mabel L. Webber, ed., *South Carolina Historical and Genealogical Magazine*, xxxi, 270, 273-74.

[81] *Economy of Human Life*, pp. 53-57.

[82] " That women adorn themselves in modest apparel, with shamefacedness and sobriety."

was extravagantly advertised by a Boston bookseller who announced that Fordyce addressed women in sober and impartial fashion, not in flattery and admiration. To quote this strong appeal to feminine purchasers—" Happy the Mothers who follow his maxims in forming the taste and manners of their daughters! Happy thrice happy the daughters who are blessed with such mothers." [83] No reprint of the sermons appeared in America until 1787 but Fordyce's *Character and Conduct of the Female Sex*, reprinted in Boston in 1781, was probably similar. Francis Hopkinson while in England in 1766 sent a copy of the *Sermons* to his sister Ann in Philadelphia remarking that they were having a great run and as far as he had read he thought them very pretty.[84] Soon after their English publication William Strahan recommended them to David Hall, Franklin's partner.[85] It was Fordyce's *Sermons* and Mrs. Chapone's *Letters* which Lydia Languish in Sheridan's *Rivals* placed in full view while she hid her favorite novels.[86] There were three American editions before 1800.[87] The *Sermons* were filled with sentimental pictures, overdrawn even for the age in which they were written, which led Mary Wollstonecraft to suspect that their popularity exceeded their deserts.[88]

The two really practical writers of this group were Dr. John Gregory of Edinburgh and Mrs. Hester Mulso Chapone both of whom wrote for the benefit of members of their own families. Judged either from the number of American edi-

---

[83] *Boston Gazette and Country Journal*, July 13, 1767.

[84] George E. Hastings, *Life and Works of Francis Hopkinson* (Chicago, 1926), p. 141.

[85] Letter of Strahan in *Pennsylvania Magazine of Hist. and Biog.*, xiii, 484.

[86] *Sheridan's Comedies*, Brander Matthews, ed. (Boston and New York, 1891), p. 97.

[87] Evans, *American Bibliography*. In 1787, 1789 and 1796.

[88] Wollstonecraft, *A Vindication of the Rights of Woman*, chap. v, sec. 3, p. 215.

tions of his book or from references to his work by American writers, Dr. Gregory was by far the most influential writer on women.   He was a physician, who had studied at Edinburgh and Leyden, and, after a period of residence in London, returned to Aberdeen and Edinburgh.   He numbered among his friends Lord Lyttleton, Lady Mary Wortley Montagu, Lord Kames and David Hume.   He published books on the work of a physician and a comparison of men with animals, but his most famous book, *A Father's Legacy to his Daughters,* was written for the benefit of his own daughters, one of whom was, for a time, companion to Mrs. Elizabeth Montagu, the famous bluestocking leader.[89]   The book was published in England in 1774 and reprinted in Philadelphia in 1775.   Evans in his *American Bibliography* lists fifteen editions published singly and two with Chesterfield's *Letters* in the next twenty-one years.   It was included in the *Lady's Pocket Library* (1792), and in other compilations.   There was an English edition of it as late as 1877 and numerous French editions.   It was well received on both sides of the Atlantic.   Ebenezer Hazard of Philadelphia commented on it in sending Jeremy Belknap, New England clergyman, a copy for use in his own family or among girls in the parish who might need it.[90]   Selections from the book appeared in periodicals with and without acknowledgment, and an article in the *Columbian Magazine* urged that the *Legacy* be placed in the hands of every young lady.[91]   The *Christian's, Scholar's and Farmer's Magazine* reprinted nearly the whole of it and the *New York Weekly Magazine* had long selections.[92]   When Mary Wollstonecraft wrote her *Vindication*

[89] " John Gregory," *Dictionary of National Biography.*

[90] *Belknap Papers,* i, 67-68.

[91] *Columbian Magazine* (Sept., 1787), p. 645.

[92] *Christian's, Scholar's and Farmer's Magazine* (1789-91), i-ii; *New York Weekly Magazine* (1796), ii, 297, 393. Also *American Museum,* viii, 169; xi, 25-26.

of the Rights of Woman, Dr. Gregory was one of the authors whom she attacked as representative of a fallacious, though possibly well meant, system of feminine education.[93]

Mrs. Chapone whose *Letters on the Improvement of the Mind*[94] (1772), written for her niece, was a practical work, though perhaps too pious from a modern standpoint, was one of a group of English bluestockings prominent during the latter half of the century. She was a close friend of Mrs. Elizabeth Carter, the noted Greek scholar, and a member of the circle which gathered about Richardson. She wrote verses and contributed to the *Gentleman's Magazine;* but the *Letters* which were her best-known work, although they first appeared anonymously, brought her many requests from distinguished persons to undertake the training of their children. She viewed life seriously and in her treatise devoted her attention to feminine duties, to moral development, and to a proper course of reading as a means of attaining these ends. She had little time for theorizing as to women's place. For her that place was established by Scripture and social convention and she gave directions for the meeting of its obligations.[95]

Rousseau's *Émile* was first published about 1762 and, by its antagonism to women, quickly became well known in this field. It was familiar to such American writers as Benjamin Rush and Enos Hitchcock, both of whom quoted it in their works on women's education. Through its influence on the writings of Lord Kames and through the opposition it aroused in Mary Wollstonecraft it had additional trans-Atlantic repercussions. Though Rousseau thought little of

[93] *Vindication,* pp. 61-66.

[94] London, 1773. First American edition, Worcester, 1783. References here are to the edition published at Hagerstown, N. Y., 1815 (2 vols. in one).

[95] See articles on Mrs. Chapone in *Encyclopedia Britannica* (14th ed.) and *Dictionary of National Biography.*

women he found it necessary for the sake of men to give them some attention in his highly theoretical scheme. The portion of *Émile* which treated of the education of Sophie, Émile's future bride, caused much comment because of the markedly inferior sphere assigned to women.

Antoine Leonard Thomas (1732-1785), a distinguished French author, at one time director of the Académie Française, was noted as a writer of eulogies. He became interested in this form of composition and made a special study of it, entitled *L'Essai sur les éloges*. Some years before the publication of this work he abstracted from it all material pertaining to women and issued that separately, summing up what he had found written in favor of women throughout the ages, and making his own comparison of the two sexes.[96] He stated that his essay was not designed as a treatise on education but as an historical picture of women showing that they were " susceptible of all the qualities which religion, society, or government, would chuse to assign them." [97]   The work had a theoretical and mildly philosophical turn found in few writings on women. It contained an extensive list of the writings on women consulted by the author, including many French and Italian volumes which from the standpoint of American influence may be dismissed as literary curiosities. A two-volume translation and enlargement of Thomas's essay was prepared by William Russell, an English miscellaneous writer, who had for a time corrected press for William Strahan, Franklin's London correspondent. This translation was published in London in 1773 and the following year Robert Aitken, the Philadelphia publisher, brought

---

[96] Sketch of Thomas in Michaud, *Biographie Universelle.* The *Essay on Woman* was first published in Paris, 1772.

[97] *Essay on Woman*, Preface (London, 1800). The full title is *An Account of the Character, the Manners, and the Understanding of Women.*

out an American edition. The introduction to this edition, reprinted in the *Pennsylvania Magazine* in 1775 under the title, " An Occasional Letter on the Female Sex," was later erroneously attributed to Thomas Paine.[98] The book met with a favorable reception in America according to Abbé Robin who wrote that when travelling with the French army he had seen copies of it almost everywhere, even among the scattered books after the surrender at Yorktown.[99]

The first point in which it is worth while to compare the views of these five authors is that of the different spheres, which they allotted to men and women, and the feminine qualities which they admired. Fordyce and Dr. Gregory were not far apart in their views on feminine character, though the picture presented by the latter was more dignified. Fordyce believed strongly that sexual differences in character made women much inferior to men and left men bound to protect women because of their weakness. As a result, most of the qualities desirable in women were valued for their effect on men. Modesty, filial piety, and affectionate sorrow were to be cultivated for the impression made on the observer as well as for their own sakes. The possession of such traits as valor or the capacity for friendship with their own sex was in large measure denied to women; timidity and sweetness were all-important. In highly sentimental fashion Fordyce said much of women's influence over men.[100] He himself did not think that he had assigned women to a subordinate place for he felt that the destiny of the sex as mothers of rational offspring, and as companions improving the pleasures and soothing the pains of men, lightening their domestic cares and setting them at liberty for

[98] Frank Smith, " The Authorship of ' An Occasional Letter on the Female Sex,'" *American Literature* (Nov., 1930), pp. 277-80.

[99] Abbé Robin, *Nouveau Voyage* (Philadelphia, 1782), p. 142.

[100] Fordyce, *Sermons* (14th ed., 1814), i, 13-18, 25-26; ii, 174.

greater duties, was high indeed.[101]   This laudatory phraseology merely served to conceal the essential narrowness of his
point of view.

Dr. Gregory's avowed belief that women were companions and equals of men, not mere domestic drudges, seems
offhand more liberal than that of Fordyce. Gregory
thought that individual women sometimes had vast intellectual possibilities.   Nevertheless he found a great difference
between masculine and feminine characteristics and strongly
urged his daughters to develop feminine traits.[102]   His fear
was that too much individual advancement might interfere
with married happiness, the great goal for women.   Mary
Wollstonecraft accused him of insincerity, especially in his
advice on religion.[103]   He said that even irreligious men
preferred to marry pious women, though this was not his
only reason for recommending religion to his daughters; it
was desirable also as a convenient solace for the inevitable
griefs of feminine existence.[104]   Then, too, the circumstances
of women's life were more favorable to the practice of devotion than those of men.   With such views it was not surprising that the doctor laid much stress on modesty and
circumspect behavior.   Though he wished his daughters to
enjoy good health, he thought it indelicate and unfeminine
to mention the subject or to display an abundance of vital-
ity.[105]   In keeping with this atmosphere of modesty, piety,
and fragility, he pictured as his ideal woman, one who
avoided large public gatherings, and took only a passive part
in conversation, save in small groups.   All his suggestions
were in this same vein, which to a modern reader appears

[101] Fordyce, *Sermons*, i, 160.

[102] Gregory, *Father's Legacy* (New York, 1775), p. 7.

[103] Wollstonecraft, *A Vindication of the Rights of Woman* (London, 1792), pp. 61-66.

[104] Gregory, *op. cit.*, pp. 9-11, 13.

[105] Gregory, *Father's Lega y*, p. 21.

likely to cause undue self-consciousness. The doctor's continued popularity, however, attests his agreement with the standards of his time.

Crossing from England to France one finds that Rousseau, who, from his other social and political ideals, might have been expected to advocate a liberal treatment of women, was in this respect an arch-conservative and even a reactionary. Placing women intellectually on a far lower plane than either Fordyce or Dr. Gregory, he scarcely conceded to them the possibility of possessing genius or talent, quite apart from the wisdom of developing such gifts. He held in theory that the superiority of men over women was never called into question since the sexes were designed for different ends, but the result of his teachings, if put into practice, would have been almost complete subordination for women. He found women's taste sound in physical matters or those depending on the judgment of the senses but that of men preferable in matters of understanding.[106] Since there was no common standard for the sexes certain traits which were defects in men were essential in woman.[107] One must be strong, the other weak, a refined way of saying that power belonged to men.[108] By the law of nature men's obligation to please was less strong than women's. Therefore women's purpose in the world must be to render themselves agreeable to men.[109] They were to accept religion entirely on authority, either that of their parents or of their husbands; even should the faith thus accepted prove false, docility in submitting to the wills of others would take away women's errors in the eyes of God.[110] Rousseau considered the opinion of the world nearly as high a criterion of feminine conduct as religious

[106] Rousseau, *Émile* (*Emilius and Sophia*; by the translator of Eloisa, 4 vols., London, 1783), iii, 128-129.

[107] Rousseau, *Émile*, iii, 177.　　[108] *Ibid.*, iii, 163-64.

[109] *Ibid.*, iii, 165-68.　　[110] *Ibid.*, iii, 211-12.

teaching. He found the sanction for his beliefs in a purely physical basis. Marital obligations were less binding on men than on women who must preserve them in appearance as well as in fact.[111] By these doctrines he closed many intellectual and physical occupations to women, complaining that Plato in providing the same pursuits for both sexes in his ideal state had subverted the natural order.[112]

Thomas, unlike the other writers, discussed women in a philosophical fashion without giving detailed instructions for education or behavior. His account of various feminine traits was balanced by references to the corresponding qualities in men though he found the characteristics of the sexes far from identical. Women's talents were imaginative because the circumstances of their life did not give them men's opportunities of attaining a knowledge of the world. They reflected but did not create, and though love was their strongest passion, they were powerless to describe it as men had done.[113] The restraint placed on the expression of women's sentiments weakened their feelings until they could not be uttered forcibly. Women's knowledge of mankind and of character, gained through observation of society, enabled them to manage lesser passions easily but in the government of nations where great views and the choice of principles were necessary men were more expert because of their wider knowledge of the world. A few women had proved themselves excellent rulers but even the brilliant reign of Queen Elizabeth had showed traces of femininity.[114] In general women's minds were more pleasing than strong; it was questionable whether they had the continuous attention needed for serious learning. This quality of concentration,

111 *Émile*, iii, 170-73.
112 *Ibid.*, iii, 175-76.
113 Thomas, *Essay on Woman* (London, 1800), pp. 111-16.
114 *Ibid.*, pp. 119-25.

rare in men, was perhaps never found in women, though in mere memory the sexes were equal.[115] Women surpassed men in religious virtues because of their deeper sensibility, stronger longing for another world, and greater docility in the performance of their duties; or because of the close alliance of religious and domestic responsibilities.[116] Since their minds were narrower in interests and less adapted for the general love of mankind women were not so capable of friendship as men; one man was more to a woman than a nation.[117] Thomas's final pronouncement was that only one who combined the physician, the anatomist, and the philosopher, and was at the same time impartial, was competent to pass judgment on the superiority of either sex.[118]

The work of the one woman writer of this group, Mrs. Chapone, was significant more for its educational plans than for theories on women's place. She presented quite unlike concepts of the ordinary duties of the sexes. Whatever she thought of women's potential abilities she did not feel that the average woman needed an education as extensive as that of most men—a fact which is of peculiar interest in view of the circle of highly educated women in which she herself moved. The position which she assumed for her sex was one of some dignity for she attacked affectation and over-emotionalism, chiefly on moral grounds. She made a careful distinction between the active fortitude desirable in men and the passive courage which women ought to display in daily life.[119]

[115] Thomas, *Essay on Woman*, pp. 110-11, 117.

[116] *Ibid.*, pp. 128-34.

[117] *Ibid.*, pp. 135, 144-47. Thomas stated that he was quoting from Montaigne.

[118] Thomas, *op. cit.*, p. 158.

[119] Chapone, *Letters on the Improvement of the Mind* (Hagerstown, 1815), p. 80.

After a writer had formulated his ideas of the respective spheres of the sexes he naturally developed the plan for the education of women which would best carry these ideas into practice. The minor writers, mentioned at the beginning of this section, had not denied women all opportunity for learning though in general they offered only conventional catalogues of studies and accomplishments. Their whole theory regarding women was such as to exclude the notion of advanced study. Kenrick discouraged the idea of much knowledge in women and Chesterfield used the term " learned woman " as a reproach.[120] Mrs. Muilman and the Abbé d'Ancourt suggested little not already found in the pages of Fénelon and the Marquise de Lambert. To the important writers, however, feminine education was more than a list of studies.

The bulk of Rousseau's work on education dealt with men but he outlined the training necessary to make women effective subordinates. The prevailing faults of feminine education he laid at the door of the mothers for no one interfered with their bringing up their daughters as they chose. His interest in the matter came from the necessity of entrusting the early part of masculine education to women, who must therefore possess some knowledge. The duty on which he felt most strongly was the physical care of infants which, he thought, should be performed by the mother herself and not by a hired wet-nurse.[121] According to Rousseau, there were two reasons for making women's education relative to that of men; first, that the constitutions of children depended on those of their mothers and second, that men's tastes and pleasures were largely derived from women. This meant a training far from identical for the two sexes. The more women were educated like men, the less power

[120] Chesterfield, *Letters*, p. 257.
[121] Rousseau, *Émile*, i, 2 note, 22-27.

they had over men.[122]   The important factor in the training of men was independent thought, in that of women reliance on public opinion.[123]

To please, to be useful to us, to make us love and esteem them, to educate us, when young, and take care of us when grown up, to advise, to console us, to render our lives easy and agreeable; these are the duties of women at all times, and what they should be taught in their infancy.[124]

Girls should be taught to bear restraint in order to render them tractable throughout life since they were continually in subjection either to one man or to the opinions of mankind. Desirable feminine qualities were therefore sweetness of temper and ability to bear injustice and even insult from a husband.   Perverseness and ill nature in women merely aggravated their misfortunes.[125]   Young girls should be governed in their ideas of good and evil entirely by those about them but might be permitted to escape obedience through artifice, a practice useful to them later in life.[126]   Afterwards they should be taught to depend on innate sentiment and on the opinion of the world.[127]   Women should learn something of the rules of society; this would aid them in meriting masculine esteem.[128]   Abstract truths and principles of science were not for feminine study; neither was anything else which tended to generalize their ideas.   Women had neither the possibility of genius nor the power needed for the study of science.[129]   They must not set themselves up as literary

[122] Rousseau, *Émile*, iii, 177-78.

[123] *Ibid.*, iii, 180.

[124] *Ibid.*, iii, 181.

[125] *Ibid.*, iii, 191-94.

[126] *Ibid.*, iii, 195-97.

[127] *Ibid.*, iii, 221-22.

[128] *Ibid.*, iii, 224.

[129] Rousseau, *Émile*, iii, 233.

critics.[130]   Their training should be threefold, to fulfill immediate duties, to study men, and to perfect themselves in the lighter accomplishments.   There was no reason why they should not continue these accomplishments after marriage, thereby adding to the pleasures of their husbands.

Fordyce, like Rousseau, believed that women had, as a rule, less mental vigor than men so that they were not ordinarily competent to venture into broad fields of learning.   Masculine women rashly pleading for a share in science and philosophy simply did not understand their own true interests, for those who pursued learning would lose in softness what they gained in force.[131]   If women sincerely wished to read and study it was their own fault, and not men's, that they failed to utilize their opportunities.[132]   A real genius might undertake the severer studies to any prudent length but even so she was bound by many limitations which did not affect the other sex.[133]   Fordyce warned against the character of the "learned lady" but admitted that it was rare in women.[134] In spite of the danger he thought that intellectual accomplishments were useful in excluding many temptations and that a proper use of mental attainments enabled women to appear to advantage in society and added to their happiness in life.[135] Like most moral writers Fordyce condemned conventional social life and fashionable boarding schools as turning feminine energy to the wrong ends; but except for additional stress on domestic duties his own recommendations did not differ greatly from the courses offered in such schools.

[130] *Émile*, iii, 128-29.

[131] Fordyce, *Sermons*, i, 210-11, 220, 231.   Compare the character of Mrs. Selwyn in Fanny Burney's *Evelina* with Fordyce's picture of the " learned lady."

[132] *Ibid.*, i, 223.

[133] *Ibid.*, i, 220.

[134] *Ibid.*, i, 19, 220, 231.

[135] Fordyce, *Sermons*, i, 220.

Appropriate studies for women were the attractive accomplishments which led to matrimony and the lighter and more polished branches of knowledge, which they needed since their talents were not argumentative but sentimental. For serious reading Fordyce offered the usual suggestions.[136] In lighter literature he praised Richardson's work, especially the character of Clarissa whom he regarded as perfect in every particular but one, probably her first clandestine correspondence with Lovelace. Few novels by other writers were safe to read; the older type of extravagant romance was less dangerous than the novel of the day but the taste for works of imagination could best be gratified by select dramatic readings, poetry and fables. The *Spectator* was excellent for feminine perusal.[137]

Much of Fordyce's advice lacked originality; he had evidently rummaged in the works of earlier writers before preparing his sermons. His remarks on dress and cleanliness might easily have been drawn from Swift and the writers of the *Spectator;* his opinions on feminine friendships from Montaigne.[138] The paragraphs in which he questioned women's ability to attain the same intellectual development as men and those in which he blamed them for their own ignorance were reminiscent of Rousseau's work.[139] His observations on female pedantry as the result of too little learning suggested Swift's comment on women's knowledge.[140]

Fordyce, as a popular preacher, prepared his work for a large audience. Dr. Gregory, on the other hand, wrote primarily for his own daughters and treated their problems in a more personal way. His attitude on study was rather two-

[136] Fordyce, i, 212-14.   [137] *Ibid.*, i, 215-17.

[138] Compare Thomas, *Essay on Woman*, pp. 135-39.

[139] *Émile*, iii, 233-34 and Fordyce, *Sermons*, i, 211-12, 220; *Émile*, iii, 177 and *Sermons*, i, 223-24.

[140] Fordyce, *Sermons*, i, 232; Swift, "Letter to a Very Young Lady."

faced.   He did not think advanced work beyond their ability, but he questioned the wisdom of exerting that ability.   He did not object to serious reading for a girl who had a natural bent in that direction but if she lacked such inclination he would not urge upon her an interest which might prove embarrassing.   He begged his daughters not to display their good sense or any learning they might have, certainly not to men, lest they suffer for it.   Most men were jealous of feminine learning; those who were not would give women credit for more knowledge than they possessed if the discovery of it were accidental.[141]   His daughters were of course to avoid all books and conversation which tended to shake their religious faith, but with that caution observed there was no impropriety in their reading history or cultivating any art or science to which they were inclined.[142]

There were at this time a number of brilliant women in England among whom were Elizabeth Robinson Montagu, Mrs. Elizabeth Carter, poet and translator of Epictetus, Mrs. Vesey who held literary salons in London, Miss Talbot, Mrs. Chapone and others.   Some of these women were noted as leaders of educated society, others as scholars.   At a later period, Hannah More and Fanny Burney were members of the circle.   Though many of the women carried on extensive correspondence, only the literary work of Mrs. More, Miss Burney, and Madame Chapone had much influence in America.   All these women had a social standing which should have rendered unimportant any attacks on them as "learned ladies."[143]   In spite of the character of

---

[141] Gregory, *Father's Legacy*, pp. 15-16.

[142] Gregory, *Father's Legacy*, p. 22.

[143] *Letters from Mrs. Elizabeth Carter to Mrs. Montagu* (3 vols., London, 1817), and *A Series of Letters between Mrs. Elizabeth Carter and Miss Catherine Talbot* (3rd ed., 3 vols., London, 1819), picture the activities of these women.

this group in which Mrs. Chapone moved she reserved extended learning, especially in the classical languages, for women of genius. Her objections to such studies were the disproportionate amount of time they consumed and the risk of pedantry they involved.[144] She believed in a sound moral and practical education for girls of ordinary ability which was to be obtained principally through well directed and systematic reading of the Bible and through a carefully prescribed course of history, both of which she outlined in detail. Her directions were on the whole sensible for she began Bible study with New Testament precepts and Old Testament history and deferred the study of the prophecies and the book of Revelation until the student had reached maturity.[145] In history also Mrs. Chapone laid out a course, naming specific text books and chronologies.[146] For general reading she recommended the poetry of Shakespeare, Milton, Homer, and Virgil, and the moral philosophy of the *Spectator* with other periodical essays, but she urged that any fiction read be chosen with extreme care.[147] She assumed that her niece would study French, an agreeable language containing many worthwhile books, and she mentioned Italian as a suitable study for any who found it interesting.[148] Outside the realm of books she made fewer suggestions although she remarked that the study of nature was pleasant and ennobling and that dancing was a useful social accomplishment.[149]

Thomas did not think women incapable of learning sufficient for everyday purposes, whatever might be true in fields

[144] Chapone, *Letters*, p. 195.

[145] Chapone, *Letters*, i-iii.

[146] *Ibid.* The chronologies recommended were those by Du Fresnay and Priestley. For text books see letters ix and x.

[147] *Ibid.*, pp. 199-201.

[148] *Ibid.*, p. 193.

[149] *Ibid.*, pp. 192, 204.

demanding advanced research, but he believed that many women failed to realize their own intellectual possibilities. Those who did acquire any knowledge did so as an ornament to their own wit, or from a desire to please others and not for self-instruction.[150] If ignorance in women had ever been desirable in the time of the world's first innocence, which was doubtful, it was so no longer. Women must now be educated to take a place in society and to protect themselves. Molière's *Femmes Savantes* though useful in ridiculing feminine follies was unjust in not comparing its shallow heroines with women of sense and proper education.[151] There were still women in the world who joined a strong mind to a cultivated understanding and were charitable and affectionate wives and mothers. Thomas drew an attractive picture of such a polished and modest woman, saying that if all women returned to a life of virtue the sex would regain its lost empire.[152]

When they came to discuss the question of marriage, most writers allowed the lady the privilege of refusing a suitor who was not personally agreeable to her though the more conservative left the choice of candidates to her relatives.[153] Mrs. Chapone, who thought that the final choice should rest with the woman, believed that parents should begin negotiations for marriage. She wished selections made on practical grounds; though she disapproved marriages based on mercenary considerations, she thought personal liking an insufficient foundation. There must be parental approbation in order to secure the divine blessing without which no marriage could be happy. Both she and Dr. Gregory, though deprecating the single life, pointed out that it had

150 Thomas, *Essay on Woman*, p. 204.

151 *Ibid.*, pp. 176-81.

152 *Ibid.*, pp. 181, 210-13.

153 Kenrick, *Whole Duty of Woman*, pp. 67-70. D'Ancourt.

many compensations and could be a position of dignity and respect, much worthier than an unhappy marriage.[154] Dr. Gregory's view of marriage, like Mrs. Chapone's, was practical rather than romantic. It was rare in his opinion that women married for love. Love ought to result entirely from the man's attachment to the woman, for nature had given women greater flexibility of taste in this matter than men. "A man of taste and delicacy marries a woman because he loves her more than any other. A woman of equal taste and delicacy marries him because she esteems him and because he gives her that preference." [155] It was grossly indelicate for women to believe it essential to their happiness to be married, yet the married state was much the happiest in life. Dr. Gregory permitted his daughters to choose their own husbands and devoted a part of his book to directions for their guidance in this choice.[156]

Fordyce, too, thought women should and usually did have the right of choosing their husbands. He warned his readers against associating with men of unknown character or those who were the companions of infamous women. In common with almost every other writer he pointed out that reformed rakes did not make the best husbands, a saying which must have enjoyed wide currency from the pains taken to refute it.[157] He thought women should avail themselves of every decent attraction leading to matrimony, the state for which they were manifestly designed.[158] They should avoid a gay and dissipated way of life which made it harder for them to settle down after marriage.[159] They were

[154] Chapone, *Letters*, p. 119; Gregory, *Father's Legacy*, p. 38.

[155] Gregory, *op. cit.*, pp. 31-40.

[156] *Ibid.*, pp. 30-31.

[157] Fordyce, *Sermons*, i, 102-104.

[158] *Ibid.*, i, 3.

[159] *Ibid.*, i, 104-110.

always to submit to harsh or unreasonable parents except in rare cases when the latter tried to force their daughters into marriage with men whom they could not love.[160]   Fordyce believed that most ill treatment of wives by their husbands was really the fault of the ladies themselves who should have behaved more gently and tolerantly.   The wife ought to study her husband's humors and overlook his mistakes. Fordyce would not absolutely exonerate men for grave delinquencies but surely women must have provoked them to such conduct,[161] a belief which Mary Wollstonecraft attacked most vehemently.[162]

In statements such as these one sees most clearly the difference between eighteenth and twentieth-century standards of marriage and of women's position.   Economically and socially, marriage at this period was almost forced upon women.   If they failed to marry they remained dependents in the homes of relatives and were persons of little importance to society.   Women had relatively fewer opportunities for making social contacts than did men.   Hence many persons thought it better for women to marry men whom they respected and who offered them economic security than to wait for the possible chance of romantic love.

Rousseau in spite of the subordinate rank which he assigned to women had liberal ideas on choice in marriage. He thought that young people should make their own selections on the basis of mutual attachment; this must be done with discernment and some respect to financial condition. They should reverse the customary French procedure by making their own choice but consulting their parents.[163] If there were any question of inequality in rank it was better

160 Fordyce, ii, 148.

161 *Ibid.*, ii, 208.

162 Wollstonecraft, *Vindication*, chap. v, sec. ii, pp. 206-14.

163 Rousseau, *Émile*, iii, 267.

for the man to marry beneath him since he raised his wife to his own state.[164] Rousseau wished to alter existing practice in another particular and allow women more freedom before than after marriage, since if they knew something of the world they would be less averse to giving it up.[165] He believed that married women should live almost as much like recluses in their homes as did nuns in a convent.[166]

With the work of the didactic writers on women that of Fanny Burney may well be considered. Miss Burney's *Evelina* presented a young lady who in most ways would have delighted Dr. Gregory and Mrs. Chapone. She was educated in retirement and when introduced to society at seventeen displayed "a virtuous mind, a cultivated understanding and a feeling heart." Though few details of her education were given it was described as excellent and designed to fit her for a quiet country life. Her chaperone, Mrs. Selwyn, a lady of intellectual attainments, was criticized as having lost the softness of her own sex in acquiring the knowledge of the other. Evelina's French grandmother, a most objectionable character, exhibited the easy manners attributed to her race. Evelina herself formed a decided contrast to most of the young ladies she met in London and Bath. The languid young lady of fashion was ridiculed as were Evelina's middle-class cousins with their aspirations towards a social life of whose usages they were ignorant. Propriety, strict attention to reputation, and gentleness were called the essentials of feminine character. Evelina took part in the amusements of the time though some of the most fashionable had little appeal for her. She enjoyed the theatre but remarked of Congreve's *Love for Love* that Angelica

[164] *Émile*, iii, 284.

[165] Some French travellers in America during the Revolution thought that this was the case in America. See chap. ix.

[166] Rousseau, *Émile*, iii, 236.

was the only character worthy of being mentioned to ladies and that even she bestowed her hand like a benefactress not a mistress.

Evelina formed an exception to the usual ban on novels. Miss Burney pointed out to possible critics that since the taste for novel reading existed it was wiser to encourage those which could be read without injury, if not to advantage. The book had a most favorable reception in England. In America it was perhaps slower in making its way. The first English edition was in 1778; four years later *Evelina* was casually mentioned in the diary of a Virginia girl;[167] in 1787 it was advertised in a New Haven paper as just imported.[168] John Quincy Adams read *Cecilia*, Miss Burney's second novel, in Newburyport, Massachusetts in 1788 though the earliest American editions of that and of *Evelina* were in 1793.[169] There were other editions of the latter in 1796 and 1797.[170] In 1797 *Camilla* was unfavorably compared with the author's other works in a way which suggested that they were widely read here.[171]   Miss Burney's influence on American ideas, however, must have come chiefly in the last decade of the century and afterwards.

[167] Emily Mason, *Diary of a Young Lady of Virginia*, p. 25.

[168] *The New Haven Gazette and Connecticut Magazine*, May 24, 1787.

[169] John Quincy Adams, *Life in a New England Town* (Boston, 1903), p. 79.

[170] The 1793 edition was published in Philadelphia, that of 1796 in Worcester, and that of 1797 in New York. See Evans, *American Bibliography*.

[171] *Huntington Letters*, ed. William McCrackan (New York, 1897), p. 143. Letter of Rachel Huntington.

CHAPTER III

European Influence after the Revolution

British influence on America, in matters intellectual, by no means ceased with the Revolution though there was a brief lull in American reprints and in importation of books.[1] In the field of women's interests the popularity of English works was, if anything, rather intensified in the 1780's and 1790's. Of the dozen or more English and French writers on women whose works were available here in those decades, only a few exerted marked influence on American thought. Prominent among them were Hannah More, Madame de Genlis, Mary Wollstonecraft, and Lord Kames, whose names appeared frequently in the pages of Benjamin Rush and Enos Hitchcock;[2] their opinions were cited freely in letters and comments on women. Mary Wollstonecraft was more often regarded with fear and distrust than with approbation but the other three were treated as authorities on female character and education.[3] Other writers in the field whose books were reprinted in America made less impression.[4] Some names like those of Mrs. Trimmer and Mrs. Barbauld are omitted here, although they had already begun to publish their work,

[1] Evans lists no reprints of works on women between 1775 and 1782 except for some editions of Gregory's *Father's Legacy*.

[2] Two leading American writers on women. See chap. v.

[3] Works of Hannah More and Madame de Genlis read in boyhood inspired *Peter Parley* (Samuel G. Goodrich) with the idea of his later writings. *Recollections of a Lifetime* (2 vols., New York, 1857), i, 171-72.

[4] Among them were John Bennett, John Burton, Boudier de Villermert, etc.

because their great influence in America came after 1800 and hence lies beyond the scope of this study.

Mrs. Hannah More, as she called herself, was an English religious writer and practical philanthropist, who, in her younger days, was noted as a poet and a wit in the circle of Reynolds, Johnson and Garrick. She had been a teacher but upon receiving an annuity from a fiancé whom she did not marry moved to London where she devoted herself to literary work. There was a gradual transition from her composition of verses and pastoral plays to a more serious type of writing in which her views on the education and duties of women occupied a large place. Her influence on standards for women reached its peak in the nineteenth century when she was, for some years, virtual arbitress on feminine duties. In the 1830's Harriet Martineau remarked that Mrs. More's works were even better known than the plays of Shakespeare to the majority of the people of America.[5] Her poetical work was published here at an early date and attracted much attention, her new books being read in American cities soon after their appearance in England. It would appear that her ideas on feminine training were at first less popular than her other work since *The Essays for Young Ladies* were not printed in Philadelphia until 1786, nine years after their first English publication. They doubtless gained wider publicity in later years through their inclusion in the *Lady's Pocket Library*.[6] They were a forerunner of the ideas on women's education which Mrs. More developed so elaborately later in the *Strictures on Female Education* and *Hints for the Education of a Young Princess*. In essence, however, her theories remained the same though her plans for the education of women grew more extensive.

[5] Martineau, *Society in America* (3rd ed., New York, 1837), ii, 310.

[6] In 1792.

The beliefs expressed in Mrs. More's *Essays* were in some ways almost reactionary and did not serve to enlarge the sphere open to women. In them, she emphasized strongly the difference between masculine and feminine character—a difference which she felt could not be too nicely maintained. The peculiar qualities of each sex ceased to be meritorious when appropriated by the other so that women never understood their own interests so little as when they affected masculine traits. Men were framed for public exhibition in the theatre of human life but women for a more retired existence as truly in intellectual as in other pursuits. The female mind did not, as a rule, seem capable of attaining as high a degree of perfection as the male.[7] Women excelled in imagination and taste but not in the abstruser works of literature. Although this position of Hannah More's was hardly advanced, in some ways she presented a dignified view of women's sphere. In her remarks on conversation she attacked the advice given to young women to conceal learning which they might possess.[8] Such an attitude was, she thought, neither reasonable nor proper. A discreet young lady would never make an ostentatious display of learning because she would be too intent on acquiring more knowledge. Moreover since women exhibited their lighter social accomplishments freely, why should they not display piety and knowledge?[9]

Madame de Genlis, member of the French nobility, whose position in the field of education was in some respects comparable to that held by Mrs. More, was governess to the children of the Duc de Chartres and wrote several books for the use of her pupils in which she anticipated many modern

[7] More, *Works* (Harper, New York, 1835), ii, 550-51.

[8] This was evidently a reference to Dr. Gregory's work although his name was not mentioned. See Gregory, *Father's Legacy*, p. 15.

[9] More, *Works*, ii, 555.

methods of teaching.   She was a most prolific writer, producing more than eighty volumes.   Her rank in society helped to make her books widely known and most of them were translated into English as soon as they appeared.   A great part of her work consisted of tales, plays and dialogues designed to afford moral and other instruction to the young. Any of her dozens of volumes afforded suggestions to those engaged in educational theorizing but her ideas were epitomized in a work entitled *Adèle et Théodore, ou lettres sur l'éducation* (1782),[10] in which through a narrative in the form of letters she outlined a plan for the education of young persons of both sexes, and of princes.   Only her views on the education of girls need be considered here.

It is interesting to compare the ideas of Hannah More and of Madame de Genlis.   Like Mrs. More, Madame de Genlis was much impressed with the importance of sex distinctions and warned persons engaged in educating women to be extremely careful not to inflame feminine minds or to raise them above themselves since women were born for a dependent situation.   For their duties in life women needed mildness, method, patience, prudence, sensibility, a just way of reasoning, and a general knowledge of affairs; their education should also provide them with resources against idleness.[11] Genius, a useless and dangerous gift for women, served merely to lift them out of their proper sphere and take them from domestic employments and the care of their children.[12] Propriety was women's special field; through its cultivation and the desire to please engendered in them by dependence, sentiment, and interest,[13] women excelled men in delicacy. Hannah More's work, at this date, was very general but

[10] English translation, 3rd ed., 3 vols., London, 1788.
[11] Compare More, *Works*, ii, 552.
[12] Genlis, *Adèle et Théodore*, i, 33.
[13] Genlis, *Le petit La Bruyère* (*Works*, Paris, 1825), p. 279.

Madame de Genlis had specific suggestions to offer. Her aims in education were to prepare women to converse with propriety on all subjects, to train them in all the accomplishments which could render them pleasing, and to develop in them a taste for reading and reflection without displaying this knowledge.[14] Accomplishments were to be taught early but reading of a weighty nature must not come too soon. Madame de Genlis believed in indirect instruction, through games, gardening, and through a judicious choice of servants and surroundings.[15] The young lady's use of her time was minutely regulated, a practice which Mrs. More also strongly recommended in her later works. Such regulation was not merely to avoid the evils of unfilled leisure but to fulfill a divine command, for every moment was a gift of God, to whom the possessor was accountable for its use. Reading of foreign languages and making extracts from books written in them had a large place in the daily program. Madame de Genlis outlined an elaborate course of reading designed to cover a period of years. Most of the authors on her list were French; among the English names were Defoe, Richardson, Mrs. Macaulay, and Hume.[16]

In *Adèle et Théodore*, Madame de Genlis made extended use of the work of earlier writers in her field. She recommended Fénelon's *L'Éducation des filles* which she thought valuable in the treatment of particular faults like carelessness;[17] his plan for the instruction of girls in the rudiments of law she also adopted.[18] She advised Madame de Sévigné's letters for the perusal of the young girl, and gave quotations from the Marquise de Lambert.[19] Chesterfield's remarks on women, she disliked, but admitted that his letters con-

---

[14] Genlis, *Adèle*, i, 33.
[16] *Ibid.*, iii, 284-86.
[18] *Ibid.*, iii, 157-58.

[15] *Ibid.*, i, 36-37; 50-51.
[17] Genlis, *Adèle*, ii, 88.
[19] *Ibid.*, i, 305; iii, 122.

tained some excellent observations on manners.[20] Except
for Richardson's novels she knew of none which contained
any morality,[21] and she condemned Voltaire's criticism of
Clarissa as arising from jealousy.[22] Of Rousseau she had
much to say which was not wholly flattering, and observed
that many of his best ideas were borrowed from Fénelon.[23]
In the matter of children's health she was inclined to follow
Rousseau's advice and that of Locke; [24] but in most respects
she was ready to argue with Rousseau. His encouragement
of artifice in women, she thought wrong, believing that nothing should be depended upon but the constant practice of
virtue.[25] In her eyes *Émile* owed its success to the enthusiastic praises of the ladies, yet no author treated women with
less respect. Rousseau denied them genius, he accused them
of deceit and coquetry, he loved but did not esteem them.
Love, apparently, served to excuse everything to the ladies.[26]

It was not only feminine writers who expressed opinions
on educational theory. Any discussion of this must include
the writing of Henry Home, Lord Kames, a Scotch lawyer
and philosopher, whose contributions were popular when
they appeared but, at least in regard to women's education,
were much overrated. If Kames's admirers had taken the
trouble to check the portion of his work on women, page for
page with *Émile,* they would have found some surprising
similarities. He himself admitted his indebtedness to
Rousseau. *Émile,* he said, was suggestive in spite of its
imperfections and was certainly superior to the other works
available on women's training. He did not like *L'Éducation
des filles* which he thought incorrectly attributed to Fénelon.
His particular dislike for this work arose from Fenelon's

---

[20] Genlis, *Adèle*, i, 149.　　　[21] *Ibid.*, i, 217.
[22] Genlis, *Le petit La Bruyère*, p. 312 *et seq.*
[23] Genlis, *Adèle*, i, 116, note.　　　[24] *Ibid.*, i, 57-58.
[25] *Ibid.*, i, 33.　　　[26] *Ibid.*, i, 118.

statement that the brain was soft in infancy and hence easily responsive to proper impressions which seemed to Lord Kames to reduce a man to a mere machine.[27] He said much of the dignity of women's vocation in the education of the young and wished to make them more widely conscious of this. For this purpose a knowledge of human nature seemed to him more important in feminine education than accomplishments.[28] His statements on this point had some value though on most topics he merely paralleled Rousseau.[29] In preparing girls for marriage Kames believed that one should restrain the development of the animal appetites as long as possible. Therefore he wished girls to be taught that marriage was a hazardous step and that the life of a single lady might be both respected and useful; but these teachings were to be used as deterrents to passion, not as real obstacles to marriage.[30]

In 1792, Mary Wollstonecraft's *A Vindication of the Rights of Woman* appeared in Boston and Philadelphia immediately following its British publication. This work was anathema to the English group of which Mrs. More was a member and to many readers in this country; its unpopularity continued well on into the nineteenth century. Partly because of the criticism it aroused, the book should not be overlooked in any study of women's status. By the law of opposites, it may have been responsible for the growing

---

[27] Kames, *Loose Hints Upon Education* (Edinburgh, 1781), pp. 27-29.

[28] *Ibid.*, p. 10.

[29] Compare condemnation of convent training, Rousseau, iii, 238; Kames, 139; health, Rousseau, iii, 180-81; Kames, 137; need for reputation as well as fact of virtue in women, Rousseau, iii, 172-3; Kames, 136; importance of training women in restraint, Rousseau, iii, 192-95; Kames, 136-37; dependence of women on opinion, Rousseau, iii, 180, 221; Kames, 135-36; early sexual differences shown in the choice of toys, Rousseau, iii, 182-89; Kames, 133-34; etc.

[30] Kames, *op. cit.*, sec. viii, and p. 221.

success of smug works like those of Mrs. More which urged women to stay in the place, "to which it had pleased God to call them," and not wander in quest of rights of which they had no need. Mrs. More's works were regarded as defenses of the established position of the sex, and as much needed social and religious bulwarks of the country. Mary Wollstonecraft's *Vindication,* despite its greater clarity of thought, was treated as an argument for deism, an attack on marriage and a means of spreading French Revolutionary ideas.[81] Part of this arose no doubt from the personal history of Mrs. Wollstonecraft which was generally regarded as scandalous and which had certainly affected her views on the position of women. Forced by circumstances to earn her own living, she had tried her hand at both teaching and writing and had reason to appreciate the drawbacks of a social and economic order which made no provision for the independent woman. The friendships she formed in London were among advanced thinkers, some of whose ideas she shared. While in France studying the progress of the Revolution she formed a connection with Gilbert Imlay, in which she regarded herself and was considered by him, for a time at least, as his wife. Imlay left her, and she later lived with William Godwin whose disbelief in the institution of marriage prevented their having a ceremony performed for some months. Not wishing to jeopardize the future of their infant, they were married a few months before the birth of a daughter, later the wife of the poet Shelley, but the mother did not long survive the birth of the child. Such a career as Mary Wollstonecraft's is of course open to more than one interpretation and those who were opposed to any of her ideas did not hesitate to

[81] For American expressions of such opinion see *Columbian Phenix,* i, 112; T. G. Fessenden, *The Ladies Monitor,* p. 59; David Ramsay, *Memoirs of Martha Laurens Ramsay* (3rd ed.), p. 45 note; Hubbard Winslow, *Woman as She Should Be,* pp. 23-25. These represent the extreme view taken after 1800.

ascribe the worst possible motives and conduct to her. In point of fact, the *Vindication* did not attack either marriage as an institution or belief in God though some remarks made by critics would lead one to think so. Mary Wollstonecraft was deeply religious, though not in a conventional way. She wrote as a woman who knew the facts confronting those of her own sex who were forced to fend for themselves, and she was thoroughly cognizant of the usual drawbacks of feminine education.[32]

The years preceding the publication of the *Vindication* were marked by serious interest in women's place—in England, France and America. The principal English books have already been discussed. French opinion ranged from the extreme conservatism of Rousseau to the liberal ideas of Condorcet who undoubtedly influenced Mrs. Wollstonecraft although his views produced no immediate response in America. On this side of the Atlantic, interest centered in the theory and practice of women's education, with occasional suggestions of the need for greater legal or political rights. After 1792, whether as a result of the emotion aroused by the *Vindication* or as a reaction against the French Revolution, most writings on women became conservative, though a few liberals like Charles Brockden Brown repeated the sentiments of Mary Wollstonecraft. There was an increase in facilities for feminine education but the possibility of greater freedom for women in other ways was temporarily forgotten. Indeed, the next widespread development of feminine interests, that of the charitable societies, was definitely conservative and under the direction of the clergy. Oddly enough, the first American reactions to the *Vindication* were not so unfavorable as those which came later.

[32] For an interesting account of her influence see Marthe Severn Storr, *Mary Wollstonecraft et le mouvement féministe dans la littérature Anglaise* (Paris, 1931). A favorable study.

Ezra Stiles, president of Yale, in his diary, referred to the book with no comment either for or against, and subjoined an account of the writer's life given by a woman who knew her.[33] One of the pupils at a public program at a school for girls in Philadelphia spoke of Mrs. Wollstonecraft as one who had asserted and vindicated the rights of her sex.[34]

The underlying theory of Mary Wollstonecraft's book is indicated in the introduction. The education of women, she wrote, had hitherto been planned by men who considered their subjects as women rather than as human beings. This error she hoped to rectify and addressed herself to middle class, instead of upper class, women, for in the former group lay more hope of results. In appealing to them openly and not pretending to address women in high society, she showed greater frankness than her predecessors.[35] She designed her book to show how the prevailing evils of feminine life might be remedied through proper education. Most earlier works dealing with women's training had been only systems of reading prefaced by a few moral remarks and characterized by subserviency to the established order of things. Few, if any, were as philosophical as the *Vindication* or attempted to reason out women's status in as clear a fashion. Mary Wollstonecraft was explicitly critical of other authors in her field, and quite familiar with their works.[36] She began her study with Rousseau's theories of the structure of society but though she admired much of his political philosophy she was far from agreeing with his theories of women. She attacked his plan for the education of Sophie because it made obedience the primary lesson of feminine character. The

[33] Stiles, *Literary Diary*, iii, 502-03.

[34] James Neal, *Essay on the Education and Genius of the Female Sex* (Philadelphia, 1795), p. 17.

[35] *Vindication* (London, 1792), p. 3, Introduction.

[36] *Vindication*, chap. v.

whole object of women's education, according to Rousseau, was to render them pleasing to men, which seemed to Mrs. Wollstonecraft a system suited to the body only. To teach the arts of a mistress in order to make women good wives was a fallacious method of procedure. She thought, with Madame de Genlis, that most women forgave Rousseau his ideas because of his susceptibility to their charms.[37] She was equally critical of other writers. Dr. Gregory's affection for his daughters and the motives from which he wrote, she respected, but she thought his work showed dissimulation and affectation in making marriage the sole end of women's education and existence.[38] Gregory's rules on behavior began at the wrong end and worked from public opinion back to conduct.[39] Mrs. Piozzi she found very wrong in saying that all feminine arts were employed to gain and keep the heart of man. To Mary Wollstonecraft such a saying was an affront to the understanding of the whole sex.[40] She was particularly scornful of Dr. Fordyce whom she thought voluptuous and affected.[41] She admitted that Madame de Genlis offered some useful hints but thought her blind submission to authority often ignored justice.[42] Mrs. Chapone, she respected, although there were points in which they disagreed, and she paid tribute to Mrs. Macaulay's judgment and literary ability. She disliked Lord Chesterfield's letters, less for their attitude towards women than for the early knowledge of the world which they afforded—a knowledge which she thought better attained by slow experience.[43]

[37] *Vindication*, p. 54 and chap. v, sec. 1, pp. 170-206.

[38] *Ibid.*, pp. 61, 66.

[39] *Ibid.*, chap. v, sec. 3, pp. 215-224.

[40] *Ibid.*, chap. v, sec. 4, p. 228.

[41] *Ibid.*, chap. v, sec. 2, pp. 206-214.

[42] *Ibid.*, chap. v, sec. 4, pp. 232-34.

[43] *Ibid.*, chap. v, sec. 5, pp. 234-36.

The end of education, according to Mrs. Wollstonecraft, was to develop one's character as a human being—to produce strength of mind and body, regardless of distinctions of sex.[44] Men complained, and with justice, of the follies of women which were in reality due to ignorance; these follies must be overcome by early education and by the development of reasoning power.[45]   Unlike most earlier writers Mrs. Wollstonecraft stressed physical development, saying that those girls often did best who ran wild.   Under the prevailing system of training, women wasted their time in acquiring a smattering of accomplishments with resultant loss of strength of mind or body.[46]   The methods then in vogue made girls either " fine ladies " or " notable women; " the former were romantic and oversensitive and the latter, though they had good sense and were useful, did not possess greatness of mind or taste.   For a well-rounded life girls should be taught the performance of domestic duties and trained to appreciate the right pleasures.   Since general cultivation of mind was needed for the successful management of a family, literature had a definite place in the feminine curriculum.   It was better to read novels than no books at all though there was a distinct danger of sentimentalism from the perusal of too many.[47]   Mary Wollstonecraft disapproved differentiation in the early education of the two sexes for though women's duties might differ from men's, both sexes were human and their training should start from the same point.   She advocated a system of national coeducation in which boys and girls should be taught together in early life, receiving later separate instruction for specialized careers.   This system, which Condorcet championed, Mary Wollstonecraft hoped to see established in France as a result of the Revolution.[48]

[44] *Vindication*, p. 34.
[46] *Ibid.*, pp. 35, 66.
[48] *Ibid.*, chap. xii, pp. 361-413.

[45] *Ibid.*, chap. iii, pp. 75-108.
[47] *Ibid.*, pp. 84, 142, 430.

In her plans for the education of women as individuals with lives of their own, Mrs. Wollstonecraft included economic training. She believed that lack of ability to support herself had a pernicious effect on the mental attitudes of the average woman, who had to adjust all her relationships in life to her dependence on the men of her family.[49] As a corrective Mary Wollstonecraft suggested training in various occupations not usually practiced by women. They should be educated to manage business affairs for themselves and their children in the event of the death of the husband or father—an idea popular also with American authors of the time and one which American women had abundant opportunity to put into practice during the Revolution.[50] Most fields open to women were menial and those like teaching, which were not, were unfortunately regarded in a servile light by many employers. If women could be educated for a wider range of occupations it would save them from the necessity of marrying for support. They might become physicians as they were already nurses; midwifery in decency belonged to them. With proper education they might undertake many sorts of business. Reading of politics and history would be desirable avocations for women in these wider fields.[51]

Mrs. Wollstonecraft had a strong conception of true morality and modesty but not a narrow one. She felt that reputation was often mistaken for morality, and strongly disapproved of a writer who criticized the study of botany by women as immodest; the women whose reason was best developed would be the most truly modest. It was wrong

[49] *Vindication*, pp. 98-101. An interesting American reflection of this is given in Judith Sargent Murray's *The Gleaner* (Boston, 1798), iii, 188-224, " The Equality of the Sexes."

[50] *Vindication*, p. 86.

[51] *Ibid.*, pp. 221-22, 338-39, 340.

to feign unnatural coldness in love and equally so to try to hold the husband's passions at a high pitch after they had cooled into friendship.[52]

The works of Mrs. Wollstonecraft and the other writers just discussed circulated in America in book form; even after the Revolution American periodicals drew heavily on trans-Atlantic sources. In addition to the selections from Dr. Gregory and the Marquise de Lambert, previously cited, the works of William Alexander, Thomas Gisborne, Mrs. Elizabeth Griffith, and John Bennett served well in filling up pages.[53] One curious volume, popular with editors, the *History of Women* (1779), was, according to its author, William Alexander, an Edinburgh physician, addressed primarily to women, not to learned men, to benefit and interest the ladies by serving as a substitute for romances and providing a history of their own sex. The book was a study of the occupations and amusements of women and of the restrictions placed upon feminine activities in many countries and at different periods in history.[54] Its popularity was no doubt enhanced for some of its readers by the lurid details which Alexander gave of life in eastern countries and in primitive eras. His discussions of women of his own time in England and western Europe, although they have some historical interest today, did not differ widely from other works of the period; most of his comments on education could be dismissed as quite the usual thing. Feminine training, he thought, should receive more attention from parents and legislatures but should not be carried too far. Women must

---

[52] *Vindication*, chaps. vii and viii, pp. 273-319.

[53] For Alexander see *Boston Magazine*, ii, 24; *Christian's Scholar's and Farmer's Magazine*, ii, 342, 470, 601; *Weekly Magazine*, i, 87, 239, 346; for Gisborne, *American Universal Magazine*, iv, 14. Mrs. Griffith, *New York Weekly Magazine*, i (whole work reprinted). Bennett, *American Museum*, x, 72, 200, 227, 307; xi, 9, 70, 91, 139, 193; xii, 17.

[54] *History of Women* (3rd ed., London, 1782), Advertisement, vol. i.

mark a narrow line between ignorance and pedantry since nature had not designed them for the severer studies; moreover men might prove jealous if rivaled in learning.[55] In his discussion of the female character, Alexander found much that was desirable in the society of women but thought that men should not frequent their company exclusively for fear of enervation. The primary traits to be developed in women were modesty and reserve. Men had more physical strength; but women had beauty, softness and persuasive force which when properly exerted put the sexes on an equal basis. Romantic ideas on the part of unmarried women were unfortunate since women were generally dependent on men for maintenance and protection. Alexander was critical of the way in which women, except those of the lower classes and a few in the middle class, spent their time. He objected especially to elaborate social life and its endless round of amusements but approved the labor forced on women by economic necessity.[56] The position of women in Europe, he wrote, seemed high because of conventional etiquette; but in actual practice women received only a slight education and were subject to strict legislation. These facts combined to keep them in a state of dependence. He gave a long analysis of the legal status of women in England. Of the marriage ceremony, he said, that it was legally binding but did not convey a right not previously possessed. Certain offenses, notably those against the social code, were punished far more severely in women than in men.[57]

Mrs. Elizabeth Griffith's *Letters addressed to Young Married Women* (1782), was a work of the conventional school. The author had supported her family by writing novels and plays, and this book, one of her later productions,

[55] *History of Women*, i, 87.

[56] *Ibid.*, i, 133-35, 145, 475.

[57] Alexander, *History of Women*, i, 319-20; ii, 480-515.

was actuated by the same motive. The letters dealt with religion, fortitude, charity and kindred topics and threw little light on women's intellectual problems. The letter on the affection due to the husband was typical of the rest. In a manner reminiscent of Dr. Gregory, Mrs. Griffith said, " A married woman should continually reflect, that her *happiness* as well as her *power,* has no other foundation but in her husband's esteem and love; so that her whole aim and study must be to preserve both." [58] Women with good sense must be cautious in displaying it, for men, even though they did not wish to preempt the whole field of learning, were jealous of much understanding in women. The wife's reading was directed to form her own taste and to entertain her husband.[59] She should cultivate those accomplishments which were most pleasing to him, a point on which Mrs. Griffith quoted much from Swift.[60] Love was transient and in the long run only good sense and knowledge could retain the husband's affection.[61]

Thomas Gisborne and John Bennett,[62] both clergymen, wrote at some length and in dull style of the duties of women. Gisborne's *An Enquiry into the Duties of the Female Sex* (1797), relegated women to a limited and almost wholly domestic sphere of action in which the importance of the female character lay in contributions to the comfort of near relatives, in improvement of the manners and conduct of the other sex by society and example, in the education of children, and in the attainment of everlasting felicity. Gis-

[58] Griffith, *Letters to Young Married Women* (Philadelphia, 1796), p. 22.

[59] *Ibid.,* p. 37.

[60] " Letter to a very Young Lady on her Marriage."

[61] Griffith, *Letters,* pp. 35-36.

[62] Bennett's name is also spelled " Bennet " in some editions. He was curate of St. Mary's, Manchester.

borne, who was a friend of Hannah More and other Evangelicals, disliked the assertions which were being made regarding the rights of women.[63] The Creator, he thought, had reserved legislation, jurisprudence, political economy, government, research, philosophy, navigation, erudition, commercial enterprise, military and naval affairs, and some additional fields exclusively to men and had endowed them with minds capable of reasoning in these branches of knowledge. Such powers were given to women with a more sparing hand but in compensation they had vivacity, imagination, and other lighter qualities. Women shone especially in tenderness, delicacy and benevolence, and bore sickness and suffering better than men. Even the faults of the two sexes were different; women were not given to intemperance or profanity but to unsteadiness of mind, fondness for novelty, habits of frivolity, dislike of sober application, repugnance to the graver studies, unreasonable regard for wit and spectacular accomplishments, a thirst for admiration, affectation, and vanity. Their education needed to be directed against this catalogue of weaknesses.[64]

Bennett expressed his ideas in two books, *Letters to a Young Lady* (1789) and *Strictures on Female Education* (1787). There were American editions of the *Letters* at Newburyport, Hartford and New York in the 1790's; the Newburyport edition was printed by subscription. It was probably one of these editions which Ezra Stiles read.[65] The *Strictures,* a less popular but more philosophical work, was reprinted at Norwich in 1792. In the *Letters* Bennett addressed young ladies themselves in the hope of recalling

[63] Gisborne, *Enquiry,* pp. 12, 19; the latter perhaps a reference to Mary Wollstonecraft's book. References are to 4th ed., London, 1799.

[64] Gisborne, *Enquiry,* pp. 21-28, 33-37. See chaps. iv and x for his conventional directions on education.

[65] Stiles, *Literary Diary,* iii, 419.

them from such faults as those in Gisborne's list and of turning them from worldly occupations to serious reading.[66] In lengthy and tedious fashion he outlined what this reading should be. It was his belief that the average boarding school instructed its pupils too much in accomplishments and too little in religion and domestic training, a grave error; for religion was especially appropriate to women whereas knowledge was of value only as an aid to piety.[67] The use which women made of their knowledge was of more importance than the knowledge itself; the customary reproaches against learned women applied only to a few viragos.[68]

Bennett was more concerned with the education of young women than with marriage, but Gisborne thought the subordinate position of women in the marital state one of great significance. The relationship of man and wife and the question of superiority had, he said, been settled immediately after the Fall and had since remained unchanged. This doctrine he reinforced by reference to the views of St. Peter and St. Paul regarding women. He explained that the obedience enjoined in the marriage ceremony was not unlimited since the wife was bound by divine laws and by the rights of any third person who might be involved. This suspension of obedience, however, was justified only in extreme cases and not in everyday affairs. One party must be dominant and the husband was obviously the one best fitted for it— an arrangement as desirable for the wife's happiness as the husband's.

It is on man that the burden of the most laborious offices in life, of those offices which require the greatest exertions, the deepest reflection, and the most comprehensive judgement is devolved.

---

[66] Bennett, *Letters to a Young Lady* (Hartford, 1798), i, Advertisement.

[67] *Ibid.*, i, 11, 12-15.

[68] Bennett, *Letters to a Young Lady*, i, 90. For his plan of reading see especially i, 94-98, 114, 122; ii, 63.

Man, that he may be qualified for the discharge of these offices, has been furnished by his Creator with powers of investigation and of foresight in a somewhat larger measure than the other sex, who have been recompensed by an ample share of mental endowments of a different kind.[69]

There were many American reprints of these books; but as an effective means of disseminating European ideas of women's sphere, one must not overlook certain popular compilations. Outstanding among them was Mathew Carey's *Lady's Pocket Library* which appeared in 1792. It included Hannah More's *Essays for Young Ladies,* Gregory's *Father's Legacy,* one of Mrs. Chapone's *Letters,* Swift's *Letter to a Very Young Lady,* Lady Pennington's *Unfortunate Mother's Advice to her Daughters,* the Marquise de Lambert's *Advice to a Daughter,* and Moore's *Fables for the Female Sex*— altogether a noteworthy collection of advice. Most of these writings have received detailed treatment in these pages. Lady Pennington's work was valuable because of the long list of books recommended to young ladies, a list which had been supplemented by the editor.[70] Moore's verses offered good advice on behavior and moral subjects. The influence of such a collection in preserving conventional ideas and establishing a European model for American women was no doubt very great.[71] Another compilation, *The Young Lady's Parental Monitor,* which was first printed in London, included the works of Dr. Gregory, Lady Pennington, and the Marquise de Lambert. It was reprinted in 1792 in Hartford, New London, and New York.[72]

In 1796 a Springfield bookseller printed a *Series of Letters on Courtship and Marriage.* The principal American

[69] Gisborne, *Enquiry,* pp. 239-44. Quotation pp. 243-44.
[70] *Lady's Pocket Library,* p. 143.
[71] Carey, however, in his autobiography lays no stress on the work.
[72] Evans, *American Bibliography.*

authors in the collection, Benjamin Franklin and Dr. Witherspoon, will be treated later;[73] British writers included Swift, Mrs. Piozzi and others with selections from the *Guardian.* Their ideas were similar to those discussed in the preceding pages. Another collection, the *American Spectator or Matrimonial Preceptor* (1797), was a work both for and concerning women. Its advertisement stated that the female mind was nowhere so well cultivated as in America where the rights of women as well as of men were acknowledged. In spite of its patriotic title the work was largely taken from a British *Matrimonial Preceptor.* It was composed almost entirely of selections from Dr. Johnson, Hawksworth, Addison, Aiken and other English writers.

Save for Mary Wollstonecraft, eighteenth-century European authors who found their way into American libraries did not hold advanced views on women's sphere, though recognition of the right of the sex to education was gradually increasing throughout the century. All but three or four writers on women discussed this subject expressing their own ideas on the proper course of reading to be pursued; but the real crux of the matter lay in the character and quality of the education they proposed and in the uses to which it was to be put. Almost without exception, whether the ideals held for women were high or low, they were regarded as inferior to men. All their training and development were designed for the service of men. The only alternative to this concept lay in describing the spheres of the sexes as different, leaving the reader to decide for himself whether women were higher or lower.

Most writers regarded literature as a convenient solace for women's idle moments or as a means of preventing worse evils. If the ladies were not permitted to leave their homes they must have some means of filling up leisure hours.

[73] See chaps. iv-v, *infra.*

These beliefs found currency even in the pages of women like Mrs. Chapone and Mrs. More who were themselves people of no mean intellectual attainments and moved in an unusual circle of women. Dr. Gregory spoke to his daughters of study for their own pleasure but dreaded the possibility that such pursuits might interfere with the more important business of marriage. The elaborate courses of reading suggested were rarely carried out. Was it perhaps a saving grace for the era that the average woman preferred the numerous volumes of novels which filled the circulating libraries to the very formal kinds of study prescribed? Or would a careful perusal of the books recommended have produced a more effective and individually developed group cf women?

A second reason offered for educating women was to fit them for companionship with men. Among thinking people, the concept of women as household drudges had passed. There were still those who regarded women as playthings but the number who thought of them as serious and helpful companions to their husbands was larger. This companionship, however, left them in a subservient position, exemplifying in advance Tennyson's—

Woman's pleasure, woman's pain,
Nature made them blinder motions bounded in a shallower brain.

For clever and alert women there was a place both intellectually and socially within the narrowly circumscribed limits of feminine life, if they chose to fill it. Many women were perhaps unconscious that their world was limited. An impetuous or radically inclined woman like Mary Wollstonecraft found herself outside the pale of society. She had achieved intellectual integrity but at a price. For the average woman, even in the upper classes, the legacy of these writers was the position of gentle but capable mistress in a sheltered home.

CHAPTER IV

EARLY DEVELOPMENTS OF AMERICAN THEORY

WHEN one has examined the mass of material produced by English and French authors in their struggle to depict the ideal woman, one wonders for a moment how much of this was assimilated into the fabric of American life. One could dismiss many of the studies, taken separately, as the musings of some pious or disgruntled individual; but, viewed as a whole, they afford some conception of an English standard which underwent a slow but decided change during the eighteenth century. In 1700, education for women and recognition of their lives as individuals were found chiefly in and through religion; their relationship to men was one of subjection, tempered, it might be, by gentleness and consideration, but still the relationship of inferiors.[1] If women sought another outlet it was in a shallow and restless social life which was a doubtful improvement on their earlier retirement. Gradually an idea of more dignity was accepted; women received education as preparation for more than mere domesticity or a life to come. Usually this was done less for their own sake than for that of the men they were to marry but the gain was real. The women of Richardson's novels were neither to be pitied nor despised. Beyond this stage many writers failed to go but a few courageous souls indicated greater possibilities for women in the future and even those who clung to the notion of a strictly feminine sphere

[1] England had some brilliant exceptions to this like Mary Astell and Lady Mary Wortley Montagu but the intellectual position of the average woman was decidedly narrow. See Ada Wallas, *Before the Bluestockings* (London, 1929).

imperceptibly increased its dimensions. At the end of the century Hannah More might refuse to read Mary Wollstonecraft's *Vindication,* but Mrs. More's conservative plan of education and the activities she thought permissible for well-bred women were liberal in comparison with those of Dr. Gregory and Dr. Fordyce. Moreover her own charitable activities in some measure counteracted the conservatism of her books.

This English development had its American counterpart which was a transplanting of European belief rather than a spontaneous growth. It was true that no single American author had read all the works discussed in the preceding chapters, but it was equally true that if he were seriously interested in women's problems he had read some of them. European influence on the American books which dealt with women was marked. The average colonial thinker was content to do his philosophizing on this subject vicariously. Perhaps he lacked leisure for it or had not reference books at hand. Perhaps, in the case of the New England divine, he found religious subjects demanding more immediate attention. Before 1795 what little speculation there was regarding women's position (apart from sermons or educational discussions) was to be found in the pages of Benjamin Franklin and in the two volumes of Enos Hitchcock, both of whom borrowed freely from the studies of Europeans; so that all in all an understanding of the European position is necessary for intelligent comprehension of American thought.

One can divide what is known of American beliefs regarding women during the eighteenth century into three periods which overlap a trifle. The first lasted until the Revolution when, in spite of the European literature on the subject which circulated in the colonies, American ideas, as revealed either in the establishment of schools for girls or in books on women, had not advanced far. There were, however, two divergent kinds of opinion regarding women which were indicated, though somewhat sketchily. The first of these which found occasional expression in the sermons of the New England clergy was a narrowly Puritan view, based on a literal interpretation of Scripture and on a profound sense of the importance of eternal salvation. The other view showed the influence of European rationalism. It did not admit women's equality with men but on rational grounds allowed them much freedom of action. This aroused an interest which slowly developed into a higher degree of education for them. This view was expounded in one or two periodical articles and in a pamphlet *Reflections on Courtship and Marriage,* by Benjamin Franklin, who had been much influenced by reading William Wollaston's *The Religion of Nature Delineated.* There was no great difference in practice under these two systems for there was nothing in Puritan usage which kept individual women from a moderate amount of study or from some forms of literary expression. New England, where the Puritan view was dominant, certainly produced as many intellectual women as the rest of the country if not more. The distinguished women of the Revolutionary era had perhaps grown away from the strict Puritan teaching but they had been brought up under its influence. The education, on the other hand, which Franklin, the liberal, provided for his own daughter was quite different from that which he gave his son and grandsons and the ideals he held for her were far from intellectual. Even the first ineffective expressions of the rationalist ideal are of interest, for in the long run that was the standard which prevailed.

The second period, which lasted approximately from the Revolution to the early 1790's, was marked by an increased interest in women's education as demonstrated by the opening of schools and academies for young ladies and by much discussion of the subject in addresses and periodicals. Numerous pens were ready to outline courses of study, to set forth the merits of classroom instruction, and to argue over the need for differentiating the studies of boys and girls. These writers, imbued with patriotism, were anxious to present distinctly American viewpoints but their claims to this were rarely justified. Speakers gave emphasis to the need of educating women to meet America's special problems and to the American desire of leading the rest of the world in education. Books were published treating of feminine education in America and American booksellers made compilations, like the *Lady's Pocket Library,* to meet the increased demand for popular British works. The religious note, although not forgotten, was no longer dominant.

In the third period two types of theory again became evident. One was that of the conservative element to whom the mere mention of Mary Wollstonecraft's *Vindication* brought a shudder. The American clergy belonged, in the main, to this group of which Hannah More was the outstanding British leader. More radical views were presented only by a few writers who, like Charles Brockden Brown, had imbibed the principles of William Godwin and Mary Wollstonecraft and were advocating economic and vocational training for women and greater freedom in marriage. Fear of radicalism and of deism undoubtedly checked many liberal tendencies which might otherwise have grown out of the educational developments of the second period so that the position of women in 1800, while more liberal than when Mather published his sermons, was little farther advanced than it had been in the decade following the Revolution.

There is a scarcity of material on the South which may sometime be supplied but which gave undue preponderance to the ideas of other areas. The thought of New England found written record from the time of the Mathers on; that of Philadelphia, less conspicuous at the beginning of the century, had abundant expression after the Revolution, but of the abstract ideas of the South regarding women little is known. Dutch influence in New York provided women with an eminently practical but not highly intellectual ideal. Such was the testimony of Mrs. Grant who had known intimately the Dutch families in the vicinity of Albany.[2] In the South there were many well-read and cultivated women but the printed sermons, addresses, and periodicals dealing with women, so abundant in the North, were lacking. From lists of books owned by planters and from the number of men who had received an English education one may infer that the views regarding women's position were in all probability those of the authors of the *Spectator* and of Richardson rather than of the more didactic writers, but this is pure inference.

I

The theoretical position of women in New England during the early part of the century bore a marked resemblance to contemporary British ideas but was not to any considerable degree derived from them. This situation, so unlike that prevailing in later colonial years, was not due to any originality of American thought but represented a return to older teachings, notably the Bible itself. New England thinking on women during the lifetime of the Mathers had probably an English origin in the seventeenth century but this was transmitted to America through direct contact rather than by literary channels, which makes it difficult to trace. The quest for scriptural authority was intensified by the fact that in this as in many matters New England theory was formulated almost exclusively by one class—the clergy or their

[2] Anne McVicar Grant, *Memoirs of an American Lady* (London, 1808), i, 33-35.

close associates. New England culture was still under the influence of the clergy and nowhere was this shown more clearly than in ideas regarding women. In early colonial days Anne Hutchinson had outraged ministers and elders almost as much by defying their authority and by stepping outside of women's appointed sphere as by her religious errors. In the eyes of the Puritan theocracy subjection was still the portion of the daughters of Eve; the clergy were not slow in reminding their feminine hearers of this. What is known today of the standards held for women at the close of the first century of colonial settlement comes chiefly from three sources, the sermons preached by clergymen at the funerals of women, particularly those of their own households or of prominent families;[3] from the diary of Samuel Sewall, Harvard graduate and intimate of the clerical and official group; and from a treatise by Cotton Mather, *Ornaments for the Daughters of Zion,* published in 1692. This last little book had a long period of usefulness. George Whitefield who discovered it on his trip through New England in 1740 recommended it to all ladies, especially those of Boston, and promised to send a copy to Benjamin Franklin, apparently with the design of having it reprinted.[4] These sources represent a limited body of opinion, it is true, but the most enlightened one of its time and place and one which set standards for many women of humbler class as well as of clerical families.

That woman's relationship to man was based on a literal interpretation of Scripture and of the early fathers did not

[3] Especially sermons by Benjamin Colman, Thomas Foxcroft, Thomas Prince and Charles Chauncy of Boston.

[4] George Whitefield, *Journals,* ed. Wale (London, 1905), p. 479. *A Select Collection of Letters of the Late Reverend George Whitefield* (3 vols., London, 1772), i, 226. Mather's book may have had even longer service. The copy in the library of the New York Historical Society was presented to the Society for the Improvement of Practical Piety in 1823.

render her position lacking in dignity or respect. She suffered, according to the preachers, the disgrace of being first in the Fall but that had been palliated by the glory of woman's bringing Christ into the world, so that men might " safely account the *Female Sex* herein more than a little Dignify'd." [5] Through religion women were raised from their low estate and given pious examples for conduct. So thought Thomas Foxcroft in styling his funeral tribute to his mother, " An Acknowledgement due to our ascended LORD, who has given such Grace, and so many Excellencies to a frail Woman; " [6] and Samuel Sewall wrote " Besides Hannah in the Old Testament and the Blessed Mary in the New, there is a numerous company of Holy Women listed in Christ's army which renders that sex honourable." [7] It was wicked not to consider women as rational creatures though " the petulant Pens of some Froward and Morose Men, have sometimes treated the *Female Sex* with very great Indignities." [8] A conscientious man would strive to provide the sex with the true ornaments which could not be taken away. Cotton Mather assured possible critics of this in his preface, setting forth at the same time his aim and his precedents—

They that shall criminate an undertaking to write a little Book for Promoting the Fear of God in the Female Sex, do but show their Ignorance of what was done by Tertullian, by Jerom, by Austin, in the Primitive Times besides what has been done by several Renowned Pens of a later date; and Perhaps, they forget, That one Book in the Sacred Bible, was written for An Elect

[5] Cotton Mather, *Ornaments for the Daughters of Zion* (Cambridge, 1692), pp. 3-4.

[6] *A Sermon ... after the Funeral of Mrs. Elizabeth Foxcroft* (1721), p. iii.

[7] Letter to John Winthrop in *Winthrop Papers* (Mass. Hist. Soc., *Colls.*, ser. 6, v), vi, 403.

[8] Mather, *Ornaments*, pp. 42-43.

Lady. As for the Manner of my own Writing, 'tis Plain, Brief, Chast; and not without an endeavour to imagine how such a subject would have been handled by a Timothy, who was to address Women, & yet be an Example of Purity.[9]

The sermons preached at funerals made no reference to works on women other than well-known passages of Scripture, but Mather's preface did not entirely exhaust his list of authorities. He offered as historical evidence a long roll of famous women whose names he had gleaned in the course of his reading;[10] referred to William Whately's book as recording many of the duties of a wife;[11] and quoted Chrysostom on the iniquity of wife beating.[12] He spoke also of a woman's legacy to her unborn child, by which he probably meant Elizabeth Joceline's book written in 1622, a volume decidedly religious in character, which advised the writer's husband, should their child be a daughter, to have her learn the Bible, housewifery, writing and good works— " other learning a woman needs not," though it was often admirable in a person of discretion.[13] In Mather's father's library there were books presenting women in a less favorable light with which he must have been familiar. Among those sent from London in 1683 were two copies of *The London Jilt, or the Politick Whore,* and *The Woman's Advocate, or Fifteen real Comforts of Matrimony.—With Satyrical Reflections on Whoring and the Debauchery of this Age.*[14] Mather's contemporaries made much use of the

[9] Mather, *Ornaments*, p. 2.   [10] *Ibid.*, pp. 33-34.

[11] *A Bride-Bush; or, A Direction for Married Persons* (London, 1619). Mather does not give the title. *Ornaments*, p. 76.

[12] *Ornaments*, p. 87.

[13] *Ibid.*, p. 90. The book was *The Mother's Legacy to her Unborn Child* (London, 1894), first printed 1624. Introduction by Lord Bishop of Rochester.

[14] Kenneth B. Murdock, *Increase Mather* (Cambridge, 1925), p. 126. This book was sent also to John Usher, bookseller as were several copies

teachings of St. Peter and St. Paul regarding women's duties but the passage in the Bible to which he himself devoted the greatest attention was Solomon's description of the wise woman in the thirty-first chapter of the Book of Proverbs.[15] He presented two views as to the authorship of this passage, first that it was Solomon's praise of his mother Bathsheba, and second that it was written by Bathsheba, for the skill displayed in household affairs carried with it a " female aspect ". This passage, Mather thought, should be used by women as a mirror, to test their own possession of the virtues enumerated. No woman, however well born, was to think herself above working flax and wool with her own hands.[16] Other clergymen were also fond of this chapter and a part of it in paraphrase appeared at the conclusion of nearly every funeral tribute to women. Thus it came about that theory regarding women's sphere had a religious rather than an intellectual basis and followed Hebrew not English guides. The spiritual kinship of Mather in this matter with Allestree and Halifax was close although there seems to be no evidence that he knew their books, which preceded his by only a few years. In view of the theocratic spirit of the American writers one is not surprised to learn that ministers in expounding women's Christian duty also laid down strict regulations for their worldly activities. Mather, speaking to an unregenerate and impious generation, gave his attention to guiding women into a pious preparation for the life to come.

The instruction of daughters, as of sons, was regarded first of all as a means of developing piety. Educational aims and facilities in this period varied decidedly with the individual. Sewall spoke of a girl who could read and spin

of *Virtuous Woman Found*. See T. G. Wright, *Literary Culture in Early New England* (New Haven, 1920), pp. 226, 231, 234.

[15] Verses 10-31.

[16] Mather, *Ornaments*, pp. 7-9.

"passing well" as knowing two things very desirable in a woman; and no doubt for some these achievements represented the whole of education. Some girls attended dame or writing schools which afforded little but elementary training.[17] One historian believes that a few girls attended public schools in Northampton and Hatfield before 1680 but that the custom later fell into disuse. In Northampton girls were not again admitted until 1802.[18] That women often acted as teachers in elementary schools is clear from old records which speak of "woman's schools" and of contracts with women as teachers.[19] These arrangements were more frequent after 1750. At a later date girls were frequently instructed by the masters of the boys,—occasionally in the same classes but often at different hours or during the summer when the older boys did not attend.[20] If home opportunities were inadequate girls were sometimes sent away but this was usually for instruction in manners and domestic arts rather than in books. Widow Margery Flynt of Braintree who died in 1687 had been noted as an instructress of young ladies, some of whom were sent to her from Boston;[21] and no doubt there were other women who offered similar training. Where the family was not strict, and social rank made domestic duties unnecessary, a young lady might

---

[17] Samuel Sewall, *Letter Book* (Mass. Hist. Soc., *Coll.*, ser. 6, i-ii), i, 19. Thomas Woody, *The History of Women's Education in the United States* (2 vols., New York, 1929), i, 140-42.

[18] Sylvester Judd, *History of Hadley* (Northampton, 1863), p. 65.

[19] Woody, *op. cit.*, i, 142-44, 164. J. B. Felt, *Annals of Salem*, i, 450; Mellen Chamberlain, *A Documentary History of Chelsea* (Boston, 1908), ii, 327-30; Town of Weston, *Records of First Precinct*, pp. 148, 157; *History of Hingham* (Hingham, 1893), i, pt. 2, p. 88; Carlos Slafter, *A Record of Education* (Dedham, 1905), p. 62.

[20] See note 19 *supra* and Charles Brooks, *History of the Town of Medford*, J. M. Usher rev. (Boston, 1886), p. 283.

[21] Charles F. Adams, *Three Episodes of Massachusetts History* (Boston and New York, 1892), ii, 604.

contrive to pass her time in idleness comparable to that decried by the British essayists. In 1760 James Murray wrote from Boston to his sisters-in-law that his fifteen-year-old daughter rose late, spent her mornings at needlework, read a little and passed the afternoons in shopping and visiting, not employing profitably, so her father thought, two hours out of the twenty-four.[22]

The education of the women of clerical families was not neglected in religious or practical ways and frequently not in intellectual interests. The daughters of Timothy Edwards, who had received a classical as well as an English education at home, a rare thing for girls, were sent to Boston to complete their studies.[23] They had later a select school in the family home at Windsor, Connecticut, where they taught " needlework, composition and various branches of mental and moral improvement," to a few young ladies, one of whom was the daughter of Eleazar Wheelock, founder of Dartmouth College.[24] That emphasis was placed on character rather than on intellectual training may be seen in a letter of Benjamin Colman, Boston minister, to his daughter Jane aged ten—

I charge you to pray daily, and read your Bible and fear to sin. Be very dutiful to your Mother and respectful to every Body. . . . Be very humble and modest, womanly and discreet. Take care of your Health, and as you love me do not eat green Apples.[25]

[22] *Letters of James Murray Loyalist* (Boston, 1901), pp. 110-11.

[23] Jonathan Edwards, *Works* (New York, 1829), i, 17, 18.

[24] *Memoirs of Mrs. Ruth Patten* (Hartford, 1834), p. 9. *Interesting Family Letters of the late Mrs. Ruth Patten* (Hartford, 1845), p. 17. In the 1790's Mrs. Patten's daughters had a successful school for girls at Hartford.

[25] Colman, *Reliquiae Turellae et Lachrymae Paternae* (Boston, 1735), p. 63.

Despite her father's silence on studies Jane became something of a scholar. A few years later after her marriage, she wrote a letter of advice to her younger sister which drew both tears and encomiums from her parents. In this Jane warned her sister against the world advising her to flee youthful lusts, and to be diligent and womanly in behavior.[26]

Cotton Mather expressed his ideas on education more explicitly than most of his contemporaries. As a young man, he made a resolution to persuade as many of his sisters as could, to spend an hour together daily giving half of it to writing and half to furnishing themselves with a knowledge of religious matters.[27] In the *Ornaments* he gave more attention to women's religious, than their intellectual, training; but under the division "Industry", he wrote of the "vertuous Maid" that she learned housewifery, needlework, arithmetic, accounts, and perhaps "chirurgery and other arts" to enable her to do good and not evil. If she had time she might study music and language but would not take pride in her skill in them.[28] These ideas he carried out in the education of his own little daughters to whom the references in his diary were frequent and affectionate. He wished them to be good mistresses of their pens and he sent at least one daughter to writing school. This drill in penmanship had a religious motive; he was preparing them to write on subjects like conversion and piety on which he gave them topics to discuss. It was probably to make notes on sermons that he wished the girls to learn shorthand. Their practice in writing evidently lapsed from time to time and was renewed, for Mather mentioned it as a "point of polite & pious Education which had somewhat languished."[29] He selected books for his daughters and other women; for the benefit

[26] Colman, p. 95.   [27] Mather, *Diary*, i, 23 (1681).
[28] Mather, *Ornaments*, p. 74.
[29] *Diary*, ii, 43, 153, 205, 276, 523.

of the family he had one member read aloud in the evenings " on some or other of the Sciences," followed by discourse and explanations on the subject.[30]   He liked especially to distribute sermons to his feminine acquaintance.   His daughters studied the catechism at home and at school, and he was accustomed to catechize the little damsels of his church, having at one time a group of one hundred assembled for the purpose.[31]   Mather had also ideas which might be classified as " vocational training " within the bounds proper for women.   To render his daughters expert housekeepers he had them prepare a new dish or a new remedy each week from instructions given in the *Family Dictionary*.[32]   He wished each daughter to understand some " beneficial Mysteries " in which she should be well instructed in order to do good to others and if necessary provide for herself.   Knowledge in physic and the preparation of medicines was his plan for the eldest, " Katy."   For the next two girls he decided to " consult their Inclinations." [33]   There was revealed in all of this a thoughtful and attentive father but not one who regarded his daughters' minds as on a level with his own.

The real learning of New England clerical ladies, when they possessed any, came not so much from the lessons of childhood as from serious reading.   The significance of suitable and systematic religious reading was realized and its performance enjoined.   What was read in other fields was more a matter of chance.   The Bible, which came first on all lists, was to be read as a regular daily duty, not to be interrupted by any other cares or pleasures.   After the Bible other books of devotional and even of doctrinal character had their proper place.   Mather encouraged women to study the Bible carefully " rather than to mispend their *houres,* and infect their *hearts,* by the revolving of such *Romances,* as

[30] Mather, *Diary*, ii, 276.   [31] *Ibid.*, ii, 85, 275, 756
[32] *Ibid.*, ii, 51.   [33] *Ibid.*, ii, 112.

commonly leave a sensible Taint upon the minds of their unwary readers." [34] Jane Colman warned her younger sister against wasting time on romances and idle poems. [35] The fulminations of Mather and others against romance reading made it fairly obvious that women did spend time on these forbidden fruits, but the bulk of the literature recorded as read by women can scarcely be dismissed as " light." [36] The absence of frivolous titles is probably due to a censorship like that exercised by Jane Colman's husband, Ebenezer Turell, who omitted her pieces of wit and humor from the writings published after her death because he felt that " her heart was set on graver and better subjects." [37]

The amount of reading done varied as well as its character. [38] Sewall's " little Betty " read one volume of the Book of Martyrs through in three months, doing it only in leisure moments at night. [39] Deborah Prince, daughter of Thomas Prince, pastor of the Old South Church, enjoyed history and divinity, especially "experimental writing." [40] Per-

[34] Mather, *Ornaments*, pp. 6, 73.

[35] Colman, *Reliquiae Turellae*, p. 95.

[36] A number of romances offered for sale in Boston before 1680 may be found in an invoice of John Usher given in Wright, *Literary Culture in Early New England*, pp. 120-21.

[37] Colman, *Reliquiae Turellae*, p. 86.

[38] Among the authors and books read by women during the first half of the century Sewall and sermon writers mention: Calamy, *The Godly Man's Ark*; Corban, *Advice to Sinners under Conviction*; Barclay, *Apology*; Vincent, *Exposition of the Assembly's Catechism*; Mather, *Jewish Children of Berlin*; Willard, *Fountain*; Mitchel, *Sermons of Glory*; Love, *Sermons*; Writings of Watts; Writings of Mrs. Rowe. Sermons by Shepard (Cambridge), William Guthry (Scotland), Stoddard (Northampton), Mather (Windsor), Flavel and Mead. Names and titles are given as cited and may be inaccurate.

[39] Sewall, *Letter Book*, i, 19. Probably by John Foxe. Sewall does not name the author.

[40] Thomas Prince, *A Sermon Occasioned by the Death of Mrs. Deborah Prince* (Boston, 1744), pp. 21-23.

haps the greatest girl reader on record was Jane Colman who before she was eighteen had read all the polite pieces in prose in her father's library and had borrowed many others from friends. After her marriage she spent the long winter evenings listening while her husband read aloud history, divinity, physic, controversy, and poetry.[41] A sister of Jonathan Edwards, Jerusha, who died at nineteen, was reported to have studied theology systematically. All his sisters enjoyed theological works and religious contemplation as did his mother who, in her old age, not only read much herself but expounded her reading to women of the neighborhood.[42] There are records of the reading done by another member of the Edwards family, Jonathan's daughter Esther, wife of Aaron Burr, second president of Princeton. After her marriage she kept a journal which she sent at intervals to her friend, Miss Prince of Boston. From this one can glean a comprehensive picture of her life and its many problems, the care of her small children, constant illness, the difficulty of obtaining servants, fears for the safety of her family at Stockbridge, and the burdens of the new college. It is easy to sympathize with her comment on her husband's suggestion that she study French—" The married woman has somthing else to care about besides lerning French tho' if I had time I should be very fond of lerning." [43] Although she had scant leisure for reading she mentioned in her journal the writings of Mrs. Rowe, Dr. Watts, Young's *Night Thoughts* and other verses, and in prose Hervey's *Dialogues,* the *Female Orator,* and Richardson's *Pamela* and *Clarissa.* Her comments on *Pamela* which she read carefully have already been noticed.[44]

[41] Colman, *Reliquiae Turellae*, pp. 78-79.

[42] Edwards, *Works* (1829), i, 18, 116-17.

[43] Quoted in *New England Quarterly*, iii, 299. The manuscript diary is in the library of Yale University where the writer was kindly permitted to examine it.

[44] See chap. ii, *supra*, pp. 51-52.

Books had also their social uses; Samuel Sewall, when courting on his own or his son's behalf, could find no better gift for the ladies than Cotton Mather's *Treatise against Antinomianism,* Walter on Christ, *Smoking Flax Inflamed,* and the *Vial of Tears;* but he judiciously interspersed these with presents of raisins, almonds, gingerbread, and shoe buckles. One cautious lady, who later rejected Sewall's addresses, was doubtful as to the propriety of accepting an election sermon lest it put her under an obligation.[45] Cotton Mather at his first wife's funeral presented a book to each of the persons, nearly one hundred in number, who had acted as watchers during her long illness. He chose for the purpose according to the condition of the recipient, either his *Ornaments for the Daughters of Zion* or *Death Made Happy and Easy.*[46]

Discussion of women's literary pursuits leads naturally to the question of the relative intellectual ability of the sexes. It is obvious that the reading and study of even the more ambitious women did not place them on a par with the men of their own families. The average preacher did not touch on this except as he made the customary quotations from the New Testament, which exhorted women to stay at home and keep silence in the churches, or as he praised some departed sister for not exceeding the bounds proper to her sex. Two leading ministers, Mather and Colman, did air their views in the matter, Mather in the *Ornaments* and Colman more quietly in a letter to his daughter. Mather apparently had a great respect for learned ladies but one qualified by religious considerations. One of his reasons for thinking women worthy of honor was the share they had had in writing those oracles " which make us wise unto salvation," among which were the songs of Deborah, Hannah and Mary, the prophecy

[45] Sewall, *Diary,* ii, 376, 378; iii, 164, 190, 202, 263, 291, 303.
[46] Mather, *Diary,* i, 449.

of Huldah, and the instructions of Bathsheba in the thirty-first chapter of Proverbs. Mather made the distinction that God had employed women to write but not to speak for the church. In the *Ornaments* he spoke favorably of Anna Maria Schurman " that most Accomplish'd Lady." [47] In a letter to his sister-in-law he mentioned the work of Mademoiselle de Gournay whom he perhaps included in his list of learned ladies though he certainly did not share her views in regard to the sexes.[48] When he remarked that the books published by women would make a library far from contemptible and that New England had not been without authors who would challenge a place in such a library he gave no names but was probably referring to the work of Anne Bradstreet.[49]

Benjamin Colman recognized that women might have as great ability as men but thought their equal education inexpedient, or so one infers from a letter to his daughter Jane. She had been almost an infant prodigy and in her 'teens produced verses which were no worse than those penned by many masculine contemporaries. At seventeen she wrote a letter to her father, whom she admired greatly, wishing that she had inherited some of his intellectual gifts. His long affectionate response recognized her natural ability but showed clearly the disadvantages under which women labored. He thought she had inherited his talent which—

in proportion to the Advantages you have had, *under the necessary and useful Restraints of your Sex,* you enjoy to the full of what I have done before you. With the Advantages of my liberal Education at School & College, I have no reason to think but that your Genius in Writing would have excell'd mine.[50]

[47] *Ornaments*, pp. 5-7. A Dutch woman (1607-1678), noted for her learning.

[48] *Diary*, ii, 325 (1715/16).   [49] *Ornaments*, p. 5.

[50] Colman, *Reliquiae Turellae*, p. 69. Italics mine.

Within the bounds of those necessary and useful restraints he advised her to improve her ability by reading and study, reserving her verse-making as an occasional indulgence for leisure moments. After her untimely death in childbirth in 1735, his two sermons on the event were published with a memoir by her husband and selections from her own writings. A remark made by her husband suggests that she was fully aware of the limitations usually imposed on women and a little impatient with them. He wrote,

I find that she was sometimes fir'd with a laudable ambition of raising the honour of her *Sex,* who are therefore under Obligations to her; and all will be ready to own she had a fine *Genius,* and is to be placed among those who have excell'd.[51]

Jonathan Edwards was more concerned with spiritual development, in which the equality of the sexes was taken for granted, than with intellectual training though one may infer that his daughters like his sisters received a better education than the average woman. The few letters to his daughters which have survived place much emphasis on religious thought and action.[52] His daughter Mary, mother of Timothy Dwight, taught her son to read before he was four, and had a large part in shaping his intellectual career.[53] Esther Edwards, wife of President Burr, had decided ideas about the ability of her sex. Richardson was not the only person whom she accused of degrading women through a wrong moral code. She had a strenuous argument lasting more than an hour with John Ewing, New Jersey College tutor, on the topics suitable for feminine conversation.[54]

[51] Colman, *Reliquiae Turellae,* p. 78.

[52] Edwards, *Works* (1829), i, 17, 126-27, 148-49.

[53] Timothy Dwight, *Theology, explained and defended* (3rd ed., New Haven, 1823), Memoir, p. 4.

[54] Ewing was afterwards Provost of the University of Pennsylvania, 1779-1802. See account in *Dictionary of American Biography.*

Ewing thought that women should confine themselves to matters which they understood and not discuss abstract ideas like friendship or society.   Mrs. Burr concluded this entry in her journal by saying that she had never met anyone so fully in Mr. Pope's sordid scheme as this young man.[55]   She recognized intellectual differences in individual women and was not happy in the feminine companionship which Newark afforded.   This lack of sympathy was perhaps religious as well as literary for she spoke wistfully of the spiritual benefits of the little circle to which her friend in Boston belonged. After the college was moved to Princeton she formed a friendship with Annis Boudinot, later Mrs. Richard Stockton, who gave her some of the companionship she craved.

The years before the Revolution did not produce many literary ladies.   The writings of Jane Colman and the few by Deborah Prince, both published with their funeral sermons, could never have reached a large circle of readers. Esther Burr's friend, Annis Boudinot, wrote occasional verses some of which Mrs. Burr transcribed in her journal. Those in honor of Colonel Schuyler were printed in the *New York Mercury,* January 9, 1758.[56]   Matrimony did not end the poetical phase of Mrs. Stockton's career, for George Washington wrote her twenty-five years later thanking her for some verses penned in his honor and urging her to continue her literary pursuits but with a different choice of subject.[57]   The efforts of the little negro girl, Phillis Wheatley (c1753-1784), who began her verse-making before the Revolution were well received.[58]   In general

[55] *New England Quarterly,* iii, 301. The "sordid scheme" was probably Pope's declaration that "Most Women have no Characters at all," and his general discussion of women in Epistle II of his *Moral Essays.* *The Works of Alexander Pope* (10 vols., London, 1806), iii, 245-68.

[56] Reprinted *New Jersey Archives,* ser. I, xx, 169.

[57] Washington, *Writings,* ed. Ford, x, 301-03.

[58] Charles Frederic Heartman, *Phillis Wheatley (Phillis Peters) A critical attempt and a bibliography of her writings* (New York, 1915).

women of the time confined their literary efforts to journals or religious writings not designed for publication. These devotional writings took either of two forms; some women wrote comments on their readings in the Bible and in devotional books, while others kept diaries of a highly introspective nature, which recorded minutely daily experiences in prayer and religious contemplation. Few of these, perhaps fortunately, found their way into print, but their existence was attested in many funeral sermons and memoirs. Towards the close of the century Samuel Hopkins, pastor of the first Congregational church of Newport, edited the writings of two former parishioners. The papers of Sarah Osborn and Susanna Anthony, from which he made selections, dated back to the revival of 1740 and were typical of the introspective class of writings. Hopkins stated that the little volume of Miss Anthony's work was chosen from over a thousand pages of manuscript.[59]

The organized religious activities of women and their efforts, in some sects, as preachers, will be given special consideration hereafter, but the theoretical aspect of women's relationship to the churches demands some treatment here. Women were, of course, expected to attend public worship regularly and not make trifling excuses for absence. Mather pointed out that the Turks barred women from worship but that Christians did not and that a Christian woman should desire to eat and drink, that is to receive the Lord's Supper, where she was not permitted to speak.[60] This was not the belief of the Quakers who held that women had been placed in subjection by the Fall but redeemed by the restoration of holiness; in Christ, they were the equals of men. This was a position for which George Fox earnestly contended.[61]

[59] Hopkins, *Life of Susanna Anthony* (Worcester, 1796), p. 165.

[60] Mather, *Ornaments*, p. 28.

[61] *Journal of George Fox*, Wilson Armistead, ed. (2 vols., London, 1852), ii, 131, 163-4, 274-77.

Except for the Quakers and the pietistic sects of Pennsylvania, most churches probably regarded women in the same light as did the New Englanders.

Samuel Sewall, defending women's religious equality, refuted an idea, sometimes found in England, that women had no place in heaven. When he ran across this notion in his reading he was greatly distressed and prepared a reply entitled "Talitha Cumi [Young Woman Arise] or An Invitation to Women to look after their Inheritance in the Heavenly Mansions." This he did from detestation of the doctrine advanced and from a due regard to his mother Eve and his own mother, in fulfillment of the injunctions of the fifth commandment. There would, he wrote, be no needless or impertinent persons in heaven, but this did not bar women as a class. They were the children of God and heaven was their country. God had no need of any creature except to show his own glory, an argument which might keep men and angels as well as women from heaven. The statement in Matthew 22 : 30 that there was neither marrying nor giving in marriage in heaven showed clearly that there were women there for the latter half of the phrase applied particularly to them. Three women would certainly rise again, Eve, the mother of all living, Sarah, the mother of the faithful, and Mary, the mother of our Lord. If these three were to rise again without doubt all women would. Eve like Adam had been created in the image of God; since millions of Sarah's descendants among the faithful would obtain the resurrection, she herself would not be left behind. As for the Blessed Virgin, Sewall wrote, that he would rather believe with the Roman Catholics that she was already in heaven than to think that she would never be. Sewall apparently believed in an intermediate state after death preceding the general resurrection for most believers. Of heaven, he observed that "the souls only of the Saints, . . . are as yet in that happy place." Women had indeed first brought sin into the world; for this they were punished with subjection and the pains of childbirth, but God had not forsaken them and after death there would be no greater change for women than for men.

Remembering Sewall's preoccupation with funerals as revealed in his diary it is interesting to note that it is from them that he derived much of his argument for women's immortality. A Christian burial, he believed, signified resurrection. The funeral of Sarah, the first recorded in Scripture, was "very considerable;" the book of Genesis covering the history of 2368 years devoted one entire chapter to this event. Of the eight funerals recorded in the book, five were those of godly women who were buried in faith and hope of a resurrection unto eternal life and glory. God had raised women as well as men from the dead thus foreshadowing their presence at the last resurrection.

Sewall's paper was most erudite. Admitting that the ancients had been divided on their views of women he thought the weight of distinguished names on his side. It would be hard, he wrote, to match Jerome, Augustine, Tertullian, and Ambrose in zeal, sanctity, or learning. The translation of the *City of God* into English a hundred years earlier should have sufficed to check attacks on women's immortality. The use of the Church of England burial service for women as well as men, the doctrines of the Church of Scotland, and of the Synod of Dort showed that those churches believed that women would share in the resurrection. Erasmus, Usher, and other divines agreed to this. If however controversies arose injurious to the rights of women they were not bound by the arguments of even the most learned men but could rest upon the words of God himself. The heavenly inheritance was inconceivably great and good and it was no small injury to have their title to it defamed but there were many women who could stand before the Lord without fear.[62]

To Cotton Mather the possibility of salvation and of religious achievement seemed open to women as completely as to men, and he believed that more women than men attained it. He explained away Solomon's statement that there was only one good woman in a thousand, balancing against it the presence of three Marys and only one John at the Crucifixion. In a Boston church of three or four hundred communicants, only one hundred were men. Women had, through religion, turned the curses of subjection and childbearing into blessings.[63] Mather's *Ornaments* was designed to insure cultivation of religious virtues, and he gave special directions for this purpose to the maid, the wife, the mother, and the widow. With Mather's rules as to the course to be pursued in each of the four states of life it is interesting to compare three characters of New England women presented by John Dunton in his *Letters from New England*. Dunton may have been influenced as much by imagination as by fact, but he left pictures of pious, virtuous and accomplished women as maiden, wife, and widow, which he professed to have drawn from Boston women.[64]

One of the baits used by Mather to lure women to piety was that they might thereby be recommended to the praise and choice of men whose good opinion it was desirable to have.[65] The virtuous maiden would not make undue haste

[62] This manuscript is among Sewall's papers in the possession of the Massachusetts Historical Society. It was written after 1711 for Sewall refers to an English book published in that year.

[63] Mather, *Ornaments*, pp. 44-45. Increase Mather's church record gave sixty-nine brethren and one hundred and seven sisters. Mather, *Diary*, i, 108 note.

[64] *John Dunton's Letters from New England* (Prince Society, *Pubs.*, iv), pp. 98-111.

[65] Mather, *Ornaments*, pp. 30-31.

to marry, and if she continued in a single state would render it blessed by caring for the things of the Lord. She would not dress to attract men but would submit proffered matches to the reasonable judgments of her parents.[66] To judge from the statements of Mather and Sewall, the women generally had some freedom of choice or at least the power of refusing persons whom the family had approved. Marriage in the better classes was usually accompanied by elaborate business arrangements though mercenary considerations were far from being the only ones. Jane Colman early laid down certain rules to guide her own choice, specifying that the man she married must have " pious and credible parents," be a strict moralist, sober, temperate, just and honest; diligent in business, prudent in manners, fixed in his religion, a constant attendant at public worship, and of a sweet and agreeable temper.[67] It may be needless to add that she became a clergyman's wife.

With the scriptural basis for women's inferiority established, it is not surprising that more was said of the duties of wives to their husbands than of the reverse, though the writings of men like Sewall, the Mathers, and Thomas Clap show real affection for their wives and daughters and some readiness to share domestic problems with them rather than to dictate to them. Increase Mather wrote that he devoted himself to study and left the management of the family to his wife, who, however, honored him too much for she always said that he was the best husband and the best man in the whole world.[68] The line of duty and honor for wives had been clearly laid down by St. Paul when he ordered them to be in subjection to their husbands, to reverence them, and

[66] *Ornaments*, p. 75.

[67] Colman, *Reliquiae Turellae*, p. 77.

[68] Kenneth B. Murdock, *Increase Mather*, p. 73. From Mather's manuscript autobiography.

to be chaste and sober, keepers at home.[69] For further details of their duties wives might consult the description of the wise woman of the book of Proverbs. Cotton Mather did not regard virginity as essential to pleasing God but thought that a virtuous wife might be equally acceptable. She was one who studied to render herself amiable to her husband, who could leave all the friends in the world for his company, and who avoided all contention with him. In every lawful matter in which she could not with calm reason convince him of his errors she submitted her will and senses to him, acting as if there were one mind in two bodies. She was careful of his reputation and faithful to him even in thought. Besides this she manifested industry, thrift, and skill in her management of the household.[70] The same testimony regarding the duties of a good wife was to be found in the brief "characters" given almost invariably at the conclusion of funeral sermons. These eulogies were stereotyped in form; a detailed tribute to the lady's religious virtues was followed by a briefer enumeration of her desirable characteristics as wife and mother. Charles Chauncy, in typical fashion, said of one lady that she had a comely body, good understanding, sprightly wit, sweet temper, and an agreeable deportment in the several relations of life.[71] Thomas Clap, later president of Yale, in a memorial of his wife, Mary Whiting,[72] described her as a faithful friend and monitor to her husband, who upbraided him only in loving and modest fashion and at the most convenient season. When they disagreed she discussed matters calmly, but not liking long debates soon acquiesced in his opinion. There

[69] I Timothy 2: 11; I Corinthians 14: 34; Titus 2: 5.

[70] Mather, *Ornaments,* pp. 76-85.

[71] *A Funeral Discourse on the Death of Mrs. Lucy Waldo* (Boston, 1741).

[72] She died aged twenty-four after bearing him six children. See "Memoirs of a College President," *Connecticut Magazine,* xii, 233-39.

was close spiritual relationship between them; and they were in the habit of praying together regularly, a custom practiced also by Cotton Mather, Jonathan Edwards, and their wives.[73] Skill in household affairs won praise from many besides Mather. Samuel Sewall, though a practical person himself, spoke of turning over his cash to his wife's management because "She has a better faculty than I at managing Affairs." [74]

Clergymen's wives and other feminine members of their households held conspicuous positions in the community, which made their moral and social duties more onerous than those of women in humbler station, while they were subject to the same burdens of household supervision and incessant childbearing.[75] They were expected to act noble and pious parts, to live above the world maintaining communion with God, and setting good examples.[76] Mather felt that it would be good for his wife and encouraging to others if she took notes on his sermons during his preaching.[77] Clergymen's wives should show constancy and fervor of devotion, ingenuity in instructing their families and instilling piety into domestics and in charity and helpfulness to the miserable.[78] Economic skill in the wife was particularly valued in clerical homes where she often held full sway leaving her husband free for spiritual affairs.[79] One minister's wife was praised

[73] *Ibid.*; Mather, *Diary*, i, 284; Edwards, *Works* (1808), i, 52.

[74] Sewall, *Diary*, ii, 93.

[75] See letter of Ebenezer Baldwin to his sister, New Haven Historical Society, *Papers*, ix, 164.

[76] Letter of Joseph Bellamy to Esther Edwards on her marriage to President Burr, *The Works of Joseph Bellamy, D. D.* (Boston, 1850), i, xv.

[77] Mather, *Diary*, ii, 97 (1711).

[78] *Ibid.*, ii, 185-86 (1712/13).

[79] Samuel Hopkins, *Life and Character of Jonathan Edwards* (Boston, 1765), pp. 49, 95.

for " Keeping every Person and Thing, as much as possible, in their own Order, Place and Business." [80]

Sermon writers also said much of the duties of mothers, though where British authors emphasized their importance in the education of their children the Americans spoke chiefly of their spiritual example and their share in religious training. Thomas Foxcroft's sermon on the death of his mother is an excellent illustration of this.[81]   Mather advised mothers to care for their children themselves, to teach children to read and write as early as possible, and to provide the other essentials of education. They were to oversee their company carefully, to give due correction, not to show too much fondness, and to manifest special zeal for their spiritual welfare.[82]

The belief in the subjection of women is clear in all these early writings and there is possibly a danger that the modern reader may mistake certain theoretical phrases for harsh or consciously unjust treatment. As the conversations with young children on death and hell which seem today peculiarly revolting grew out of the desire to protect the beloved child's eternal welfare, so the instruction to women to submit themselves to men was regarded as the fulfillment of a divine command. This did not indicate lack of affection; Mather, for instance, was sincerely grieved over the long illness and suffering of his " lovely consort " and made the well-being and education of his " desirable " daughters the subject of frequent and ardent prayer.[83]   At the same time there is little

[80] [William Williams], *A Funeral Discourse Occasioned by the Death of Mrs. Hannah Williams* (Boston, 1746), pp. 26-27. This standard had not changed in essentials at the end of the century, S. G. Goodrich, *Recollections of a Lifetime*, i, 371-73.

[81] Published Boston, 1721.

[82] Mather, *Ornaments*, pp. 93-95.

[83] Mather, *Diary*, i, 405, 447, 547; ii, 388, etc.

evidence of intellectual companionship between the sexes at this period. Those who guided the reading of their wives and daughters or corrected their literary attempts did so as superiors not as comrades. This is less surprising as the growth of education for companionship with men was slow in England until the publication of Richardson's works.[84]

II

The beginning of a rationalistic treatment of women's status came in 1722 with the publication by young Benjamin Franklin of the *Dogood Papers* in a mood very different from New England sermons. These essays, which were not entirely serious, were printed as the work of a middle-aged widow, and were in some ways reminiscent of the *Spectator*. Turning to English sources was in itself something of an innovation, for although the ideal woman of the British essayists bore a character not altogether incompatible with the portrait drawn by New England divines, yet the emphasis was different. It is doubtful whether either Mather or Colman would have recommended the *Spectator* as a guide. Franklin, believing that his points could best be driven home by an assumed character, adopted that of a normal, shrewd, and philosophical woman. The supposed widow reported of herself that she had received the instruction necessary for her sex, including needlework, writing, and arithmetic; except for imaginary evils she had led a peaceful existence married to a clergyman. Her leisure was devoted to books and the retirement of country life. Needless to say, the intense religious introspection found in many characterizations of women in sermons was lacking in Franklin's work. The *Dogood Papers* made fun of hoop petticoats much as the *Spectator* had attacked hoops and masculine riding habits,[85]

[84] Compare p. 54, *supra*.
[85] Franklin, *Writings*, ed. Smyth, ii, 20.

and they contained practical suggestions for insurance for widows, with satirical ones to the same effect for old maids.[86] Writing in this feminine guise Franklin selected women's position as a topic on which to philosophize, pleading in behalf of the fair sex that men had not only as many faults as women but were in great measure the cause of women's errors. Women who were popularly accused of idleness regarded themselves as perpetually busy; if the accusation were true men had only themselves to blame for supporting women in luxury. Feminine folly and pride were due, Franklin thought, largely to the attitude of men who encouraged them by flattery.[87] In this connection, though he did not give the author's name, Franklin quoted Defoe on the barbarity of denying learning to women and then reproaching them with ignorance. He believed in the moral equality of the sexes but did not encourage women to enter unusual fields of action. That Franklin at this period was reflecting the material which he had read was apparent, though the papers showed also his strong vein of practicality.

After Franklin's establishment in Philadelphia a letter in the *Pennsylvania Gazette* signed *Celia Single* showed his concept of a tradesman's wife. She should be as industrious as her husband, particularly if she had been married without a portion, spending her time in knitting and in attending to household duties, not in dressing her hair and attempting to pass for a gentlewoman. Another satirical letter signed *Alice Addertongue* pictured feminine gossip as a prevalent evil.[88]

One of the first secular works in America to treat primarily of women's status was Franklin's *Reflections on Courtship and Marriage,* a small pamphlet which appeared in 1746

[86] *Writings*, ed. Smyth, ii, 32-40.
[87] *Ibid.*, ii, 3-6, 14-18.
[88] *Ibid.*, ii, 186-95 (1732).

and which in style and content was not characteristic of the later Franklin.[89] The *Dogood Papers* show that he had been mildly interested in feminine welfare for many years, and in his *Autobiography* he told of an early discussion with John Collins of Boston on the propriety of educating the female sex. In this debate Franklin had taken the affirmative, alleging that women possessed a capacity for education and that study was proper for them, but he admitted later that he did so partly for the sake of argument.[90] His familiarity with the *Spectator* and its discussions of women was of long standing, and after coming to Philadelphia he had access to a number of other works on the subject. Defoe's *Religious Courtship* had been advertised in the *Pennsylvania Gazette* in 1736, and *The Ladies' Library* in 1738.[91] William Bradford offered *Pamela* for sale in 1742 [92] and Franklin advertised the same novel in 1744 with emphasis on the moral quality of the book.[93] At the time that his pamphlet appeared he must have been fairly well read in current literature dealing with women's place and education. His work commenced with arguments against marriage, based on the usual description of the feminine character, but he quickly offset these by counter arguments. In the analysis of women's position there was still more than an echo of Defoe and Steele. Taken as a group, women had many faults due to a defective education and a resultant wrong system of

[89] Listed by P. L. Ford in *Franklin Bibliography*, p. xxv with the comment—"which but for the certain proof one would hardly think could be written by him." First printed Philadelphia, 1746. Reprinted Edinburgh with Swift's "Letter to a Very Young Lady," 1750. Other editions Philadelphia, 1758, New York, 1759.

[90] Franklin, *Writings*, i, 240-41.

[91] November 18-25, 1736 and May 18-25, 1738. This latter must have been Steele's book.

[92] *Pennsylvania Gazette*, September 23, 1742.

[93] *Ibid.*, October 11, December 14, 1744.

thought, not to defects intrinsic in the sex. Such failings as too much attention to the person and false ambitions, coming from pride in accomplishments, led to superficiality rather than to substantial culture and sound judgment. The character of women thus unfitted them for the pleasures of friendship in the masculine sense. These were serious charges but all the defects enumerated could be overcome by educating women to make suitable companions for men.[94] In the past men had been largely responsible for feminine errors. Although Franklin did not give a formal program of education to correct the evils listed, he thought that men might do much to improve their wives or wives-to-be through indirect means. To do this they must in talking with them avoid flattery and the bombastic style of romances, conversing intelligently and developing friendship based on rational grounds,[95] a scheme reminiscent of Mr. B's education of Pamela. Of course such training ought not to be carried too far for Franklin, as he explained in a satirical paragraph, was no admirer of pedantic ladies.[96]

Franklin's reasoning on the position of married women brought to America for the first time English rationalistic views in contrast to well-worn scriptural arguments. The passage which developed this idea was based, as Franklin stated, largely on a paragraph in Wollaston's *The Religion of Nature Delineated,* but despite its apparently liberal views it placed married women in a position of definite inferiority to their husbands although not on religious grounds. Wollaston, it will be remembered, wished to regulate such matters by reason. Marriage viewed in this light was a contract between the parties for their mutual happiness and could

[94] Franklin, *Reflections on Courtship and Marriage* (as reprinted in *A Series of Letters on Courtship and Marriage,* Springfield, 1796), pp. 2-3, 5-6.

[95] *Ibid.,* pp. 26, 29.   [96] *Ibid.,* pp. 31-33.

be governed by no standards except those of reason and prudence. Whatever the laws of the country might say, nature gave a man no arbitrary power over his wife. If reason showed, as was usually the case, that men had more knowledge and experience than their wives, then the latter must and would submit to their rule.[97] Franklin was very sure of this superior knowledge and understanding on the part of men. He felt that our whole scheme presupposed masculine superiority, that recognition of this played a large part in marital happiness and that marriage would suffer without it.[98]

Much of Franklin's pamphlet dealt with considerations antecedent to marriage. Marriage without union of minds, sympathy of affection, mutual esteem, and friendship was contrary to reason and no one should be compelled to it. Hence parents must not force marriage upon children, for when parental authority was repugnant to moral happiness it was not binding on them. Nevertheless children should consider carefully before thwarting the wishes of their parents,[99] an opinion also expressed in the later works of Mrs. Haywood and in the writings of Richardson, though there is nothing to show positively that Franklin derived it from them. Franklin feared mercenary marriages and gave detailed reasons for their undesirability, reasons however, which resembled the complaints against pin money and jointures in the *Spectator* as much if not more than they reflected American conditions.[100] Hasty marriages based on passion were also to be dreaded.[101] Since lasting happiness came only from friendship, frankness and sin-

[97] Wollaston, *op. cit.*, p. 154.
[98] Franklin, *Reflections*, pp. 43-46.
[99] *Ibid.*, pp. 40-41.
[100] *Ibid.*, pp. 9-17.
[101] *Ibid.*, pp. 16-20.

cerity on both sides were needed before marriage in order to reveal the true nature of the parties.[102]

In discussing the respective functions of the sexes after marriage, Franklin assigned, conventionally enough, business and the improvement of fortune to the husband, and house-wifery to the wife, whose duties were subdivided into prudent frugality, neatness, and harmonious economy, each of which was discussed in some detail.[103] Care must be taken by both husband and wife to cultivate even tempers and to avoid disturbance by trifles,[104] the women being especially warned against neglect of the person after marriage. Franklin had occasion in this connection to refer to Swift's " Letter to a Very Young Lady on her Marriage," with which for the most part he agreed, although he admitted that Swift treated the ladies with unreasonable contempt.[105] He concluded his essay with a picture of the happiness which a wise and prudent wife could bring to her husband.[106]

It is easy to note the sources from which Franklin drew his material. The opinions which he thus brought together were not illiberal for the age, but they were conventional enough to satisfy the average taste, so that one may safely conclude that this early American work on women was little more than a synthesis of current British ideas arranged perhaps with a bookseller's eye to trade. There may have been some deeper significance in the presentation of the rationalistic view of marriage as opposed to the traditional religious one, though it is doubtful whether most women would find it more comfortable to submit to men through reason rather than religion.

[102] Franklin, *Reflections*, pp. 22, 35.

[103] *Ibid.*, pp. 62, 65.

[104] *Ibid.*, pp. 48-51.

[105] *Ibid.*, pp. 57-58.

[106] *Ibid.*, pp. 72-73.

Franklin's later writings on women which are better known than this essay may be mentioned here though they belong to another period in his career. They dealt with women in a different and more sensuous way, and must be regarded as satires rather than as serious treatises. The advice on the choice of a mistress, however, began with an address in favor of marriage which was, Franklin said, the most natural state of man, wherein the two sexes united to make the complete human being thus enhancing the value of each individual. The man furnished strength of body and of reason, the woman softness, sensibility, and discernment.[107] Franklin believed in early marriages when the temper and habits were still adaptable and older friends were at hand to give advice.[108] In his views of economy a thrifty wife was a real asset.

Education in New England obviously reflected the Puritan concept of women's status. To a lesser extent this was true also of the middle colonies. Before the establishment of Benezet's and Dove's schools, the education of girls in Philadelphia did not differ greatly from that in Boston, if the opportunities which Franklin provided for his daughter Sally may be considered typical. His ambition was to have her become a " notable woman," that is a capable housewife with enough business training to render her useful to her husband. He enjoined diligence in church attendance, and sent her a variety of books, directing her attention especially to Steele's *The Ladies' Library.*[109] James Logan's daughter Sally also studied French, dancing, and spinning as did Sally Franklin.[110]

Philadelphia in the 1740's and 1750's had some liberal thinkers although they did not all share Franklin's ideas.

[107] *Benjamin Franklin on Marriage* (Larchmont, 1929), pp. 8-9.

[108] *Ibid.*, pp. 18-19.

[109] Franklin, *Works*, ed. Sparks, vii, 43, 153, 166-67, 267-71; 563.

[110] *Hannah Logan's Courtship* (A. C. Myers, ed., Philadelphia, 1904), p. 8. Her father also taught her a Hebrew psalm as an experiment.

It was in these decades that schools for girls which offered something more than dame schools were established. In 1751 David James Dove announced in the *Pennsylvania Gazette* that he would open a school where young ladies "might be instructed in some parts of learning as they are taught at the Academy," the boys' academy being at that time a new institution. These subjects included English grammar, spelling and pronunciation, writing, arithmetic, and accounts. Dove spent so much of his time teaching young ladies that his work at the academy suffered and he was obliged to resign. The private school which he then opened had more boys than girls so that the cause of feminine education was not greatly advanced.[111] There was also a charitable school for girls attached to the academy which offered elementary instruction after 1753. In 1764 the trustees voted that the room used by the charity girls be devoted to other uses as the girls could not in prudence or decency be kept there "after the Youth are collected into a Collegiate Way of Life." [112] In 1755 Anthony Benezet, the Quaker reformer, kept a school for girls under the supervision of the Quakers which drew its pupils from the better classes in the city and was highly successful, Benezet being noted for his gentle method of discipline, unusual in that era.[113]

Less is known of women's education in New York than in Philadelphia or Boston in this period though the Dutch and Anglican church schools apparently taught reading and

---

[111] Dove's advertisement in the *Pennsylvania Gazette*, August 29, 1751 as quoted by T. H. Montgomery, *A History of the University of Pennsylvania* (Philadelphia, 1900), pp. 143-44. Joseph Jackson, "A Philadelphia Schoolmaster of the Eighteenth Century," *Pennsylvania Magazine of History and Biography*, xxxv, 318-20.

[112] Montgomery, *op. cit.*, pp. 444-45.

[113] Roberts Vaux, *Memoirs of the Life of Anthony Benezet* (printed Philadelphia, reprinted York, 1817), pp. 15-16. Woody, *History of Women's Education*, i, 235.

the catechism to girls as well as boys.[114] Beyond this the
education of the Dutch women was practical and barring
exceptional cases had little to do with books. Occasional correspondence throws light on the ideas of
individuals; an example may be found in a letter written by
Cadwallader Colden to his granddaughters. This letter,
which was not designed for publication, had much the flavor
of the British didactic works. Colden, who was offering advice to his granddaughters approaching womanhood, felt that
modesty was the quality most likely to make women esteemed
in society, and his entire letter was on this one trait which
he interpreted in a broad sense. A modest woman's actions
were natural and easy, he wrote, permitting her to indulge
herself in moderate gaiety, for modesty added dignity to
pursuits like dancing and was a safeguard against unbecoming liberties on the part of men. True modesty in women
corresponded to honor in men, preserving their dignity as
rational beings and safeguarding their rank in society.
Modest and honorable behavior provided the middle path
between an undue pride and an abject spirit, leading to the
true distinctions which marked the gentleman and lady.
Hence modest conduct led to true pleasure and serenity of
mind.[115] Franklin also paid tribute to modesty, urging his
sister to—

remember that modesty, as it makes the most homely virgin
amiable and charming, so the want of it infallibly renders the
most perfect beauty disagreeable and odious. But, when that
brightest of female virtues shines among other perfections of
body and mind in the same person, it makes the woman more
lovely than an angel.[116]

[114] Woody, *op. cit.*, i, 179-80, 195-97.
[115] *Colden Papers* (undated), vii, 305-08.
[116] Franklin, *Writings*, Smyth ed., ii, 87.

CHAPTER V

THEORY AND PRACTICE AFTER THE REVOLUTION

THE events of the Revolution diverted public attention into other channels temporarily but in the years between the close of the war and the beginning of the new century America developed a literature of her own dealing with women's problems and education. Trite though the ideas expressed in much of this literature were, they showed increasing interest in feminine education and an attempt to meet American needs in a distinctive way. This patriotic trend was most noticeable in the decade from 1785 to 1795. After that time there was more suggestion of controversy between radical and conservative groups within the country, possibly because of the feeling aroused by the appearance of Mary Wollstonecraft's *A Vindication of the Rights of Woman*. The post-Revolutionary era was characterized by the growth of schools and academies devoted to the education of girls, and, from a theoretical standpoint, by an increased attention to women's need for education. Though traces of the earlier idea of the subjection of women on scriptural grounds survived, the enlightened thought of the time favored the liberal education of women as companions for men and tried to meet this need by the development of schools which taught a little—if not much—besides " accomplishments." As in colonial days the larger part of the writings on women emanated from Philadelphia or New England. In the Quaker city they usually came from persons connected in one way or another with the young ladies' academies there. In New England the important commentators were Noah Webster, Enos Hitchcock, and perhaps indirectly Jeremy Belknap, though he published nothing on the subject unless anonymously. Boston had also some newspaper discussions as to the value of public schools for girls. The student of theory should turn first to Philadelphia which had in 1790 probably the most progressive school for girls in the country. In addition to Anthony Benezet's private school for girls there had been other schools in which both boys and girls were instructed, but these, unlike the new academies, seldom offered more than elementary education to girls. Special instruction in accomplishments had been available throughout the century, and girls in the towns could usually obtain individual teaching in any subject which they wished.[1] The rise of academies with a regular course of studies was, however, a decided gain. Histories of Philadelphia and of women's education often refer indifferently to the Young Ladies' Academy of Philadelphia or to Poor's Academy, failing to recognize that there were at least two academies for girls in Philadelphia during a part of the period under discussion. The best-known paper on feminine training given in America before 1790, Dr. Rush's *Thoughts Upon Female Education,* was not delivered at Poor's Academy, as is sometimes assumed, but at a school under the direction of Andrew Brown whose services in this field have been too much overlooked. Brown's methods in the education of girls attracted some attention in Philadelphia where he had the cooperation of several prominent citizens. Poor's school which was opened a year later had much the same organization as Brown's.

Brown had come to America from the North of Ireland before the Revolution and had served in the American Army. After the war he opened a young ladies' academy in Lan-

[1] Robert F. Seybolt, *Source Studies in American Colonial Education: The Private School* (Univ. of Illinois, Bureau of Educational Research, Bull. no. 28), pp. 72, 74, 81-82. Woody, *History of Women's Education,* i, 198-202, 225.

caster which was regarded as very liberal, but he soon moved to Philadelphia. At the time when Brown announced his new institution for the education of young ladies, the *Pennsylvania Gazette* referred to him as well known for his success in conducting an English education.[2] The school was under the patronage of a board of visitors who after the first year were elected annually by the parents of the pupils. According to Dr. Rush, Philadelphia was the first city to have an academy managed in such a fashion for the education of young ladies. Rush thought the plan excellent since it restrained the power of the teacher and extended the objects of education.[3] This arrangement should have proved favorable to Brown's institution for among the men who served on the first board of the school were William White, first bishop of Pennsylvania, Timothy Pickering, Dr. Gerardus Clarkson, and Benjamin Rush, a list which unlike that of Poor's Academy was not predominantly clerical.[4] The visitors held quarterly examinations to which parents were invited. It was customary following these tests to award premiums and to have an address delivered; the addresses which have survived supply excellent material on liberal training for girls. Apparently the school prospered for in the summer of 1787 Dr. Rush stated that there were more than one hundred pupils.[5] Tuition was thirty shillings a quarter with no entrance fee. The school hours were from nine to twelve in the morning and three to five in the afternoon. The principal feature of the curriculum was the teaching of English grammatically and of reading with special attention to pronunciation. The children were taught

[2] *Pennsylvania Gazette*, April 19, 1786 under the heading Philadelphia. See also Brown's advertisement in the same paper, August 27, 1788.

[3] Rush, *Thoughts upon Female Education* (Philadelphia, 1787), p. 23.

[4] Advertisement in *Pennsylvania Gazette*, May 10, 1786.

[5] Rush, *Thoughts upon Female Education*, p. 24 note.

a catechism designated by their parents, though lists of awards mention only the Episcopal and Presbyterian; there was daily Bible reading. Writing, arithmetic, geography, and spelling were also included.[6] Vocal music was taught at the academy by Andrew Adgate who was much interested in the promotion of musical instruction in Philadelphia and was noted for his Uranian Academy established in 1787.[7] Perhaps the most unusual study offered at the school was a series of twelve lectures on chemistry and natural philosophy which Dr. Rush gave in 1787.[8]

Brown's career as instructor ended in the summer of 1788 when he resigned to devote himself to newspaper editing. Of his success as teacher there are conflicting estimates. Certain biographical dictionaries, beginning a few years after his death, referred to teaching as a profession unsuited to one of uncommonly irritable temper and suggest that Brown had abandoned it for this reason.[9] These charges probably resulted from the political feeling aroused by his newspaper articles for at the time of his resignation the board of visitors passed a laudatory resolution, commending his abilities as an instructor.[10]   At his death in 1797 Dr. Samuel Magaw of Philadelphia who had been closely connected with the academy referred to Brown's excellent service as principal, and his efforts on behalf of women's education. Magaw spoke strongly of Brown's advanced ideas on this subject saying, " Before him, perhaps, no one in this country, had

[6] *Pennsylvania Gazette*, May 10, 1786.

[7] O. G. Sonneck, *Early Concert Life in America* (Leipzig, 1907), pp. 103-120. Account of Adgate in *Dictionary of American Biography*.

[8] Swanwick, *Thoughts* (1787), p. 24; *Belknap Papers*, iii, 381, letter of Rush.

[9] Articles in Hardie, *New Universal Biographical Dictionary*; Allen, *American Biographical and Historical Dictionary*; Appleton's *Cyclopedia of American Biography*.

[10] *Pennsylvania Gazette*, August 20, 1788.

ever contemplated female education in so proper a view, or conducted it on so good a plan, as he did. His very soul was in this business, and he did it honour." [11] The school continued for a year after Brown's resignation and perhaps longer but ceased to be an important exponent of new theories.[12]

Mr. John Poor's Academy for Young Ladies, according to statements made when the academy was incorporated, was opened June 4, 1787 with a board of sixteen visitors, the majority of whom were clergymen, and none of whom except possibly Dr. Henry Helmuth had been on the board of Brown's academy. The school under Poor's direction soon had pupils from a dozen states.[13] The first recorded program was given in December. It was the practice there, as at Brown's school, to hold a "Commencement" once or twice a year at which premiums were given to the pupils who excelled in the various subjects. In 1792 Poor's academy was legally incorporated and after that time diplomas were awarded to those students who on completing their work had passed an examination before the principal and a selected number of trustees. These programs which were events of some moment were usually held at the Moravian church. The young graduates made salutatory and valedictory addresses in addition to the longer discourses of outside speakers. The students' speeches were usually short and fairly reeked with platitudes although one damsel gave a vigorous outburst against the teachings of St. Paul on the position of

[11] Samuel Magaw, *A Discourse ... delivered February 5, 1797* (Philadelphia, 1797).

[12] John Swanwick, *Poems on Several Occasions* (Philadelphia, 1797) contains a poem referring to the school in 1789.

[13] *The Rise and Progress of the Young Ladies' Academy of Philadelphia* (Philadelphia, 1794), p. 5; Woody, *History of Women's Education*, i, 333-38.

women[14] It is a little odd to see the note of defense which crept into many of the speeches delivered at the two academies. Even Dr. Rush in dedicating his address to Mrs. Elizabeth Powel observed that it contained opinions so contrary to the general prejudice that he could not offer them to the public without the patronage of a respectable female name.[15]

Affording a decided contrast to these two academies was the Moravian Seminary for Young Ladies at Bethlehem, one of the best-known boarding schools of the time. The Moravians had long maintained a school of sorts for the daughters of their members but in 1785 it was opened to pupils from other denominations and three years later had received a number from several states and from the West Indies. Its pupils were of good families, the daughters of General Greene being among the number. In contrast to the Philadelphia schools it gave much emphasis to domestic training. The dialogues delivered on special occasions by the pupils of the school all had a religious tone, stressing also the beauty of industry and the necessity of domestic accomplishments. The Moravians made no contribution to the theory of feminine education although the school was an excellent one according to earlier standards.[16]

Three addresses given at Brown's academy were published, those of Samuel Magaw, John Swanwick, and Dr. Benjamin Rush. It is worth while to note something of these men and of their ideas regarding women. Magaw was an Anglican clergyman, graduate of the College of Philadelphia, rector of St. Paul's Church and from 1783 to 1791 vice-

[14] *The Rise of the Young Ladies' Academy*, p. 93 in the address of Miss Priscilla Mason dealing with the right of women to speak in public.

[15] Rush, *Thoughts upon Female Education*, Dedication.

[16] William C. Reichel, *A History of the Rise, Progress, and Present Condition of the Moravian Seminary for Young Ladies at Bethlehem* (2nd ed., Philadelphia, 1870), pp. 32-77.

provost of the University of the State of Pennsylvania.[17]
He was elected to the board of Brown's academy in 1787 and
was later president of the trustees of Poor's school.   John
Swanwick, merchant and congressman of Philadelphia, who
served on Brown's board as secretary and some years later
on Poor's, composed highly sentimental occasional verse,
some of the poems dealing with occurrences at the school.[18]
There were other speakers at Poor's school, mostly clergymen, whose literary efforts in academy programs have been
preserved; but their addresses were decidedly conventional.[19]

The most famous expounder of women's capacity for education was no doubt Dr. Benjamin Rush, a noted physician,
member of the American Philosophical Society and of other
organizations, and one of Philadelphia's leading citizens.
He was much interested in the education of women and
had at least one brilliant woman in his family connection,
for he had married Julia, the daughter of Annis Boudinot
and Richard Stockton.   Mrs. Stockton's literary efforts and
her friendship with Esther Burr have already been discussed.
Rush had also an interesting contact with British writers on
women.   Writing to Mrs. John Adams in 1778 he spoke of
sending a little book which he hoped she would present to
her daughter on his behalf.   This book, Rush said, was
written by Dr. Gregory, one of his former masters and a
worthy physician of Edinburgh.[20]   He did not give the title
but the book could hardly have been other than Dr. Gregory's
Father's Legacy, the work so popular in America.[21]   Rush's

[17] William Buell Sprague, *Annals of the American Pulpit,* v, 246 note.

[18] Swanwick, *Poems,* pp. 24, 98.

[19] Summaries of a number of these may be found in *The Rise and
Progress of the Young Ladies' Academy.*

[20] Excerpts from this letter are in *Pennsylvania Magazine of History
and Biography,* xxix, 16.

[21] *Supra,* p. 60.

speech at the academy became well known under the caption, *Thoughts upon Female Education,* though it did not show great originality. Harry G. Good in *Benjamin Rush and his Services to American Education* has shown the close relationship between the ideas of Rush and those recorded by Archbishop Fénelon in *L'Éducation des filles* a century earlier.[22] Rush did not mention Fénelon's name but he referred to Rousseau and quoted from the educational writings of Lord Kames.[23] A close comparison of Rush's address with one which Dr. Magaw had delivered at the school a few months earlier shows some striking similarities. Rush was nevertheless regarded as something of an authority in the field. His *Thoughts* were cited favorably in an essay in the *Pennsylvania Gazette* where praise was given principally to the American tone of the work.[24] Rush described his paper as hastily put together; but he thought well enough of it to send a copy to Jeremy Belknap which became the entering wedge for a correspondence between them.[25] Rush's work reached other New Englanders besides Belknap, for Enos Hitchcock asked for advice before publishing his own treatise on feminine training.[26]

Another volume which grew out of the activities, or the needs, of the Philadelphia academy was James A. Neal's *An Essay on the Education and Genius of the Female Sex,* published in 1795 with a report of the commencement held by the academy in December 1794. Neal's essay was not an address but was written to interest the Pennsylvania legislature in a lottery which Mr. Poor, the principal, wished to

[22] Good's work was published by the Witness Press, Berne, Ind., 1918.
[23] Rush, *Thoughts upon Female Education,* pp. 13, 24 note.
[24] *Pennsylvania Gazette,* August 15, 1787.
[25] *Belknap Papers,* i, 494; iii, 381.
[26] See letter of Rush to Hitchcock in Rhode Island Historical Society, *Publications,* n. s. vii, 95-97.

have held for the school.[27]   Neal himself was a teacher and in 1802 was principal of the academy.[28]   Though it is not clear just what position he held at the time he wrote, his work was hardly disinterested.   He pointed out the importance of feminine education to society and urged that Poor's efforts should be encouraged.   The plan of his work was a little like that of Thomas's *Essay on Woman,* so well known in America.   He began with historic instances of famous women and traced women's activities down to modern times. Among successful authors of his own century he named Mrs. Chapone, the Marquise de Lambert, Lady Pennington, and Hannah More, all of whom, he said, had written upon female education.   He did not expressly state that he had read their works but since his book appeared only two years after the publication of Mathew Carey's *Lady's Pocket Library* containing extracts from those authors, it is easy to surmise the sources of his information.

An important event in the educational history of the early republic was the opening of a law course at the University of Pennsylvania and in this, too, women had some share.   The first lecturer was James Wilson, noted lawyer of Philadelphia and signer of the Declaration of Independence.   His opening lecture, given on December 15, 1790, was a brilliant affair attended by President Washington with many ladies and gentlemen of fashion.   There were so many women in the audience that Wilson addressed the concluding portion of the speech directly to them, discussing their function in society and the activities they might undertake while the men were receiving professional instruction.   Wilson's phraseology was highly laudatory but it was obvious that he did not

---

[27] The *Pennsylvania Statutes at Large* for 1794-1797 do not show that such a lottery was ever authorized.

[28] John Watson, *Annals of Philadelphia* (3 vols., Philadelphia, 1898), i, 292 quoting the *City Directory* of 1802.

wish women to stray far from their appointed sphere and thought their influence should be exercised through the home. In keeping with the remarks to the ladies, the published speech was dedicated to both President and Mrs. Washington.[29]

In New England, also, during this period interest in women's position was primarily concerned with education and was manifested by many persons in the upper classes. The clergy still formed an influential though not a completely unified group, and their testimony was for the most part in favor of additional educational facilities for women. These were secured to some extent, both in public and private schools during the last decade and a half of the century; but it is doubtful whether any one of the New England schools was as progressive as Brown's and Poor's academies. Clerical influence in favor of better schools or more thorough training at home made itself felt in several ways—through the criticism and comments of Jeremy Belknap and his kinsman John Eliot of Boston, through the book of Enos Hitchcock, and through actual teaching done by the young theological student, Jedidiah Morse, and by Timothy Dwight. The clergy thus aligned themselves in favor of women's education, but the very fact of their support made it probable that strange ideas like those of Mary Wollstonecraft would not be harbored.

The exact period at which institutional education for New England girls, outside of Boston, became common is not clear. Town records and local histories show that girls often shared in the advantages of the village schools though they

[29] James Wilson, *An Introductory Lecture to a Course of Law Lectures* (Philadelphia, 1791). *The Works of James Wilson* (Chicago, 1896), i, pp. xvi, 29-35. Excerpts from the part of the speech addressed to the ladies are in *American Museum*, ix (January, 1791), 21-24.

did not always attend at the same hours as boys.[30]   In Medford, in 1766 girls were admitted to the town schools for two hours a day after the boys were dismissed.[31]   In 1793 the Salem school committee was authorized to provide tuition for girls in the town writing schools.[32]   The Derby school at Hingham, opened in 1791, offered the common branches to fifty girls.   This instruction was given by the master of the boys; they had also a mistress who taught needlework.[33]   In 1794 the town of Hingham had five " female schools " for six months each in a different part of the town.[34]   These village schools in some ways corresponded to later public schools but usually offered only reading, writing, arithmetic and perhaps religious instruction.   In 1772 and later, Salem had writing and sewing schools and instruction in accomplishments such as French and dancing.[35] In cities, private day schools were available for elementary studies and large towns often had evening schools some of which were open to girls.[36]   Boarding schools had more elaborate curricula including needlework and music.[37]   Most of these schools were not productive of new theories in fem-

[30] Robert F. Seybolt, *The Private School*, p. 69. Woody, *History of Women's Education*, i, 144-48. For description of such a school in the 1790's see, S. G. Goodrich, *Recollections of a Lifetime*, i, 34, 36.

[31] Charles H. Morss, " The Development of the Public Schools of Medford," *Medford Historical Register*, iii, 1-41, esp. pp. 15, 21.

[32] Felt, *Annals of Salem*, i, 456.

[33] Ezra Stiles, *Extracts from the Itineraries of Ezra Stiles* (New Haven, 1916), p. 415.

[34] *History of the Town of Hingham*, i, part 2, p. 89.

[35] Felt, *op. cit.*, i, 451, 452.

[36] Seybolt, *The Private School*, pp. 70-71, 73.   *The Evening School in Colonial America* (University of Illinois, Bureau of Educational Research, Bulletin, no. 24, Urbana, 1925), pp. 17, 56, 57; Woody, *History of Women's Education*, i, 149-53.

[37] Seybolt, *The Private School*, p. 72.

inine education. It is difficult to estimate what percentage of girls actually attended the available schools.

In Boston and nearby towns there was a growing consciousness that conditions were unsatisfactory. The diary of Anna Green Winslow written about 1772 affords a clear picture of the educational opportunities offered to girls of good family. She attended sewing and writing schools but her attendance was broken by illness, bad weather and even social calls. Though she read widely for a child of ten or twelve there was little stress on formal education.[38] Early in the Revolution Abigail Adams testified to the general neglect of women's education including her own though it was obvious that through her reading she had done much to supply the deficiency. At Newburyport in 1788 John Quincy Adams sententiously remarked that female education was such that few young ladies could carry on a satisfactory conversation.[39] Jeremy Belknap and John Eliot added the weight of clerical authority to such complaints and in 1782 Belknap apparently took steps to bring the matter to public attention. About February 1, of that year there was a letter signed Civis in the *Boston Evening Post,* which was probably the work of Belknap. In this letter the author, after discussing several aspects of education, ended by wishing that the female mind might enjoy some of the benefits of public education and as a result be dignified with the principles of wisdom and virtue while the external form was graced by the usual polite accomplishments. Eliot in commenting on the need for reform said that Boston women were taught nothing but dancing and a little music, except in the private writing schools whose instruction enabled

[38] *Diary of Anna Green Winslow,* ed. Alice Morse Earle (Boston and New York, 1894), pp. 12, 15, 28, 34, *et passim* (1771-72).

[39] Adams, *Familiar Letters,* p. 213 (August 14, 1776) and *Letters of Mrs. Adams,* i, 130-31 (June 30, 1778). John Quincy Adams, *Life in a New England Town,* p. 60.

women merely to write a copy or sign their names. It was an exceptional woman who could write a page of commonplace sentiment with correct spelling and elegant style. Eliot felt, however, that people were becoming sensible of their neglect.[40] No doubt he and Belknap had helped in bringing about the changed attitude. Belknap's comments on the books of Hitchcock and Dr. Gregory and his correspondence with Benjamin Rush showed some acquaintance with progressive thought on the subject. Boston had no good private school for girls until Caleb Bingham offered them instruction about 1784. In 1789 some provision was made for public education for girls. What schools there were, made less parade of their activities than did those at Philadelphia.

The question of opening public schools for girls in Boston was discussed in an interesting series of letters in the *Massachusetts Centinel* in the spring of 1785. They began on a serious plane but finally descended to complaints of the futility of instructing servant girls who were thereby enabled to write love letters and neglect their proper duties. The arguments adduced in favor of educating women were mainly of the familiar sort—their capacity for learning, their importance in the education of children, and their function as the companions and partners of men.[41] The value of business education in the event of widowhood was also discussed.[42] One letter opposing public schools for girls suggested that there were few women whose intellects were capable of much cultivation and that a general plan of female education would subvert the social order.[43] Others spoke of the unfairness of educating boys and not girls, of the injustice to the taxpaying fathers of daughters, and of the

[40] *Belknap Papers*, iii, 223-24.

[41] Letters of Humanus, March 2, 1785, and Daphne, February 26.

[42] Humanus, March 9, Lorenzo, April 6, 1785.

[43] Tantabogarus, March 30, 1785.

wrong done the women themselves from the standpoint of justice, humanity, and sound policy. *Humanus* wrote that such a condition did not prevail in any other town in the state.[44] Another writer, however, asserted that no maritime city in the United States provided public education for girls and that the instruction offered in the villages was nominal.[45] The opening of schools was bound up with the question of town finances, but since a new school for boys was opened during the period when the city could not afford one for girls this argument may well be discounted.[46]

Bingham's school for girls may have been in connection with one for boys though biographical sketches of him do not refer to this. His notices in the *Massachusetts Centinel* in April 1785 and April 1786 informed the public that his school was now open for young ladies from six to seven thirty or eight in the morning and from five to six in the afternoon; probably he instructed boys in the intervening hours.[47] Bingham taught reading, writing, spelling, arithmetic and English grammar but apparently did not go into *belles-lettres.* One of his most famous textbooks, the *Young Lady's Accidence,* was written to meet the needs of his feminine pupils. In 1790 he gave up his private school to become a master in the reorganized public school system which made provision for girls.[48] Hours like those mentioned in his advertisement were common at other reading

[44] *Massachusetts Centinel*, February 19, 1785.

[45] Philomathes, March 5, 1785.

[46] *Ibid.*, also letters of Mechanick, March 12, and Humanus, March 9, 1785.

[47] *Massachusetts Centinel*, April 16, 27, 1785 and April 19, 22, 1786.

[48] William B. Fowle "Memoir of Caleb Bingham" in Barnard's *American Journal of Education*, v, 325-49 and Earl L. W. Heck, "Caleb Bingham and his Textbooks," *Education*, xlvii (June, 1927), 612-18; Woody, *History of Women's Education*, i, 146.

and writing schools in Boston where girls often attended between the periods of instruction for the boys.[49]

William Woodbridge who graduated from Yale in 1780 spent much of his life teaching young girls and in his old age wrote an account of feminine education in New England. He regarded himself as the pioneer in modern instruction for young ladies, especially in the school which he conducted in New Haven in the winter of 1779-1780 where he offered arithmetic, geography and composition as novelties. Woodbridge believed that before the period of female academies women had developed their character by natural logic and the careful reading of a few books. Among these few were Milton, Watts, Young, Hervey's *Meditations,* the *Tatler,* the *Spectator, Pamela, Clarissa,* and *Robinson Crusoe,* but especially the Bible, titles certainly familiar enough in pre-Revolutionary writings. He reported that he had given a " collegiate exercise " in which he advocated the importance of " Improvement in the Education of Females." After his graduation from college he taught for several years in the new academy for boys at Exeter and in 1789 opened a young ladies' academy in Medford which he believed was the first of its kind in New England. He afterwards taught in several Connecticut schools.[50]

This was a period of new academies, some taught by men later famous in other ways. Unfortunately we do not have adequate records of their educational service. Connecticut seems to have had more such schools than Massachusetts. In 1786 Ezra Stiles listed among the Connecticut academies

[49] Advertisements in *Massachusetts Centinel,* April 16, 1785, April 26, 29, 1786 by George Richards and November 11, 1786 by Andrew Campbell.

[50] For Woodbridge's life see *National Cyclopedia of American Biography,* x, 104; Dexter, *Biographical Sketches of the Graduates of Yale College,* and two articles which Dexter attributes to Woodbridge in *American Annals of Education ... for the Year 1831,* i, 97-98, 521-26.

two coeducational schools, Dwight's at Greenfield and Kingsbury's at Waterbury.[51] Dwight's school was established in 1783 and extended in 1786 to include young ladies. According to the advertisement mentioned by Stiles it offered work in *belles-lettres,* geography, philosophy and astronomy.[52] Dwight continued the academy until he became President of Yale twelve years later. During these twelve years he gave six hours a day to the school and had over 1000 pupils.[53] It is uncertain what percentage of his students were girls; in 1787 he advertised in the *New Haven Gazette and Connecticut Magazine* that three or four young ladies could be received into his family and school if early application were made.[54] One biographer writing in 1823 observed that Dwight instructed his feminine pupils in many branches of literature not previously offered to their sex, and informed the ladies of his own day that they owed Dwight a debt of gratitude for developing women's education as that of intelligent beings capable of mental improvement.[55] John Kingsbury, just graduated from Yale, taught the new academy in his native town of Waterbury for the year 1786-1787 before beginning the study of law.[56] The advertisements of his school emphasized college preparatory courses rather than the instruction of young ladies though their attendance was solicited.[57] Hartford had, from 1785 to 1807

[51] Stiles, *Literary Diary*, iii, 248.

[52] *Ibid.*, ii, 451, iii, 247. Dwight had previously taught young ladies at Northampton.

[53] Sketches of Dwight's life in *Dictionary of American Biography*; Dexter, *Graduates of Yale College* and Sprague, *Annals of the American Pulpit*, ii, 155.

[54] October 18, 1787 repeated weekly till November 29.

[55] Memoir of Dwight in *Theology Explained and Defended*, i, 17.

[56] Dexter, *Graduates of Yale College*, iv, 487 and Henry Bronson, *History of Waterbury, Connecticut* (Waterbury, 1858), p. 422.

[57] *New Haven Gazette and Connecticut Magazine*, June 21, 1787.

and afterwards, a school for young ladies, taught by the Misses Patten, granddaughters of Eleazar Wheelock. This school was of the old-fashioned variety where the time was allotted to study, painting, embroidery, and needlework, each young lady taking a " handsome framed peice " home to her parents at the end of her course. The pupils made extracts of their reading which included geography, history, astronomy, and theological commentaries; but their reading was not very profound since one of the reasons given by Mr. Patten in 1807 for the opening of a Literary Institution for both sexes was to enable young ladies to enjoy more advanced study than the girls' school had offered.[58]   There was also a school for young ladies advertised in Hartford in 1788 by a Mr. Lathrop.[59]

Jedidiah Morse, after graduating from Yale in 1783, remained in New Haven to study theology; but in order to earn money, he taught a day school for young girls with many pupils from the best families. His geography was first written for these pupils. He had also a class for young ladies two evenings a week but his teaching in New Haven was apparently limited to the winter of 1783-1784.[60]   In 1785 he was in Norwich as preacher and teacher and while there had some feminine pupils, perhaps in his capacity as teacher in the Norwich academy.[61]   Noah Webster also had a select school for young ladies in Sharon, Connecticut, in 1782.[62]   During a part of this period a Miss Pierce taught such a school in Litchfield. There were other schools, and

[58] *Interesting Family Letters of the Late Mrs. Ruth Patten*, pp. 18-20.

[59] William D. Love, *The Colonial History of Hartford* (Hartford, 1914), p. 274.

[60] William B. Sprague, *The Life of Jedidiah Morse*, p. 6, Sidney E. Morse, *Memorabilia in the Life of Jedidiah Morse* (Boston, 1867), p. 7.

[61] Sprague, *Annals of the American Pulpit*, ii, 247.; F. M. Caulkins, *History of Norwich* (1866), p. 542.

[62] Dexter, *Graduates of Yale College*, 1778, iv, 66 *et seq.*

continuations by other instructors of those already mentioned. Teachers of boys conducted girls' schools at irregular hours or during the summer. In April 1785, Abel Morse, bookseller in New Haven, opened one which he advertised as furnished with a library of about two hundred volumes well adapted to female pupils.[63] Examples might be multiplied but it is obvious that Connecticut girls at this period could find a number of private schools offering more than elementary instruction.

Jedidiah Morse in the 1794 edition of his *American Geography* viewed the position of women in a more cheerful light than had the Bostonians a few years earlier, observing that many women in New England had good educations. His ideals were not wholly intellectual for he stated that the women of this region were taught domestic concerns early and that ladies of the first rank superintended the affairs of their own households, idleness being universally disreputable.[64]

The pages of Ezra Stiles's diary afford glimpses of a few women and their activities though they can scarcely be accepted as typical. In 1783 he told of examining Miss Lucinda Foote, aged twelve, in Greek and Latin. Finding her well qualified to enter the freshman class of Yale " *nisi Sêxus ratione* ", he gave her a certificate to that effect.[65] The principal subject of study of the girls of Stiles's own family appears to have been the Bible. Of their efforts in this direction he made frequent notes in the diary—as that his granddaughter at the age of eleven had read it through five times and one of his daughters had read it fourteen times in eighteen years.[66] His daughters and his second wife studied geography with him using the globes.[67] The

[63] *Connecticut Journal*, April 6, 1785.
[64] Morse, *American Geography* (1794), p. 279.
[65] Stiles, *Literary Diary*, iii, 102-03.
[66] Stiles, *Literary Diary*, iii, 499.
[67] *Ibid.*, iii, 513.

wife also did a little studying of Hebrew, reaching the point
of translating and parsing the first psalm. This she undertook for her own amusement and late in life.[68]   Stiles said
little of the formal education of his daughters; the youngest
was for a time under the tuition of a clergyman's daughter
in Hebron.[69]

At Yale even before Stiles's administration the position
of women was occasionally discussed.   At the commencement of 1773 two graduates debated, " Whether the Education of Daughters be not without any just reason, more
neglected than that of Sons? "[70]   Stiles encouraged his
students to discuss such topics.   One of his standard themes
for " forensic disputes " among the Seniors was, " Whether
Women ought to be admitted to partake in civil Gov't
Dominion & Sovereignty." [71]   In 1782 he had a similar
discussion on " whether female academies would be beneficial? " [72]   It is tantalizing to the student of theory not to
find any indication of the views presented.

In spite of the growing attention given to women's education, few New Englanders actually put their ideas into print.
Among those who did Noah Webster was perhaps most
familiar with what had been done elsewhere.   He doubtless
knew much of women's educational activities in Philadelphia,
before he published his essays, for he had been in that city
during 1787, was a friend of Andrew Brown, and had more
than once visited the young ladies' academy.   On July 28,
he noted in his diary that he had been to " Hear Mr. Brown's
young Misses read Dr. Rush's Dissertations on female

---

[68] Stiles, iii, 315.

[69] *Ibid.*, ii, 548, 557.

[70] Dexter, *Graduates of Yale College*, iii, 466.

[71] Stiles, *Literary Diary*, ii, 490 (1781) ; iii, 15 (1782) ; iii, 167 (1785).

[72] *Ibid.*, iii, 10.

education." [73]   His copy of the address delivered by Samuel Magaw at Brown's school in the same year is now in the New York Public Library. Lexicography was far from being his only interest; being, as Jeremy Belknap described him, " critick and coxcomb-general of the United States," [74] he was quite ready to discuss the training of women in his addresses and to devote some space to it in the pages of his *American Magazine*. One topic advertised in his Boston addresses of 1786 was " the Importance of Female Education, in domestick Life, in Society, and in Government." [75] In 1790 his discussion in the *American Magazine* was reproduced in a volume of essays, some of them in the simplified spelling in which Webster then delighted. [76]

The longest American work dealing with women which appeared before 1800 was also a New England production. Enos Hitchcock, a clergyman of Providence, gave, under a thin veil of narrative, a comprehensive and didactic plan of feminine education. Hitchcock, the pastor of the Benevolent Congregational Church in Providence, who in later life exhibited Unitarian tendencies, was generally regarded as a liberal, and in his *Discourses on Education* published in 1785 he advocated free public schools. [77]   His work on the training of girls, entitled the *Memoirs of the Bloomsgrove Family,* was published in 1790. He was familiar with European authors on the subject and quoted frequently from *Émile*

[73] E. E. F. Ford, *Notes on the Life of Noah Webster* (New York, 1912), i, 217.

[74] *Belknap Papers*, ii, 233.

[75] *Massachusetts Centinel*, July 26, 1786.

[76] Noah Webster, *Collection of Essays and Fugitiv Writings* (Boston, 1790).

[77] Account of Hitchcock in *Dictionary of American Biography*, and his diary in Rhode Island Historical Society, *Publications*, n. s. vii (1900), which deals chiefly with his experiences as army chaplain in the Revolution but has valuable notes by William B. Weeden.

though he preferred Rousseau's abstract theories to his educational methods.[78] He also referred to Lord Kames's book on education and repeated Locke's ideas on the physical care of children although not with entire approbation. His authorities on female education were Madame de Genlis, Mrs. Chapone, and Richardson whom he thought valuable for young readers though he did not name him as the source of any of his ideas.[79]

Hitchcock, like the European Utopians, described an ideal household where the son and daughter were trained in accordance with the elaborate system which he advocated. This was a plan used by Fénelon in *Télémaque*, by Rousseau in *Émile*, and by Madame de Genlis in *Adèle et Théodore*. Benjamin Rush, to whom Hitchcock had written asking his advice, observed that it was a new scheme in this country, which should " ensure it a more extensive usefulness." Rush assured Hitchcock that he was pleased to find the subject taken up by a gentleman of Hitchcock's principles and character in the literary world; but he was disturbed by the selection of a family of only two children to illustrate the system, pointing out that five or six was a more common number in most households. He thought the larger family afforded a good opportunity for instruction in fraternal respect and proper subordination in the family order. Rush suggested a simplification of Hitchcock's title, which finally appeared as *Memoirs of the Bloomsgrove Family, In a Series of Letters to a respectable Citizen of Philadelphia. Containing Sentiments on a Mode of domestic Education, Suited to the present State of Society, Government, and Manners, in the United States of America: and on the Dignity and Importance of the Female Character. Interspersed with a*

[78] Hitchcock, *Memoirs of the Bloomsgrove Family* (2 vols., Boston, 1790), i, 52; ii, 43.

[79] *Ibid.*, ii, 42, 44-46.

Variety of interesting Anecdotes.[80] The publication of Hitchcock's book evoked some comment in the correspondence of Jeremy Belknap and Ebenezer Hazard. Hazard was pleased with Hitchcock's general style of writing and with the system he suggested; but Belknap drily observed that it was a piece of patchwork as were all Hitchcock's productions. Belknap commented especially on the author's indebtedness to Lord Kames, but he agreed that the plan outlined was not unreasonable for a man who had never had a family upon which to experiment. Hitchcock had lost an only daughter some years before but Belknap grumbled that " Bachelors' wives and old maids' children you know are always the best educated and best behaved of any in the world." Hazard's criticism, that Hitchcock's methods would require more time and attention than the average parent had to give, was better justified. Both these critics agreed that the book had been too much puffed.[81]

From so wide a range of schools and individuals one could not expect unanimity of opinion, but in describing what the " female character " should be, American authors at this date were fairly well agreed. Their viewpoint was more liberal than that of older British works like the *Whole Duty of Woman* or than the ideas of the Mathers; but the separate sphere assigned to the sex was still a subordinate one and the inheritance from the older writers is easily traced. The end of character training was to have women reach their highest development for the sake of men. This could be done without injuring their domestic character, for their place was to make men happy and thus enable them better to bear the cares and burdens of the world; women's study should prepare them for this task for which the Creator had

[80] Rhode Island Historical Society, *Publications*, n. s. vii, 95-97 gives Rush's letter.

[81] *Belknap Papers*, ii, 228, 232, 238 (August-October, 1790).

manifestly designed them.[82] Women's importance in the
world lay in their influence over men. Even the young
speakers at the commencements of Poor's Academy pointed
out that war and politics were not women's field, that their
work was the performance of household duties and the care
of their children.[83] Theorists still excused defects in feminine character by attributing them to false standards set by
men or to a faulty education which men had imposed on
women. Neal in his essay on female genius complained
especially of the way in which men had withheld educational
advantages from women.[84] Such discussions led naturally
to comparison of the position of the two sexes. In the opening address of his law course James Wilson admitted that
women were not inferior to men in virtue or honesty and
probably not in wisdom. It would be impossible to find three
men of greater talents than Semiramis, Zenobia and Elizabeth; but he would not call any of these three women, accomplished female characters, a term far more important to
women than that of successful ruler. Wilson nevertheless
placed women lower than men. They were created to shine
in domestic society, to embellish and refine social life. They
could aid the development of education through teaching their
daughters, and forming the virtues of their sons.[85] Noah
Webster, much more than Wilson, believed in the natural inferiority of women, and exhorted them to concern themselves
only with domestic affairs and social life. He argued from
observation that men were pleased when their wives showed
them deference but that women despised husbands who exhibited any signs of inferiority. This showed natural jus-

[82] Swanwick, *Thoughts on Education*, p. 26 and his address bound with
Neal, *Essay on the Education and Genius of the Female Sex*, pp. 22, 26.

[83] Neal, *Essay*, pp. 19-20.

[84] *Ibid.*, pp. 2-5.

[85] Wilson's address, as printed in *American Museum*, ix, 21-23.

tice in the subordination of women although in individual traits some might prove superior to men.[86]

Enos Hitchcock spent some time in combating the idea of female inferiority but concluded by saying that as there must be a head in every society, it should be man. This masculine headship, he found based on nature and designed only for the honor and security of the fair sex. Since the restraint needful for women was offset by their power over the wills and affections of men, there should be no servility in women's attitude.[87] Hitchcock, in this part of his work, by his somewhat specious doctrine on women's position, just missed the opportunity of endorsing their full development and expansion as individuals. Liberal though he was he felt the influence of older ideas. In so far as Rousseau and other European writers proposed to classify woman as an inferior species or to insist on her surrender of natural rights Hitchock challenged their position. He was especially scornful of the notion that women should submit to masculine caprices because of men's superior physical strength; he believed that the natural modesty of women arising from weakness made them look to men as protectors. Any decent woman would be mortified at having it said that she ruled her husband especially if it were true.[88] For the sake of society women must be habituated to restraint.[89] They might rule through command of men's affection and through persuasion, but their lower place was established by natural law to preserve the equilibrium of society.[90] Hitchcock's book contained a letter, supposedly from a Philadelphia lady, thanking him for denying the necessity for blind submission by women and for giving them rational grounds for

[86] Webster, *Essays*, p. 411.

[87] Hitchcock, *Bloomsgrove Family*, ii, 15-17.

[88] *Ibid.*, ii, 43-44. [89] Compare Rousseau.

[90] Hitchcock, *Bloomsgrove Family*, ii, 17, 44-46.

conduct.   She attributed feminine weakness to flattery and to a wrong education imposed by men.[91]   Therefore she was pleased with Hitchcock's design of rescuing female character from the state in which the pride or inattention of men had kept it too long.[92]

Some letters which George Washington wrote at this period regarding the education of his niece Harriet afford an interesting supplement to the formal ideas of Hitchcock and others.   Washington urged Harriet to remember that as she was being stamped with a character which would last a lifetime she should be careful of her company, and accept the advice of the cousins with whom she was living.   Since she was not wealthy she should supply her want of fortune by cultivating submissiveness, industry, usefulness and frugality, traits of benefit not only to her but to the man she might marry.[93]   John Adams favored more advanced education for women than did Washington, perhaps because of his pride in his wife's intellectual attainments and his admiration for the wide knowledge and brilliancy of the women he met in France.   He disliked the *femme savante,* but since the charges made against her applied equally to the male pedant, he did not regard the danger of pedantry as a reason for neglecting feminine education.[94]

American writers did not doubt that women had the capacity for a high degree of education and declared that popular objections to feminine training came only from little minds.   In general the idea of schools for girls aroused little hostility although Samuel Magaw found it necessary to explain that the Philadelphia institution was not designed to take girls from home.   Private instruction was, he said, often impracticable, and when this was the case the school

[91] Hitchcock, ii, 19-20.   [92] *Ibid.,* i, 17.
[93] Washington, *Writings,* W. C. Ford ed., xii, 84-86, 200.
[94] Adams, *Familiar Letters,* pp. 219, 330.

offered the culture necessary for women, with such additional studies as taste and fortune permitted.[95]   Commentators found historical examples in abundance which showed women's capacity for learning.[96]   Study was good for women since it made them more attractive and useful to men and better able to see for themselves the limits beyond which they must not go.   The right training made them more amenable to government instead of less so, for the more they were trained in reasoning the less likely they were to defy authority.[97]   Their chief defects could be removed by education, as Defoe, the *Spectator,* and Franklin had pointed out long before.   As rational beings, women ought to be instructed in the light of reason and Christianity.[98]   Thus no American theorist wished to deny them the opportunity of learning; but this did not mean that there was entire unanimity either on details of instruction or the extent to which it should be carried.   One writer thought that the heart should be the chief object of attention since defects in women's intellect were less noticeable than in men's;[99] but others agreed with John Adams that there was no art or science beyond the reach of the female sex.[100]   Much was said of educating women that they might be better able to train their own children, undertaking the entire education of their daughters and if necessary supervising that of their sons.[101]   In 1789 an essay in the *Columbian Magazine* suggested that well-informed ladies might with propriety render public service by assisting vol-

[95] As quoted in *American Museum,* iii, 25-28.

[96] Neal, *Essay,* pp. 2-5.

[97] Rush, *Thoughts upon Female Education,* p. 25.

[98] Unsigned article in *Columbian Magazine,* September, 1787, p. 643.

[99] Article in *Columbian Magazine,* September, 1787, p. 643.

[100] *Warren Adams Letters,* i, 115.

[101] Jefferson, *Writings,* H. A. Washington, ed. (New York, 1854-55), vii, 101; *Journal and Correspondence of Miss Adams* (2 vols., New York, 1841), i, 205.

untarily in the education of their own sex; the writer highly praised a Philadelphia lady who had given such service.[102]

The course of study advocated by the writers just mentioned began as a rule with a knowledge of English in its various branches, penmanship, some arithmetic and bookkeeping or elementary accounts. This last subject had been suggested a hundred years earlier by Fénelon and as recommended by Rush and others, was perhaps a direct heritage from the archbishop. Geography and chronology were to be taught as tools for use in the reading of history, biography, and travels.[103] There was a difference of opinion as to the value of " accomplishments." Rush, for instance, favored the study of vocal music, which he considered health giving but objected to instrumental music as expensive and wasteful of precious time.[104] He opposed the study of French, because of the time expended, and the failure to carry the work to an advanced stage, believing moreover that there was ample literature in English for women's attention.[105] John Adams on the other hand urged his daughter to learn French but advised her not to mention her study of Latin grammar to many people, " for it is scarcely reputable for young ladies to understand Greek and Latin." [106] John Swanwick, unlike Rush, believed in instrumental music and thought that French, though less essential here than in Europe, was still a desirable accomplishment which might prove necessary in the future. He also recommended dancing.[107] Webster agreed with Rush in counting French a

---

[102] *Columbian Magazine* (1789), p. 330.

[103] Rush, *Thoughts*, pp. 7-13; Swanwick, *Thoughts on Education*, p. 9; Webster, *Essays*, pp. 27-30; Magaw in *American Museum*, iii, 26.

[104] Rush, *Thoughts upon Female Education*, p. 15.

[105] *Ibid.*, p. 17.

[106] Katharine M. Root, *Colonel William Smith and Lady* (Boston, 1929), p. 12, a letter written April 18, 1776.

[107] Swanwick, *Thoughts on Education* (Philadelphia, 1787), pp. 10-23.

luxury, which is interesting since almost all girls of the better classes spent some time on it; even the Moravian Academy offered it as an extra.[108] French instruction had been available in Boston and Philadelphia throughout the century.[109] Drawing, which was not greatly emphasized by Rush, was given a prominent place by Swanwick who thought it could be used in the artistic development of needlework.[110] Thomas Jefferson heartily recommended the cultivation of dancing, drawing, and music as " the ornaments of life for a female." [111] There was general agreement that time devoted to accomplishments should be governed by the taste and income of the individual.

Little instruction was offered in science and that little was mostly for pleasure. Cadwallader Colden, a quarter of a century before the Revolution, had taught his daughter Jane botany, but he had valued the study as a pleasant way of spending leisure time rather than as an essential of education. Letters from his friends also treated the matter as an agreeable but somewhat unusual amusement for a young lady.[112] The lectures given at Brown's academy by Dr. Rush on chemistry and natural history were probably the first formal attempt to instruct American women in science.[113] Scientific interest increased so rapidly that early in the nineteenth century it became fashionable for women, particularly in New York, to attend lectures on chemistry, botany and allied subjects.[114] Oddly enough astronomy was regarded as the

[108] Webster, *Essays*, pp. 28-30.

[109] Seybolt, *The Private School*, pp. 1, 14, 15, 18, etc.; Woody, *History of Women's Education*, i, 290-92.

[110] Swanwick, *op. cit.*, p. 21.

[111] Jefferson, *Writings*, vii, 101-02.

[112] *Colden Papers*, iv, 406; v, 29-30, 37, 139, 203.

[113] Swanwick, *Thoughts on Education*, p. 24.

[114] Lambert, *Travels through Canada and the United States* (3rd ed., London, 1816), ii, 95.

most appropriate science for women since it tended to exalt their ideas of the Creator.[115]

No discussion of educational aims was complete without a reading list, though American authors did not produce quite such ponderous and extensive ones as did their British brethren. Going back a few years one finds that Franklin saw to it that his daughter had at her disposal, *Pamela*, the *World*, the *Connoisseur*, the *Whole Duty of Man*, and *The Ladies' Library*.[116] Silas Deane recommended to his step-daughter the works of Pope, Addison, Young, Harvey, and Thompson.[117] Jefferson's list added Dryden, Shakespeare, Molière, Racine, and Corneille. The only exceptions to Jefferson's ban on novels were the moral tales of Marmontel, Miss Edgeworth's novels, and some of Madame de Genlis's work.[118] At this time Franklin also recommended the writings of Madame de Genlis to his friend, Mrs. Hewson, who was educating her own children.[119] Few novels were admitted by any theorists to be desirable reading, a point wherein practice and theory were far apart. Jefferson thought novel reading not only wasted time which should have been instructively employed but poisoned the mind against wholesome books.[120] Dr. Rush disapproved novels as inadequate mirrors of American life.[121] The writings of Smollett were condemned as unpolished. Hitchcock thought even Richardson's books questionable, since young readers would probably pay more attention to scenes of passion than to those dealing with the understanding; this was also held

---

[115] Anonymous article in *Boston Magazine*, ii, 213.

[116] Franklin, *Works*, Sparks ed., vii, 153, 166-67.

[117] Letters of Deane in *Correspondence and Journals of Samuel Blachley Webb*, W. C. Ford, ed. (3 vols., New York, 1893-94), iii, 229-31.

[118] Jefferson, *Works*, vii, 102.

[119] Franklin, *Works*, Sparks ed., ix, 230.

[120] Jefferson, *Works*, vii, 102.

[121] Rush, *Thoughts upon Female Education*, pp. 11-12.

to be true of Fielding's books.[122]   Timothy Dwight at the
end of the century observed that the reading of girls was
regularly lighter than that of boys.   If the boys' standards
were lowered those of the girls declined proportionately.   The
grave danger in reading romances, Dwight thought, was
in allowing girls to live in an ideal world.   When faced with
reality they were unable tõ accept everyday conditions and
experiences.   Romances also weakened their taste for Bible
reading and left readers unprepared for meeting sorrow.
By keeping the mind from vigorous thinking novels exposed
womeri to the dangers of modern philosophy.[123]

Although none of the American authors proposed any
radical departure from old-world traditions, most of them
claimed to be developing certain American distinctions.
Rush pointed out that the education of women should be
adapted to the society and government of the country in
which they lived.   He gave five reasons why education in
America should differ from that in England.   First, early
marriages here cut down the time available to women for
study.   Again, American men were so busy that women
must be trained as guardians or stewards of their husbands'
property.   This second idea was not new but probably came
directly from Fénelon.   In the third place, because of the
many and varied occupations of men, women must assume
responsibility for the education òf children, a suggestion
found earlier iri the writings of Locke and Richardson.   The
American form of government made it necessary for mothers
to educate their sons in the principles of liberty and government in order to prepare them for public office.   Finally
the scarcity of servants and the absence of a permanent
servant class in America must affect the training of daugh-

---

[122] Hitchcock, *Bloomsgrove Family*, ii, 86-89.

[123] Timothy Dwight, *Travels in New England and New York* (4 vols.,
London, 1823), i, 474-77.

ters in domestic pursuits.[124]   In this patriotic vein Rush tried to emphasize the value for American women of history, travels, moral essays, and poetry rather than novels.[125]   His exclusion of instrumental music and French from American schools, was on the ground of the short time available to American girls for study.[126]   He observed that we copied Britain in education as in fashions but he condemned the practice.[127]

Others besides Rush, who were connected with the academy at Philadelphia, also sounded an American note.   James Neal dedicated his essay to the " American Fair " and talked of the importance of feminine education as a service to the country.   The ode sung at the Philadelphia Academy commencement in 1794 had a patriotic tone.[128]   Swanwick in his address in 1787 spoke much of the future of America, arguing that since no one could tell what twenty-five years might bring forth in this country we should look beyond our present needs and give our young ladies a polished education.[129]   He claimed the institution of seminaries for young ladies as a development peculiar to America and as one of which the country might be justly proud, a new proof of our civilization and a bulwark of the constitution.[130]

Not all writers were optimistic over the state of American womanhood.   Governor Livingston of New Jersey, from a conservative standpoint, brought up another aspect of the problem of American education.   He was alarmed by the importation of French and English fashions and felt that the young women of the country had departed from the

[124] Rush, *Thoughts upon Female Education*, pp. 5-7.

[125] *Ibid.*, pp. 11-12.   [126] *Ibid.*, pp. 15, 17.

[127] *Ibid.*, p. 19.

[128] See Neal, *Essay*, pp. 24-26 for words.

[129] Swanwick, *Thoughts on Education*, p. 23.

[130] Speech in 1794, given in Neal, *Essay*, pp. 22-23.

standards of their grandmothers. Families were neglected for dissipation, wives were no longer industrious, and French dancing masters had replaced spinning wheels. He quoted the whole passage on the wise woman from the book of Proverbs to show his countrywomen what was expected of them. A few years later, however, the French traveller, Bayard, wrote that Livingston's advice was ignored by the women of America.[181] Noah Webster wished to make the country truly American in education as in speech though his plans to that end were not strikingly original. Since American women often educated their own children he believed they should receive practical training in preparation for this duty. As one might expect he thought it important to teach women the correct use of their mother tongue.[182]

Hitchcock and Rush both implied in the titles of their books an education suited to the existing state of America. Hitchcock dedicated his work to Mrs. Washington as the first lady of the land, possibly the earliest instance in which this was done. The tone of the dedication was significant of the desire for an American expression of opinion on the training of women. European systems were, Hitchcock thought, unsuitable for this country since they were designed for a life different from the American. The country needed to become independent in education, dress, and manners, as it already was in laws and government.[183] He gave some attention also to problems arising from the American practice of early marriages, stressing the need for industry and economy as the only means to wealth which America offered and one in which women could be of marked assistance.[184]

[181] Livingston, "Our Grandmothers," *American Museum* (March, 1791), ix, 143-44; Bayard, *Voyage dans l'intérieur des États-Unis* (2nd ed., Paris, 1791), p. 253.

[182] Webster, *Essays*, pp. 27-30.

[183] Hitchcock, *Bloomsgrove Family*, i, 16-17.

[184] *Ibid.*, ii, 31.

An interesting appeal to the ladies themselves appeared in the *Pennsylvania Gazette* at the time when the new federal constitution was being debated.

It is the duty of the American ladies, in a particular manner, to interest themselves in the success of the measures that are now pursuing by the Federal convention for the happiness of America: They can retain their rank as rational beings only in a free government. In a monarchy (to which the present anarchy in America if not restrained, must soon lead us) they will be considered as valuable members of society, only in proportion as they are capable of being mothers for soldiers, who are the pillars of crowned heads. It is in their power, by their influence over their husbands, brothers and sons, to draw them from those dreams of liberty under a simple democratical form of government, which are so unfriendly to that order and decency, of which nature has made them such amiable examples. As the miseries of slavery will fall with peculiar weight upon them, they are certainly deeply interested in the establishment of such a government as will preserve our liberties, and thereby preserve the rank—the happiness—the influence, and the character in society, for which God intended them.[135]

After their brief years of education were over, marriage was the accepted destiny of young women. American writers in this decade said more of women's education at school and of their later duties in the home than of marriage as an institution and the choice of a husband. Domestic training in preparation for marriage was usually regarded as a function of the home, not the school, although the Moravian Seminary at Bethlehem instructed its pupils in household duties. The writers connected with the Philadelphia academies said little of marriage save that young ladies should have the necessary training in housewifery and kindred duties. Hitchcock insisted that mothers should not allow their daughters to wed

---

[135] *Pennsylvania Gazette*, June 6, 1787 under " Philadelphia."

until they were qualified to be true and faithful wives.[136] Travellers reported that customs governing marriage and the choice of partners were less rigid here than in Europe, women being more likely to have their own way. It is interesting to note that George Washington once said he would never advise a woman to marry without her own consent.[137] Some of the young graduates of the Philadelphia academy spoke pessimistically of the expected loss of power to regulate their own lives, after marriage.[138] The general conclusion was that marriage, although it did not always prove happy, was women's lot and should be accepted as such.

There were few elaborate discussions of marriage, nothing at all comparable to the detailed attention given to education, but there was one notable exception. The " Letters on Marriage " written by Dr. John Witherspoon, president of the College of New Jersey, at the beginning of the Revolution were reprinted later in the *American Museum*. Witherspoon showed no great interest in women as individuals but emphasized the institutional aspect of marriage as of great importance to society. He also discussed marriage in his classroom lectures, observing that the marriage contract was for life and was equally binding on both parties. Witherspoon noted differences of opinion as to men's superiority. If they really possessed it, they must use it cautiously allowing their wives as much liberty as possible. Most nations gave men the right to dispose of property, a right Witherspoon did not find objectionable. He said that marriage could be dissolved only for adultery, desertion, or incapacity,[139] and in his " Letters on Marriage " he complained of attacks on that institution as attacks on society itself. He

---

[136] Hitchcock, *Bloomsgrove Family*, ii, 33.

[137] Washington, *Writings*, Ford ed., x, 318.

[138] See speeches in Neal, *Essay*, p. 35.

[139] John Witherspoon, *Works* (2nd ed., Philadelphia, 1802), iii, 424-27.

found the usual description of married life too exalted, since the outward charms of the ladies were overrated—partly because of the excessive reading of romances and plays. Physical beauty, the least important quality in a wife, was no compensation for other unfortunate traits. In marriage there was less happiness and less unhappiness than was generally supposed, but much genuine satisfaction was possible. To attain this satisfaction in the lower classes financial circumstances should be easy enough for comfort. Marriages were likely to prove successful where there was something like equality in age and rank, though women could marry beneath them with more safety than men. Marked superiority of understanding on one side and good nature on the other made for peace; but specific traits were of less importance than a similarity of qualities in the persons concerned. Good sense was even more important than good nature and overmuch delicacy was undesirable. The larger share of responsibility fell to men since they had the power of selection.[140]

Despite the increased educational opportunities of the period the number of women writers was not large. After 1770 there were several letters and journals not designed for publication, and unknown save to a few contemporaries, which show that their authors were not lacking in literary ability. Among narratives of the Revolution were the journal of Sally Wister (Pennsylvania), that of Mrs. Hannah Drinker (Philadelphia), Margaret Morris (New Jersey), Mrs. Mary Gould Almy (Rhode Island), a letter of Mrs. John Winthrop describing her flight after the Battle of Lexington, and one of Sarah Deming dealing with occurrences in Boston.[141] There is other material of this sort but few women were avowedly writers or attained literary dis-

---

[140] Witherspoon, *Works*, iv, 161-83, " Letters on Marriage."

[141] For details of these see Bibliography.

tinction. The Negro poet, Phillis Wheatley, died in 1784. Annis Boudinot Stockton penned verses to celebrate the surrender at Yorktown but she was never more than an occasional writer. Elizabeth Graeme Fergusson was still living in comparative retirement and discouragement because of the charges made against her of aiding the British; but there were occasional traces of her literary interest in her letters to her friends.[142] Certain new names were becoming conspicuous. The two best known today are those of Abigail Adams, and Mercy Otis Warren. Mrs. Adams made no claim to be an author, but her letters were known among her husband's friends and she had several distinguished correspondents; when she quoted from famous poets or produced political maxims she was no doubt aware of the effect on the reader.[143] Mercy Otis Warren (1728-1814) was a recognized writer of drama, verses, and later of history. The views of these two women had their greatest significance in the field of politics and will be discussed in some detail in that connection. Two women who became professional writers were beginning their work at this time. Hannah Adams (1755-1831) of Medfield, Massachusetts, began her literary career in 1784 with an *Alphabetical Compendium of the Various Sects Which Have Appeared from the Beginning of the Christian Era to the Present Day.* Partly from economic necessity she determined to make writing a profession, and spent much of her time for several years in preparing *A Summary History of New England* which appeared in 1799.[144] Another woman who devoted herself seriously to writing was Judith Sargent Murray whose work is discussed in the following chapter.

[142] *Pennsylvania Magazine of History and Biography,* xli, 386-98.

[143] John Adams, *Works,* ix, 625, to F. A. Vanderkemp (1809).

[144] Article on "Hannah Adams" by Harris E. Starr in *Dictionary of American Biography.*

CHAPTER VI

THE CLOSE OF THE CENTURY

AT the end of the century all American theorists on
women's sphere were affected either directly or indirectly by
the controversy arising from the publication of Mary Wollstonecraft's work and by American reaction to the events of
the French Revolution.   Authors placed themselves definitely
on the radical or the conservative side and, although the
educational developments of the preceding fifteen years were
not forgotten, fear of radicalism tended to check feminine
advancement.   Women's position and education were, however, treated in several books.   Two of the more liberal
school appeared first in periodicals.   In *Alcuin, a Dialogue,*
Charles Brockden Brown, the novelist, discussed the rights
of women in a way which showed clearly the influence of
Mary Wollstonecraft and William Godwin.   This dialogue,
published in 1798 in the *Weekly Magazine* of Philadelphia,
appeared in pamphlet form in New York in the same year.
The Gleaner, a collection of the essays of Judith Sargent
Murray, which among other topics discussed women's training in a liberal spirit, was reprinted from the *Massachusetts
Magazine* for which she had written for several years.
Brown was apparently passing through a stage of youthful
radicalism, but in the case of Mrs. Murray it is interesting to
speculate on the possible connection between her advanced
views and the religious teaching of her husband, one of the
founders of Universalism in America.

Brown's work took the form of conversation with a lady
on the subject of women's political and other rights.   This

discussion, in the main favorable to the extension of women's rights, followed closely the thought of Mary Wollstonecraft with occasional borrowings from Godwin. It was assumed that the admitted differences between the sexes were as nothing to the differences in individuals of the same sex which arose from circumstances and education. Women's way of life in the past had produced some bad effects in their character; for instance, their addiction to scandal was explained, though not excused, by the fact that their natural curiosity had been denied all outlet but gossip. To remind women, however, that their sex had produced no Pythagoras or Socrates was unfair since the opportunity for such careers had been denied. The only acceptable apology for the prevailing inferior position of women lay in the fact that some part of the community had to be condemned to servile occupations and that it perhaps made little difference whether such assignment was based on sex or on some other distinction. Women were in reality the equals but not the superiors of men. A trace of Mary Wollstonecraft's ideas regarding coeducation appears in Brown's statement that the customary separation of the sexes after early childhood had the injurious result of making the ideas, pursuits, systems of morality, and even the meanings given words by men and women different. Relationship between the sexes was thus constrained, neither being able to express its true sentiments.

Legal conditions, Brown went on to say, reduced married women to a state of unlimited obedience though the yoke was lighter in America than in most countries. Moreover laws made by men had perhaps done as much to protect women in the past as to injure them. As women's occupations were to some extent dependent on their legal rights, Brown explained that the law did not bar them from trade or wage earning, if they wished to undertake such work. Churches did not permit them to enter the ministry but there was nothing to keep them from attaining sanctity. The excuses given for not allowing women to be physicians, lawyers, or religious leaders were, Brown thought, poor. He went into some detail on the reasons why women had not hitherto taken part in politics and he presented arguments on both sides of the question without reaching any definite conclusions. The masculine belief was that, although women were excluded from participation in government, their happiness was consulted in the decisions reached. The woman's response was, that so long as she was conscious of willing and moving she would not consent to be treated as nothing whatever politicians might say. Despotisms existed only because of the subservience of the slaves under them. Men were barred from voting by shortness of residence, poverty, youth or color; but mere sex was too purely physical a circumstance and had too little influence to be accepted with patience as a barrier to women's participation in government. Even though property considerations might arise with married women there were many others who were independent and could take part in government. The man's response to this was that women in public office would only arouse feelings of regret and disapprobation, that the sexes were different but women were superior in their own sphere.[1]

A continuation of this dialogue, not printed in Brown's lifetime, was published by Dunlap in 1815 in his life of Brown.[2] It would be interesting to know whether fear of popular opinion on the subject restrained Brown or whether the omission was merely fortuitous. The discussion did not accord with many popular ideas of propriety. In it Brown pictured a Utopian society in which no distinction between

[1] *Alcuin: A Dialogue* (New York, 1798). Also *Weekly Magazine*, i (1798), 198, 231, 271, 298.

[2] William Dunlap, *Life of Charles Brockden Brown* (Philadelphia, 1818), i, 71-105.

the sexes save the physiological one was recognised. They received the same education, dressed alike, and followed the same pursuits. Both took part in the provision of food and shelter but beyond that might occupy themselves as they pleased. Most of this later section was concerned with marriage and was really a discussion of William Godwin's views to which Brown subscribed only in part.[3] In this portion of the dialogue the lady upheld marriage as an institution, although she attacked many of the evils which had grown up in connection with it. The gentleman followed more closely the ideas of Godwin, who wished to abolish marriage. Both agreed that the inequality of the sexes under prevailing conditions was unjust. Women by marriage were made slaves and in large measure lost their own property. The debaters did not agree on the necessity for sharing the same domestic establishment nor on the effect of unlimited divorce on public morals although such divorce was thought desirable. The most extreme statement made was that marriage was based only on custom regarding sexual intercourse and that one might decide for one's self the correct procedure when the type of marriage prescribed by law did not conform to one's notion of duty. Brown ended with the more cautious definition of marriage as a union based on free and mutual consent which could not exist without friendship and personal fidelity; a relationship which ceased to be just when it ceased to be spontaneous.[4]

Mrs. Judith Sargent Murray under the name " Constantia" produced a number of essays which appeared in the *Massachusetts Magazine* and other periodicals. The articles in the *Massachusetts Magazine* were later reprinted in three volumes under the title, *The Gleaner,* a book dedicated to John

[3] Brown also discussed Godwin's views on marriage in his novel *Ormond.* See pp. 199-200, *infra.*

[4] Dunlap, *Life of Brown,* i, 105.

Adams.[5]   The collection, which included two plays and a novel of sorts, had a number of familiar essays in avowed imitation of the *Spectator,* some of them dealing with women's problems.   The essays as they first appeared had purported to be the work of a man but the sex of the writer was admitted in the preface of *The Gleaner.*[6]   In the essays were descriptions of women who conducted themselves with exceptional propriety, pleas for simplicity in dress, and for the development of American fashions in clothes and literature.[7]   The novel contained much similar material; the whole book, though didactic in tone, yet showed liberal ideas.   One long paper on women's interests which, though not notably original, was valuable as an exposition of current thought, was offered as a supplement to a paper on the " Equality of the Sexes " which had appeared in the *Massachusetts Magazine* in 1790.   Mrs. Murray began this paper by congratulating her countrywomen on the revolution of thought in recent years which made it possible for them to devote time to studies other than the needle.   The " Rights of Women," she thought, were just beginning to be understood in their true sense.   The younger generation must now show that the enlarged scope of female education had been justified.   Mrs. Murray drew a glowing picture of this new and more enlightened era in female history, which was to manifest itself in the intellectual development of women free from romantic ideas of marriage and ready to act as enlightened and thoughtful mothers.   She believed that women might become as independent as Mary Wollstonecraft had wished, if they were taught to earn their own living and to regard matrimony only as a probable contingency.   Education for economic independence would enable women to make choices in marriage

[5] Published Boston, February, 1798.

[6] *The Gleaner,* Preface, viii-x.   See also i, 13; iii, 313.

[7] *Ibid.,* iii, 110-13; 261-2, etc.

with' much greater freedom. Moreover the united efforts of men and women for support might save many families from destruction—a situation in which the writer had had practical experience. She closed her article with descriptions of several women who had been notably successful in business ventures of their own.[8]

Mrs. Murray regarded the idea of women's incapacity in any field as inadmissible in the new age. She enumerated women's talents in many different directions illustrating her statements with historical and geographical examples. Where women had failed of accomplishment in the past it was because of masculine restrictions rather than fundamental limitations, for their minds were naturally as capable of improvement as men's. Mrs. Murray developed a number of examples of equality between the sexes. Among these were ingenuity, resourcefulness, the capacity to endure hardships, heroism, patriotism, energy, eloquence, faithfulness, influence in public affairs, ability to support the toils of government with honor, and literary skill. In the list which she presented of successful women of her own time most of the names were those of English authors including both. More and Wollstonecraft. American names were Warren, " Antonia," " Euphelia," and " Philenia." [9]

The writings of Brown and Mrs. Murray represented radical thought, but there was more material to be found on conventional lines. The organization of women's charitable societies, beginning just before 1800, which gave an appearance of progress, really represented an intensification of conservative thought, as seen in the published sermons delivered before the societies. One exponent of the old school was Charles Stearns, a New England clergyman, who speaking

---

[8] *Gleaner*, iii, 188-224. For an account of Mrs. Murray's life and work see Vena B. Field, *Constantia; a Study of the Life and Works of Judith Sargent Murray* (*University of Maine Studies*, ser. 2, no. 17).

[9] The pen name of Mrs. Sarah Apthorp Morton.

in verse rather than from the pulpit, proffered advice to the fair sex in a poem entitled the *Ladies' Philosophy of Love*.[10] Similar ideas pervaded the memoir which Dr. David Ramsay wrote of his wife, Martha Laurens, and which, though it appeared after 1800, dealt with this decade. In 1797 Mrs. Hannah Webster Foster, author of the famous novel, *The Coquette,* issued proposals for printing by subscription, *The Boarding School,* " By a Lady of Massachusetts," designed to improve the manners and form the character of young ladies. In the guise of farewell talks given by the teacher of a small and select school to her pupils as they approached womanhood, Mrs. Foster gave her own detailed and highly conventional views on the education and duties of young ladies. They were in keeping with her position as the wife of a New England clergyman and with the style of morality found in her novel.[11]   A more normal view of the situation, and one not designed for publication, was presented in the letters of Eliza Southgate Bowne, schoolgirl and young lady during this decade.

As an expression of opinion in which women themselves played a large part, it may be worth while to turn first to the charitable societies. The earliest of these appears to have been the " New York Ladies' Society for the Relief of Poor Widows with Small Children," founded in December, 1796. The Boston Female Asylum followed in 1800 and in the next five years there were similar organizations in Baltimore, Philadelphia, Providence, Salem, one in Troy or Albany, and several in New England including Hanover, N. H.[12]   Hart-

[10] Leominster, Mass., 1797.

[11] Article on Mrs. Foster in *Dictionary of American Biography* and advertisement of *The Boarding School* in *Columbian Centinel,* September 6, 1797.

[12] Timothy Alden, *Sermon to the Portsmouth Female Asylum* (1804), p. 9. Alden refers to Troy but perhaps meant Albany where Eliphalet Nott preached to such a group in 1804.

ford women formed a society in 1809. The annual sermons preached to the Salem and Boston societies were printed regularly and those of the other organizations occasionally so that there are abundant data on their work. The ladies contributed small dues, often a cent a day, for the care of widows and orphans, especially for the education of young female orphans in the paths of domesticity and religion until they were of an age to be placed in service.[13] Usually they were placed out at the age of ten to remain until grown. The plan obviously had a practical as well as charitable aspect in furnishing a supply of cheap but trained servants. There was some gain in having women organized for any purpose but the influence of these societies was on the whole conservative. Under their plans they provided, with the approbation of the preachers, that the orphans under their care should receive at least a modicum of education. This instruction in plain sewing, reading and perhaps writing was no greater than that usually given apprentices.[14]

Funeral sermons at this time continued to emphasize the place of woman as a crown for her husband, praiseworthy in so far as she manifested the qualities attributed to the wise woman of the book of Proverbs.[15] Amos Chase of Litchfield preaching in 1791, on the death of his wife Rebecca, gave a long discussion on character in women, emphasizing goodness, sincerity, modesty, humanity, industry and piety as traits to be cultivated; he called a prudent wife the gift of

[13] See Appendix A for list of such sermons. In Portsmouth dues were two dollars a year. At Hartford twenty-five cents a quarter.

[14] Compare Robert F. Seybolt, *Apprenticeship and Apprenticeship Education in Colonial New England and New York* (New York, 1917), chaps. ii-iv.

[15] John Devotion, *Sermon on Madam Griswold* (1788), pp. 23-24. Joseph Lathrop, *Sermon on Mrs. Gay* (1796), pp. 19-20; Nathaniel Emmons, *Sermon on Mrs. Bathsheba Sanford* (1800), pp. 17-18.

the Lord.[16]   Many sermons delivered before charitable societies went no farther in their discussion of women's position
than to stress the peculiar appropriateness of charitable work
for women and its enhancement of their charms, but others
went into more detail.   William Bentley, who in most
matters was regarded as liberal, wrote that he found from
observation of women that social influence was more power-
ful than intellectual in shaping their character, that their best
traits depended on love of home, cheerful economy, and
pleasant family associations.   The worthy women of history,
he thought, were usually found in domestic not public life.
He did not wish women to suffer as a result of their position
saying—

Let us flatter ourselves, that in some things we can do better for
woman than she can do for herself, still let us confess that she
is our companion, our friend, and our equal.   If we hold the
power let us value the riches of our subjects as our own, and
esteem it honourable to supply all the knowledge and the hope,
which can render a woman deserving of admiration and praise.[17]

John S. J. Gardiner of Boston made his sermon in 1809
a plea for the more serious education of women in general.
He felt that women's customary inferiority to men in reasoning and judgment arose from faulty education with too much
emphasis, on the manual exercises of painting, music, and
embroidery and too much reading of novels.   To prepare
women for the duties of discreet wives and prudent mothers,
he recommended solid education in grammar and arithmetic
to strengthen the mind.   Women need not undertake studies
designed to prepare for activity outside the home but should

[16] Extracts from Chase's sermon may be found in an article by Kate
Woodward Noble in *Connecticut Magazine*, x (1906), 81-91.

[17] *Discourse delivered to Salem Female Charitable Society* (Salem,
1807), p. 24.

read classical authors in English and French if they had time.[18] This could hardly be called an advance in liberal ideas.

The aims of Mrs. Foster in the education of young ladies may be best set forth in her own words—

to polish the mental part, to call forth the dormant virtues, to unite and arrange the charms of person and mind, to inspire a due sense of decorum and propriety, and to instill such principles of propriety, morality, benevolence, prudence and economy, as might be useful through life.[19]

She presented a detailed daily program whose principal feature was needlework accompanied by reading and discussion. She laid stress on sewing well as a means of livelihood in distress and a help in acts of charity.[20] In accordance with the prevailing sentiment Mrs. Foster described novels as the favorite and most dangerous form of reading. Thinking perhaps of her own work she explained that some novels conveyed lessons of moral improvement through pictures of virtue rewarded and vice and indiscretion punished.[21]

Charles Stearns's *Ladies' Philosophy of Love,* a didactic poem, was written according to its author in 1774, but it was not published until almost the end of the century and gives evidence of revision after the Revolution. His primary emphasis was on the occult sympathy between the sexes and the value of virtue in attracting a lover. Penelope was to his mind the great example for women. He wished to give directions for the training of girls which should enable them to obtain and hold the right sort of husbands, and especially he wished to help them to avoid the dangers of seduction.

---

[18] Gardiner, *Sermon* . . . *the Boston Female Asylum* (1809), pp. 14-18.

[19] *The Boarding School,* p. 7.

[20] *Ibid.,* pp. 11-15.

[21] *The Boarding School,* pp. 18-24. Compare Fanny Burney's address to possible critics at the beginning of *Evelina.*

His directions for education were most conventional adding nothing to other British and American works.[22]   His views on marriage were more liberal.   Since true marriages came only from mutual love he believed that parents had no right to force children into a hated match.[23]   Marital happiness arose from constancy, the use of reason, and the preservation of the lover's respect, and young women must be prepared for this situation.[24]

The average American was too busy to comment much on the theoretical side of feminine training; but Aaron Burr, writing in 1793 to his wife regarding the education of their nine-year-old daughter, Theodosia, gave some of his views. He feared above all things that his daughter might become a mere fashionable woman; but if this could be avoided, he hoped to convince the world through her, " what neither sex appear to believe—that women have souls."   He thought women capable of genius; their defects were due to education, prejudice, and habit.   He praised Mary Wollstonecraft as an able advocate of her sex and regarded her book as a work of genius.[25]   At the age of ten Theodosia, who was already reading Terence, began the study of Greek and soon read Lucian.   She devoted much attention to history on which her father recommended Millot's work as better than Rollin's which he characterized as tedious and superstitious nonsense.[26]   Burr's interest in feminine education is sometimes regarded as a means of self-glorification through his

[22] *The Ladies' Philosophy of Love*, pp. 21-23.

[23] *Ibid.*, p. 12.

[24] *Ibid.*, p. 49 *et seq.*

[25] Matthew L. Davis, *Memoirs of Aaron Burr* (2 vols., New York, 1869), i, 361-63.

[26] *Correspondence of Aaron Burr and his Daughter Theodosia*, Mark Van Doren, ed. (New York, 1929), pp. 12, 19, 27, 41, 47. Rollin and Millot were well-known French writers of ancient history. Millot wrote also on the history of England and France.

daughter's accomplishments. Whatever her father's motives in educating her, Theodosia was by no means lacking in the gifts of the brilliant family to which she belonged.

In referring favorably to Mary Wollstonecraft, Burr was going counter to the views of most of the clergy who were prone to attack her teachings and those of William Godwin.[27] Hannah More on the other hand was generally approved.[28] The preachers of charity sermons tried to counteract the evil influence of radical Europeans as far as they could. Daniel Dana declared in a sermon at Newburyport that—

The philosophy which discards all distinction of sexual character, is itself fit to be discarded with mingled indignation and contempt. Had this sage discovery of the eighteenth century been permitted to die in its birth, it had been better.[29]

Dr. David Ramsay, physician and author of South Carolina, was thoroughly in accord with clerical ideas. His wife, Martha, daughter of Henry Laurens, received most of her education in England and France and read widely. After her death there was published a little volume containing a sketch of her life by her husband, with selections from her correspondence and religious writings. Dr. Ramsay perhaps unconsciously epitomized a widespread view of a wife's proper relation to her husband, in his description of Mrs. Ramsay's attitude toward the duties of a wife.

In the same manner she had determined what were her conjugal duties. She was well acquainted with the plausible reasoning of modern theorists, who contend for the equality of the sexes; and few females could support their claims to that authority on better grounds than she might advance; but she yielded all

[27] See sermon preached by Joseph Eckley before the Boston Female Asylum in 1802, p. 8.

[28] Dana, *Sermon* (1804), pp. 13-14.

[29] Dana, *Sermon*, p. 18.

pretensions on this score, in conformity to the positive declarations of holy writ, of which the following were full to the point, and in her opinion outweighed whole volumes of human reasoning.[30] . . . In practice as well as theory, she acknowledged the dependent subordinate condition of her sex; and considered it as a part of the curse denounced on Eve, as being the 'first in the transgression.' I Tim. ii, 13, 14. The most self-denying duties of the conjugal relations being thus established on a divine foundation and illustrated by those peculiar doctrines of revelation on which she hung all her hopes, the other duties followed by an easy train of reasoning, and were affectionately performed.[31]

In a note to this passage Ramsay added—

Such were the principles and conduct of a wife who had read Mary Woolstoncraft's *Rights of Women,* but studied her Bible with care and attention, as the standard of faith and practice.[32]

It is a relief to turn from formal works on women to the letters of Eliza Southgate Bowne written between her departure for school in 1797 and her death in 1809. She belonged to a New England family and received part of her education at Mrs. Rowson's school at Medford, which in itself meant greater educational opportunities than were given to the average girl.[33] Mrs. Susanna Haswell Rowson, famous as the author of *Charlotte Temple,* over which thousands of readers wept, began her career as actress and writer in England and America, but left the stage in 1797 and opened a school in Boston which she later moved to

[30] At this point Dr. Ramsay quoted Genesis, iii, 16, Ephesians, v, 22, 23, 24.

[31] Ramsay, *Memoirs of the Life of Martha Laurens Ramsay* (3rd ed., Boston, 1827), pp. 41-42.

[32] *Ibid.,* note p. 43.

[33] *A Girl's Life Eighty Years Ago* (New York, 1888), Introduction, pp. iv-v.

Medford.[34] Perhaps she encouraged her pupils to read works on women. In any case Miss Southgate had read Mary Wollstonecraft's book and it is clear from her letters that she must also have been familiar with Gregory's *Father's Legacy*, or some work closely akin to it. Eliza Southgate was no theorist in the sense of consciously writing material for publication; but in a series of letters to a young cousin, Moses Porter, she compared the qualities of the two sexes and gave her views on marriage in great detail. Though she expressed few sentiments not rehearsed in the preceding pages, her letters afford an excellent view of the ideas of a well-read young woman of the time.

Discussing the difference in the mental qualities of the two sexes Miss Southgate decided that women were sprightly and men profound, a difference emphasized by the character of their education and their pursuits in later life. Women had no reason for undertaking profound research and the desire of study for pleasure only was rare. Since women lacked incentives to action, the presence of even an occasional ray of genius in them was thought surprising. Women excelled men in imagination but this again might be the result of the different training of the sexes, for persons of sound judgment would not possess such an imaginative flow of ideas as did most women. Women had minds which must have been designed by the Creator for use and cultivation. Certainly the pursuits of the sexes should vary but the development of women's natural qualities would not infringe on masculine prerogatives, for there was no reason to suppose that, given education, women would assume the right of command. Educated women would remain under the same degree of subordination as before because they would see

[34] Mary E. Sargent, "Susanna Rowson," *Medford Historical Register*, vii (April, 1904), 25-40.

the necessity of submission.[35] Censure would, Miss Southgate felt, follow any woman who attempted to vindicate her
sex. She devoted a paragraph to Mary Wollstonecraft,
many of whose sentiments she thought admirable, although
she feared the application of her principles might lead to
the wrong sort of conduct. Any good which might come
from Mary Wollstonecraft's work was likely to be prevented
by prejudice against her.[36]

Having disposed of women's education Eliza Southgate
went on to consider marriage. The reader of eighteenth-
century English works on this subject will not be surprised
to learn that women could not expect to wed the men whom
they would prefer above all others, that marriage followed
gratitude more often than love, that gratitude was the usual
foundation of the esteem a wife felt for her husband and so
on.[37] Although Miss Southgate presented these as popular
sentiments on the matter she felt that they were not enough
for her. Therefore she resigned herself to the single life
as being more dignified than marriage without love. This
problem did not long trouble her for she was happily married
at nineteen.[38]

British influence was still markedly felt in this period but
was itself divided into two schools. The difference in tone
between Brown's work and that of Dr. Ramsay was very
nearly the difference between the teachings of Mary Wollstonecraft and of Hannah More. In spite of our boasted
Americanism, British writings still circulated here and
received increasing attention from our periodicals, though
the desire for an American standard was occasionally men-

---

[35] Compare Hitchcock, *Bloomsgrove Family*, ii, 43-44; Rush, *Thoughts upon Female Education*, p. 25 with these ideas on submission.

[36] *A Girl's Life*, pp. 58-62.

[37] Compare Gregory, *Father's Legacy*, pp. 30-31.

[38] *A Girl's Life*, pp. v-vi, 37-41.

tioned. An instance of this may be found, curiously enough, in the foreword of a compilation entitled *The American Spectator, or Matrimonial Preceptor,* which was really taken from an English book of similar title;[39] but the advertisement contained a few phrases designed to gratify American patriotism—

The female mind is, probably, no where, so generally cultivated, and adorned with that knowledge and sentiment, which qualify for conjugal, and parental relations. THE RIGHTS OF WOMEN, as well as of MEN, are acknowledged and (a few instances excepted, in which the application of *American* or *Republican* to the title of *Husband* is a mere solecism) they are caressed as the first and dearest friends of their partners.[40]

In spite of this pleasant phraseology it is obvious that the women of 1800 were seldom regarded as the intellectual equals of the men to whom they were allied.

[39] The American volume was printed for David West, Boston, 1797.

[40] *American Spectator,* vi, Advertisement.

CHAPTER VII

Women in Early American Literature

I

THE women of fiction and drama are significant for the social historian in two ways; they may serve as actual pictures of women of their time showing them as they were, or they may present patterns for the feminine reader to follow or to avoid. The numerous second-rate novels of romantic adventure so frequent in eighteenth-century England did neither of these things and in spite of their popularity in revolutionary America are of little importance to the student of the period. This also holds true of early American romances written in the same style. On the other hand the work of Richardson with its idealized heroines set standards for British and American theory and his books formed an essential part of the education of many women; English dramatists also left their impress.[1] Our own literature developed so slowly that there were no American novels until after the Revolution, but when these did appear many of them had heroines resembling Harriet Byron and Clarissa Harlowe.[2] The American productions, although inferior in literary quality to Richardson's books, did not depart widely from his ideals, which persisted in the heroines of American fiction well into the nineteenth century, and served indirectly as patterns for the young girls of this country.

[1] *Infra*, p. 45, *et seq.*

[2] Because of this late development some novels are included in this discussion which were not published until after 1800.

Among the first novels written in America, three, which had enough in common to be treated collectively, bore many resemblances to Richardson's work. These were: Mrs. Rowson's *Charlotte Temple; The Coquette* by Mrs. Hannah Webster Foster; and *The Power of Sympathy.*[3] Although Mrs. Rowson's book was written in England, she had spent her girlhood in America and passed the latter part of her life in New England, so that her work, with its New York setting, may well be considered an American novel.

Each tale had a basis in fact, in the cases of Mrs. Rowson and Mrs. Foster taken from relatives of the authors.[4] Each dealt with a young woman of good family and education who through some minor slip on her part fell into the power of a designing man, was seduced, and died soon afterwards in a repentant state. In *The Power of Sympathy* this was not the experience of the heroine herself, whose tragedy was of a different nature, but that of her dead mother. *The Coquette* and *The Power of Sympathy* both told their story, as Richardson had done, by means of letters exchanged between the characters. All three authors emphasized their moral purpose; the title page of *The Power of Sympathy* stated that the book was designed to represent the " specious causes and to expose the fatal consequences of seduction." [5] Mrs. Rowson and Mrs. Foster made similar apologies for their productions. Recording personal tragedies for moral effect was not, however, confined to novels. A letter reprinted in

---

[3] Probably by William Hill Brown. See Milton Ellis, " The Author of the First American Novel," *American Literature*, iv, 359-68.

[4] See Introduction to 1905 edition of *Charlotte Temple*. For *The Coquette*, see Caroline Dall, *Romance of the Association* (Cambridge, 1875), esp. pp. 69-80 and Charles Knowles Bolton, *The Elizabeth Whitman Mystery* (Peabody, Mass., 1912). The 1854 edition of *The Coquette* (Boston), pp. 3-30 has an historical preface by Jane E. Locke which is very inaccurate.

[5] Boston, 1789, Isaiah Thomas, 2 vols.

the *Independent Chronicle,* Boston, on September 11, 1788, referred to Miss Whitman's tragic death, on which the plot of *The Coquette* was later based, as "a good moral lecture to young ladies." [6] The novels contained many edifying comments, though it was probably their sentimental rather than their moral qualities which attracted their numerous readers. There was a strong effort to play upon the emotions, but the stories lack verisimilitude, partly because of the tendency to make characters types of some particular virtue or vice rather than to show them as individuals.

There was a marked difference in the reception of these stories. *The Power of Sympathy* contained a detailed account of a scandal in a prominent Boston family whose names were so thinly disguised that apparently everyone in Boston knew on what the episode of Ophelia was based. The members of this family were much distressed and attempted to suppress the book by buying and destroying all copies within reach. [7] The rest of the story was not generally approved, since the hero, though in ignorance of the relationship, was in love with his half-sister. This was discovered in time to prevent their marriage but the heroine soon died of grief. After her death the brother committed suicide, another reason for viewing the book with disfavor. All in all, the work seemed designed to appeal to a lurid popular taste rather than to carry out the high moral sentiments which the author professed. *Charlotte Temple* unlike *The Power of Sympathy,* enjoyed widespread popularity and has continued to be read even in the present century. More than a hundred American editions were published between 1794 and 1905. The reputed grave of the heroine in Trinity

[6] C. K. Bolton, *The Elizabeth Whitman Mystery,* pp. 59-60.

[7] See note 2 in this chapter and Emily Pendleton and Milton Ellis, *Philenia: The Life and Works of Sarah Wentworth Morton (University of Maine Studies,* ser. 2, no. 20), pp. 32-40.

churchyard, New York, was often visited by emotionally affected readers.[8] *The Coquette* though it hardly attained an equal success was popular enough to justify reprints as late as 1854, and had in all more than thirty editions.[9]

Of what type were the women over whom so many tears were shed? They were all young and attractive, with a fair education; none of them was wealthy. Their unfortunate associations arose from minor faults and from the vicious character of the men they met. Too much novel reading and, in the case of Charlotte Temple, the intrigues of a French governess, embodying all the supposed faults of her nation, contributed to their downfall. Eliza Wharton of *The Coquette* had indeed persisted in a mild degree of flirtatiousness and independence against the advice of her friends, but her behavior contained nothing which would be thought startling today. As foils to their misguided heroines, all three books had minor female characters who followed the conventions strictly and were rewarded with happiness and good reputations.[10] Such literature emphasized the need of a sheltered life for women, and above all their observance of every detail of propriety. Sweetness and submission rather than vigor and ability marked the heroines, with the possible exception of Eliza Wharton. They copied, perhaps unconsciously, Clarissa Harlowe, as their happier friends resembled Harriet Byron and their seducers Lovelace.

All three novels discussed women's status with advice as to their behavior and training. This material formed no integral part of the plots but was inserted either with genuine moral purpose or to win the approval of the graver sort of

[8] *Charlotte Temple*, F. W. Halsey ed. (New York, 1905), gives the bibliographical history of the book.

[9] Dall, *Romance of the Association*, and Bolton, *The Elizabeth Whitman Mystery*, pp. 149-55.

[10] These were Lucy Sumner and Julia Granby in *The Coquette*, Mrs. Beauchamp in *Charlotte Temple*, and Myra in *The Power of Sympathy*.

critic. The author of *The Power of Sympathy* in a long
discourse on the choice of books for women's reading, treating novels as generally unsuitable, ascribed the downfall of
one young woman, whose name he gave, to notions derived
from too much reading of romances.[11] He also recommended a not very original list of readings,[12] with some
remarks in praise of American literary ladies, urging others
to enter their ranks. In *The Coquette* appropriate amusements for the ladies of Boston were discussed. Readers
were told that tragedies were too distressing to be attended
and that a circus, especially with female performers, was not
suitable for the delicacy of ladies. Museum exhibitions were
thought proper because they added to one's knowledge.[13]
The duties of wives were discussed chiefly through implica-
tion, though in the account of Eliza's relations with Boyer
there was some hint of the special traits expected in a minister's wife.[14] Both the *Power of Sympathy* and *The Coquette* treated the question of parental interference in marriage. In the former the father of the hero objected to the
early marriage of his son. In the latter the heroine at the
request of her parents acquiesced in her betrothal to a man
to whom she was indifferent. The authors agreed on the
propriety of obedience but thought that parents should not
force the issue.

With these novels should perhaps be included a work by
" Constantia ", Mrs. Judith Sargent Murray. Her story of
Margaretta, first published in the *Massachusetts Magazine*,

[11] *Power of Sympathy*, i, 50-52 and note. This was Elizabeth Whitman,
the original of Eliza Wharton in *The Coquette*. See also *The Coquette*
(13th ed., Boston, 1833), p. 168.

[12] *Power of Sympathy*, i, 57-67; ii, 4-19.

[13] *The Coquette*, pp. 173-74.

[14] *The Coquette*, pp. 41-42, 52, 127. Boyer was supposed to be Joseph
Buckminster, a noted clergyman. See Dall, *Romance of the Association*,
pp. 16-17, 65.

was reprinted in *The Gleaner*. Obviously didactic in purpose, its good advice was borne along by a stream of narrative composed of uncertain love affairs, threats of seduction, marital complications, and the reappearance of long-lost relatives. The heroine was most carefully brought up by her foster parents whose methods of educating her and bringing about a happy and appropriate marriage filled many tedious pages. This didactic material was neither new nor very attractively presented but it may have served readers whom the more formal works on education would not have reached.

These first American novels leave one with a renewed sense of women's limited sphere. Women could not wander from the bounds of domesticity and conventionality without danger of criticism. The influence of Richardson was still apparent, with no sign that American ideals for women differed from those current in Great Britain.

Two American satirical novels, Hugh Henry Brackenridge's *Modern Chivalry* (1815), and Royall Tyler's *Algerine Captive* presented good pictures of certain phases of American life but paid little attention to women, though Tyler gave a short sketch of a lady for whom Fielding's Mrs. Western might have served as prototype. Among other intellectual feats she claimed to have read Dr. Johnson's *Dictionary* through in two days.[15] One satire, *Female Quixotism*, probably suggested by the English *Female Quixote*, described the ridiculous adventures of a woman unbalanced by too great addiction to novels.[16] These experiences were given an American setting, but the heroine, unlike Mrs. Lennox's Arabella, was not cured of her follies in time for a happy marriage and had some of her most ludicrous experiences as she approached old age.

[15] Tyler, *Algerine Captive* (2 vols., Walpole, N. H., 1797), i, 112-116.

[16] [Tabitha Tenney], *Female Quixotism: Or, the Extravagant Adventures of Dorcasina Sheldon* (2 vols., Boston, 1829, first ed., probably 1808).

There were occasional American novels of romantic adventure in which the heroines showed no greater force or self-assertion than did the young ladies of the English Gothic romances. Melissa in *Alonzo and Melissa*,[17] torn by her cruel father from a lover who had met financial reverses, was imprisoned in a stone mansion with mysterious nocturnal visitants. She was sent secretly to South Carolina, and only escaped the machinations of her father by spreading a false report of her death. She was described as beautiful and apparently received a conventional education, but she remained throughout a vague and unreal figure. This book like its many British counterparts has little value as a picture of feminine existence or as a reflection of contemporary ideals.

A few novels, however, showed capable and sensible women with resourcefulness in emergencies. They had a more or less genuinely American setting and to some extent revealed the realities of American life, though the English tradition was still apparent. The most important of these were the novels of Charles Brockden Brown but at least two others gave fair pictures of American women. One of these was from the pen of Mrs. Sally Sayward Borrell Keating Wood who signed herself " A Lady." In her preface she discussed women's place which was, she wrote, in the home. She believed, however, that time was better spent in serious writing than in amusement and dissipation; through such efforts women might develop virtue for themselves and renown for their country.[18] She advocated Americanism in literature and independence of Europe in manners and fashions.[19] Her purpose was both patriotic and moral, her

---

[17] Daniel Jackson, Jr. [Isaac Mitchell?], *Alonzo and Melissa: or the Unfeeling Father* (1811). First published as *The Asylum*. See *Cambridge History of American Literature*, i, 292.

[18] *Dorval* (Portsmouth, N. H., 1801), Preface, p. iv.

[19] *Ibid.*, pp. iii-iv, 80.

novel being chiefly designed to expose the evils of speculation. The villain and principal character, in her *Dorval or the Speculator,* was supposed to have been drawn from life. The story of *Dorval* did not describe the heroine's downfall but depicted Aurelia as one who maintained her own integrity and supported others through a variety of trials. Among Aurelia's misfortunes were the elopement of her betrothed with her best friend, the loss of her father's property, his subsequent imprisonment and death, the loss of friends, and her mother's marriage to the villain, to say nothing of robbery, illness and murder in her immediate circle. When the family troubles came she accompanied her father to prison, and later when Dorval married her mother and drove Aurelia from her home, she supported herself in Philadelphia by needlework. She had also the shock of learning that the parents to whom she had been so devoted were only foster parents. In the end, her real father and her unknown half-brother appeared, her supposedly dead lover returned, and the wedding was celebrated with a feast at which the poor were not forgotten. Throughout all her trials, Aurelia displayed fortitude, consideration for others, industry and resourcefulness; her distrust of the speculation which gave the book its title showed some business acumen. She was not markedly frail and clinging, though in spite of Mrs. Wood's efforts in behalf of Americanism her character had a Richardsonian touch. She had been carefully educated by an aunt, who proved later to have been her true mother, and who was herself a gracious and accomplished person. This aunt, anticipating the possibility of poverty in the family, gave Aurelia a practical as well as elegant education so that at an early age she was capable of directing household tasks or performing them herself, and her days were well filled. In times of prosperity, she studied dancing, drawing, and music under expert masters, and also learned arithmetic, languages, geography, and needlework. Her annual allowance she used with liberality and economy for though she enjoyed amusements her fondness for retirement and active duties enabled her to pass her time comfortably away from society.[20] Like a dutiful daughter she received her lover's addresses only with her father's consent and insisted upon a long interval between betrothal and marriage to test the lover's constancy.[21]

The other women of the novel were quite different. Miss Wilson, aunt of Aurelia's foster father, was a dignified and intelligent old maid.[22] Mrs. Morley, the supposed mother of the heroine, was a weak woman, overfond of show, gaiety and social life and easily misled.[23] The accomplishments of Aurelia's real mother have already been noticed; the tragic but innocent circumstances surrounding Aurelia's birth had reduced this lady to a profound melancholy though she still found enjoyment in books and in the care of her child.[24] The hero's mother was a good widow with a cultivated mind, elegant manners and a gentle cheerful disposition, who had refrained from remarriage in order to promote the happiness of her son. She managed his support on a limited income and educated him herself even to the extent of preparing him for " Providence College." [25]

The book gave evidence of the author's familiarity with English writers on women's training. Aurelia, in a passage like one in Dr. Gregory's *Father's Legacy,* discussed the possibility of friendship with a sensible and refined man with-

---

[20] *Dorval*, pp. 14-18.
[21] *Ibid.*, p. 62 *et seq.*
[22] *Ibid.*, pp. 8-9.
[23] *Ibid.*, pp. 10, 21.
[24] *Ibid.*, p. 10 *et seq.*
[25] *Ibid.*, pp. 71, 186.

out thought of marriage.[26]   A minor character in the book was stigmatized as a disciple of Mary Wollstonecraft, who, it appeared, was endeavoring to shake the foundations of female happiness and teach women to trample upon duty and virtue. The *Vindication* was as injurious to female happiness as Tom Paine's *Age of Reason* was to the cause of religion, for Mrs. Wollstonecraft laughed at the institution of marriage and wished to deprive mothers of their best and sweetest employment.[27]

Samuel Woodworth, who wrote at a somewhat later date, presented in the *Champions of Freedom* (1816), normal though slightly idealized American girls. The hero's sister shared her brother's education and recreation along with certain feminine accomplishments. His sweetheart Catherine, the daughter of immigrants, studied practical and serious subjects first and ornamental accomplishments afterwards in a manner which would have done credit to any English didactic writer. The other women of the book, though active and well read, were conventionalized figures in the story which was, in the main, a history of the War of 1812. The position of women was exalted in a fashion more eulogistic than practical;[28] but with this high praise of virtuous women there was much condemnation of a young lady who, after marrying in deference to the wishes of her parents, allowed an earlier love to revive. Her marriage to a man she did not love was thought permissible, but by such a marriage she had bound herself thenceforth to sacrifice feeling to duty. Failing in this she lost her reputation completely and through her plots for revenge nearly ruined the lives of the principal characters. The book emphasized propriety; a masquerade held in Boston was placed under

[26] *Dorval*, pp. 30, 49-50. Compare Gregory's *Father's Legacy*, p. 29.
[27] *Ibid.*, pp. 46-47.
[28] *Champions of Freedom* (2 vols., New York, 1816), ii, 99-101.

amusingly strict direction to prevent the evils attributed to similar English entertainments. Parents confided in the prudence of their daughters and, with the exception noted above, did not interfere with the girls' choice in marriage save by friendly advice.

The novels of Charles Brockden Brown formed a group by themselves; their literary quality was higher than that of most of the volumes previously discussed, with more variety in the types of women presented. Brown's women were individuals with problems of their own, not mere bundles of conventional virtues. Some of his books, however, can be set aside as of no great importance in the study of women. In *Edgar Huntley,* women played only minor parts, and although the narrator of *Wieland* was a woman her character was not made especially vivid. In *Clara Howard,* Clara and Mary Wilmot exemplified the problem of love against duty in marriage. The hero was obliged to choose between the two women; most of the letters of which the book was composed dealt with his changeable feelings and emotional struggles. The concept of marriage illustrated in this story was on a high plane, the two women being intelligent and interesting figures, not stereotypes of perfection; but unfortunately the book as a whole was dull and unreal.

Arthur Mervyn presented women of many sorts, from the coarse and designing servant who entangled the affections of Arthur's father to the English Jewess whom the hero finally married. There were even some foreign women in the story, introduced primarily to lend color and add to the mysteries of the tale. The Quaker farmer's daughter who was sweet and intelligent but lacked breadth of culture, the young music teacher proud of maintaining herself by her own industry, the lady who aided her brother in his work as a copyist, were all clearly individualized figures exhibiting certain American traits.

In *Jane Talbot* the life story of a young widow was told in letters with an attempt to analyze moods and motives. The book was concerned with certain ethical problems; Jane wished to marry an avowed freethinker in defiance of the desires of her foster mother. Her first marriage had taken place in deference to the wishes of her family but she had come to think such an arrangement an inadequate basis for marriage. The problems propounded were not really solved in one sense, for the second marriage was postponed until after the mother's death and the lover had in the meantime changed many of his radical ideas, but the discussion of such problems at all showed a changed attitude.

Constantia Dudley in *Ormond* was an even more forceful character than Jane Talbot. She believed that actions should be governed by the dictates of truth, and that marriage was a life contract not to be entered upon hastily nor in extreme youth but only when one's character had become permanent.[29] For this reason she rejected the first suitor who offered himself, a rejection which proved later to have been wise. She also refused a man of wealth, inferior to her in education and understanding, since she thought poverty less constraining than the circumstances of such a marriage, and did not believe that she could conscientiously take the marriage vows with such a partner. Her father also proved himself liberal, for although he would have gained much by the marriage he made no attempt to force her.[30] Constantia, who was in all other particulars a dutiful daughter, especially in times of illness and misfortune, willingly gave up her own opportunities and possessions to devote herself to the care of her family. She was obliged to support them by needlework, for her own education had been in Latin and mathematics, subjects so unfeminine that they offered her no opportunity of employment.

[29] *Ormond* (Philadelphia, 1887 in *Works*), p. 20.
[30] *Ormond*, pp. 81-84.

Ormond, a sinister and mysterious individual, came to play a large part in Constantia's life, though she never regarded him as a lover. He held various unorthodox ideas to some of which Constantia was receptive since, although herself a religious person, she had not been firmly grounded in any creed. Ormond's views on marriage, extensively discussed in the description of his relations to his mistress, were an adaptation of the ideas of William Godwin, which Brown neither accepted nor rejected entirely. Ormond believed marriage absurd because of the incurable imperfection of the female character and the irrevocable nature of the vows taken; he was not looking for a household superintendent and did not wish to forego the liberty of choosing his companion at will. Helena, his mistress, though neither ignorant nor intellectual, possessed the qualities which Ormond desired for sensual gratification. Since however her education had not taught her to reason on the principles of human action or the structure of society, he did not think her qualified to be his wife. She accepted the terms of her relationship to Ormond voluntarily but was not happy in it. Constantia, who believed it Ormond's duty to marry the girl, was unable to convince him of this, and after his desertion Helena committed suicide.[31] Having expounded Ormond's philosophy at great length Brown demonstrated its falsity by subsequent developments. Ormond regarded himself as the instrument of destiny for the control of Constantia's life, even going so far as to instigate the murder of her father. Constantia finally stabbed him to preserve her honor.

Brown's women, far from being figureheads, were not ignorant of developments in contemporary philosophy and though they might blunder could at least think for themselves.

[31] *Ormond*, pp. 116-28, 168. Compare William Godwin, *Enquiry concerning Political Justice* (4th ed., London, 1842), ii, 243-45 and Brown's own ideas in the latter part of *Alcuin*.

While they were hardly to be taken as models for young girls, they marked an altered attitude toward women; Brown's radicalism, however, limited the range of his influence. This was not entirely a matter of chronological development, for *Ormond* was written only two years after Mrs. Foster published *The Coquette*. It is perhaps not too much to say that these two novels represented attitudes toward women as sharply contrasted as those of Hannah More and Mary Wollstonecraft.

II

Plays were frequently presented in this country by companies of travelling players from about 1749; [32] but it is difficult to estimate the importance of any one author. Plays produced by three or more companies may be assumed to have had some influence on American ideas and usage.[33] Among those frequently presented, some, like *Venice Preserved* or Addison's *Cato*, approximated the classic tragedy and had probably little effect on the American comedy of manners or on social behavior, though Marcia in *Cato* combined beauty, dignity and wisdom. Shakespearean heroines were too much apart from everyday types to serve as models, as, for a different reason, were the women of the popular *Beggar's Opera*. Most comedies of manners, however, dealt with women in more normal fashion; though sometimes merely amusing, such plays served to depict current usage and occasionally to change standards. Mrs. Centlivre in *The Busy Body* ridiculed the Spanish custom of keeping women under lock and key. In *A Bold Stroke for a Wife* the plot centered about the need for winning the consent of

[32] George O. Seilhamer, *History of the American Theatre* (3 vols., Philadelphia, 1888-89), i, 2-4. For earlier theatrical performances in New York and other cities see George C. D. Odell, *Annals of the New York Stage*, i (New York, 1927), pp. 1-31.

[33] Detailed accounts of the companies of players and of the performances offered may be found in the first volume of Seilhamer's book.

four guardians.   The heroines of Farquhar's plays were far less dignified than the women in Richardson's novels; particularly they were not averse to playing off men against one another.   Silvia in *The Recruiting Officer* disguised herself as a boy and enlisted in the army as part of a ruse to gain her father's consent to her marriage.   The women in Congreve's *Love for Love* and Vanbrugh's *The Provok'd Husband* were for the most part such types as the country girl, the lady of doubtful reputation and the misguided young wife.   Vanbrugh presented many women who regarded married life as a means of furthering their own amusement and power. Convention, however, did not allow this attitude to triumph and the heroine was made quiet, home-loving and dignified, with many of the qualities found later in Richardson's characters.[34]

Plays of a slightly later date influenced American productions like Tyler's *The Contrast*.   Chief among these was Sheridan's *The School for Scandal; The Rivals* and Goldsmith's *She Stoops to Conquer* were also popular.   Goldsmith's play was given in New York in 1773, *The Rivals* in 1778 and *The School for Scandal* in Baltimore in 1784 and in New York in 1785.[35]   These plays were free from the coarseness of Congreve and Vanbrugh and from the excessive sentimentalism of Richardson.   Sheridan subtly mocked the sentimental type of girl in Julia of *The Rivals* and made the romantic notions of Lydia Languish the source of much amusement.   *The School for Scandal* aptly portrayed current social life.   Sheridan's work was much cleverer and more finished than that of his American imitators.[36]

[34] *The Complete Works of Sir John Vanbrugh* (4 vols., Bloomsbury, 1927).   Compare the characters of Lady Grace and Lady Townly in *The Provok'd Husband* for two ideas of women's place, iii, 186, 225.

[35] Seilhamer, *American Theatre*, i, 318; ii, 36, 108, 185.

[36] *Sheridan's Comedies*, Brander Matthews ed. (Boston and New York, 1891), pp. 20-21, 68-69, 201.

The drama as it developed in this country affords interesting pictures of American women, though it must be admitted that, with minor differences of setting and social customs, the heroines of many American plays would have been equally at home in an English cast. All plays produced in colonial days were of European origin except Thomas Godfrey's *Prince of Parthia,* presented in Philadelphia, April 24, 1767, which was the first play written by an American to be given in America by professional actors.[37] The experiment was not repeated until the production of *The Contrast* by Royall Tyler in New York City, April 16, 1787.[38] After this, American dramas became more numerous, though it was not until the second decade of the next century that an extensive repertoire was available. Some of the first American plays have little to interest the student of women. Mercy Otis Warren's satire, *The Group,*[39] and other plays of Revolutionary and political interest had no female characters; and when they had, as in James Nelson Barker's *André,* their women were of little importance. A play with a remote eastern setting, like Godfrey's *Prince of Parthia,* could hardly be regarded as having any typically American character.[40] There were several romantic Indian plays based on the legend of Pocahontas, but in these white women had only minor parts.

For the study of American types one must turn to the comedy of manners, the most important of which was Tyler's *The Contrast* written in 1787, soon after he first witnessed *The School for Scandal.* One editor says of *The Contrast*

[37] Arthur H. Quinn, *Representative American Plays* (New York, 1922), p. 3.

[38] *Ibid.,* pp. 45-46.

[39] 1775. Reprinted in Montrose J. Moses, *Representative Plays by American Dramatists* (3 vols., New York, 1918), i, 219-32.

[40] Moses, *Representative Plays,* i, 19-108.

that it was written in *terms* of the Battery, New York, but
in the *spirit* of London.[41]   This might well be true without
rendering the play an inaccurate description of certain classes
of American society, for at that date imitation of British
customs and manners was still attracting unfavorable comment.[42]   Although *The School for Scandal* inspired the play
the influence of Richardson was not wanting; indeed his
books were said to have profoundly affected the conduct of
the heroine.   The plots of *The Contrast* and other comedies
were almost invariably concerned with the difficulties attendant upon a desired marriage.   These problems which arose
from lack of fortune, family prejudice, intrigue and other
complications were usually solved by the reappearance at the
opportune moment of long-lost friends with abundant funds,
or by some equally simple method.   Then, a wedding, perhaps a double or triple one, took place and the curtain fell
upon a scene of happiness.

The important feminine characters in the early American
comedies were of two classes.   There were heroines with all
the virtues set forth by Richardson and the didactic writers,
who conducted themselves with grace and propriety in the
most distressing circumstances.   Then there were other
women with less strength of character who deviated in
various ways from these ideals.   They might be merely weak
and vain or they might exhibit certain malicious traits.   Of
the first type, the idealized heroine, Maria Van Rough in *The
Contrast* was the outstanding example.   Others of this type
were Harriet Trueman in *The Politician Out-Witted*,[43] Eliza
Clairville in *Virtue Triumphant*,[44] Miss Felton in Dunlap's

[41] Moses, i, 433, 437.

[42] See pp. 165-67, *supra*.

[43] Samuel Low (New York, 1789).   Reprinted in Moses, *Representative Plays*, i, 351-429.   Apparently never produced.

[44] Judith Sargent Murray, *The Gleaner*, iii, 13, 15-87.   Performed
once.

The Father,[45] and Louisa in *Tears and Smiles.*[46] They all belonged in the class of Richardsonian heroines, and were educated in accordance with his recommendations. Some of them were obliged to struggle against paternal prejudice and interference in their choice of husbands as Clarissa had done. Of Maria, it was said, that having read *Sir Charles Grandison, Clarissa, The Sentimental Journey,* and the writings of Shenstone she had formed her ideas of love and marriage upon those models. She was ready, as a dutiful daughter, to marry as her father wished although his choice was contrary to her inclination and judgment. In her soliloquies on her unfortunate fate she said that, although she could overlook awkwardness or poverty in a husband and even endure mental weakness, she dreaded joining herself to a depraved wretch whose only virtue was his polished exterior and who devoted his time to reading Lord Chesterfield and putting the author's maxims into practice. The complications which confronted her reduced her to a state of melancholy in which she found diversion in study, in song, and in reflecting that in woman's helpless condition the only safe asylum a woman of delicacy could find was in the arms of a man of honor.[47] She was much pleased at being addressed by a man of sense but dutifully refused to receive his advances until she had her father's permission. Her father who sniffed contemptuously at ideas derived from story books had little sympathy with her attitude toward marriage or with her studies, holding that " if a woman knew how to make a pudding, and to keep herself out of fire and water, she knew enough for a wife." [48] Her

[45] In *Dunlap Society Publications,* no. 2. Reprinted from *Massachusetts Magazine,* October and November, 1789.

[46] James Nelson Barker. First acted 1807. Printed in Paul H. Musser, *James Nelson Barker, 1784-1858* (Philadelphia, 1929), p. 138.

[47] Quinn, *Representative American Plays,* p. 54.

[48] *Ibid.,* 54.

father and she presented two frequent but opposite ideas of women's position. Maria's views were Richardsonian. Her father belonged to an earlier school, possibly that of Lord Halifax, though it is unlikely that the old gentleman ever troubled his head with treatises on the subject. Maria on the other hand was much concerned over feminine status; some lines from her meditations, usually omitted in the stage presentation, read almost like quotations from formal English writers in the field. She concluded that women were—

Formed of the more delicate materials of nature, endowed only with the softer passions, incapable, from our ignorance of the world, to guard against the wiles of mankind, our security for happiness often depends upon their generosity and courage :— Alas! how little of the former do we find.[49]

Harriet Trueman and other heroines who bore a close resemblance to Maria added but little to Tyler's skilful delineation. Harriet Trueman who believed strongly in common sense and propriety professed herself weary of mere fashionable politeness and the society of coxcombs. She thought the "hearing" a good play, a rational enjoyment and a happy way of satirizing the vices and foibles of human nature. She was determined, though an obedient daughter, to marry the man she loved, if necessary without her father's consent, which he had given and withdrawn. Eliza Clairville, in Mrs. Murray's work, displayed great restraint in refusing to involve her lover in her own vicissitudes.

The second type of feminine character was probably in closer affinity with the women of *The School for Scandal* and other English comedies than with Richardson's Harriet Byron and Clarissa. Charlotte Manly in *The Contrast* was the outstanding figure of this class though Maria Airy in *The Politician Out-Witted* was likewise noteworthy. With

---

[49] Quinn, *Representative American Plays*, p. 54.

them belong also dissatisfied or misguided young married women like Augusta Bloomville [50] and Mrs. Racket.[51] Charlotte Manly devoted her attention to dress and various petty measures to attract masculine notice. She scorned the followers of Richardson with their serious view of life, saying— "Why I'll undertake with one flirt of this hoop to bring more beaux to my feet in one week, than the grave Maria, and her sentimental circle, can do, by sighing sentiment till their hairs are gray." [52] She offered the *Spectator* as authority for her use of feminine modesty and blushes to attract men. In spite of her ardent desire for a husband she like others of her class regarded the giving of the heart as the least important consideration in marriage and despised Richardson's recommendations. Gossip, scandal, and the newest fashion filled their conversation; fashion must be attained, though beauty and comfort were sacrificed in the effort. The end of the play brought signs of reformation in these characters who represented in dramatic form the evils against which moralists delighted to warn young people.

Since the earliest plays had usually town settings the country girl, who should have been a distinct American type, was rarely depicted. When such plays appeared with an attempt at dialect, Americanisms were more frequent in the speech of the men than of the women. One of the best portrayals of country women, *The Forest Rose,* was not written until 1825 [53] and so lies beyond the scope of this study; but another play, written as late as 1819, may be included here because it shows interesting traces of feminine independence in contrast to older views. Christine, the heroine of Noah's *She*

[50] Of *Virtue Triumphant.*

[51] Of *The Father.*

[52] Quinn, *Representative American Plays,* p. 51.

[53] By Samuel Woodworth.

Would Be a Soldier,[54] either because of her country upbringing or in spite of it, had an independent mind and masculine
accomplishments. She received a good general education
and her father, a retired French soldier, taught her to hunt
and shoot so that she could crack a bottle at twelve paces with
a pistol.[55] When he offered her an ignorant farmer as a
husband she refused saying that, though she had always been
obedient in other affairs, in marriage she must consult her
own happiness. Her astonished father observed that " times
have strangely altered; when young women choose husbands
for themselves, with as much ease and indifference, as a
ribbon for their bonnet." [56] The attitude of her rejected
country suitor was essentially conservative. When making
his proposal he magnanimously stated that he did not " mind
how larned she was " though the idea of her ability in shoot-
ing and hunting disturbed him a trifle.[57] He asked—" Can
she milk—knit garters—make apple butter and maple sugar
—dance a reel after midnight, and ride behind her husband
on a pony, to see the trainings of our sogers—that's the wife
for my money." [58] To the astonishment of her father and her
suitor, Christine ran away disguised as a boy and, believing
the officer whom she loved to be faithless, joined the army
where her training in the use of firearms stood her in good
stead.[59] At length the deception was discovered, matters
explained, and Christine was happily married to her officer.

These plays had many minor female characters, usually
conventionalized types, among them the domestic servant, of

[54] In Moses, *Representative Plays*, i, 629-78.

[55] *Ibid.*, i, 651.

[56] *Ibid.*, i, 653.

[57] *Ibid.*, i, 649.

[58] *Ibid.*, i, 651.

[59] She had precedent for this. At least one woman in disguise served
in the army during the Revolution.

country origin, who after moving to the city became sophisticated and gave herself airs,[60] and the gossiping and trouble making old maid, still in quest of a husband.[61] The over-trustful girl betrayed by her lover appeared occasionally, though less frequently in plays than in novels.[62] There was at least one presentation of a dignified and helpful older woman who though unmarried was respected and admired.[63]

Women in the drama still retained their conventional sphere, usually with a fair education and some freedom of choice in marriage. Most plays had at least one character who held the older and more subservient conception of women's place and tried to enforce it. There were no women in these first American dramas who represented very liberal thought or were exponents of the ideas of Mary Wollstonecraft.

III

The American periodical, especially at the close of the eighteenth century, revealed women and their interests in dual fashion. In the first place, in the essays, "characters" —a popular form of short description—and, to a lesser extent, in the fiction which the magazines published, the reader was given a composite picture of women of the upper classes. This picture, neither so idealistic nor so stilted as that drawn by the didactic writers, was reminiscent of the pleasant, mildly satirical, sketches of women which had appeared in the *Spectator* three-quarters of a century before. Secondly, besides these popular portrayals of women, often very English, the literary tastes of women themselves are suggested by the

[60] Jenny in *The Contrast*; Dolly in *The Politician Out-Witted*.

[61] There were two such in *The Politician Out-Witted*; also Miss Starchington in *Tears and Smiles*.

[62] Clara in *Tears and Smiles*.

[63] Matronia Aimwell in *Virtue Triumphant*.

material provided for their enjoyment. Scientific and political articles were designed in the nature of things to interest men; but the remainder of the magazine, notably poetry and fiction, had a wider audience. Editors in planning those departments considered the feminine reader for whose perusal material in fiction and in *belles-lettres* was generally intended. One may not always approve the editor's taste but one cannot doubt that his selections had a wide appeal for women of moderate education. A few articles were inserted with a view to improving women's condition, but on the whole the periodical mirrored popular opinion rather than molded it.

In the other class of periodical, the newspaper, women played a less important part, although before 1776 there were occasional essays or descriptions with a similar appeal to women.[64] Parker's *New York Gazette* of March 5, 1753 had an unsigned essay on women which discussed the fallacy of regarding men as superior to women. This article, which was probably English in origin, gave a number of historical instances of women of unusual ability; particular reference was made to Mary Astell though not by name. The essay is significant merely as it showed popular interest in the subject rather than because of its own content. During the Revolution patriotic appeals for feminine support were sometimes made in the newspapers,[65] and later the *Massachusetts Centinel* published a number of letters on women's education.[66]

Magazines, however, played a leading role. The English *Lady's Magazine* which was popular here helped to set

[64] *Boston Gazette*, March 30, 1767, "Essay on a Wife"; *New York Gazette*, December 4, 1760, "Letter to a Lady"; January 15, 1750, "The Specific: or, a Cordial for the Ladies"; *Pennsylvania Gazette*, June 2-9, 1737, selection from the *London Magazine*.

[65] *Boston Evening Post* and *Boston Gazette*, February 12, 1770.

[66] At frequent intervals from February to April, 1785.

American standards. There were few magazines on this side of the Atlantic before the Revolution but even these early efforts contained some material of interest to women. Of this it is difficult to tell how much was adapted from British articles and how much was original. *The American Magazine and Historical Chronicle* published in 1744 two poems, perhaps English, purporting to be a complaint by a young lady with the reply of a masculine friend. The lady protesting against woman's perpetual subjection to man, in early life to father and brother and later to her husband, begged fate to give her a slavish mind that she might wear her fetters more cheerfully. The response asserted that woman's life was free from care and woe, that masculine guardians constantly afforded her protection, and that she had great power to wield through love.[67] A paper in the same magazine entitled " In Defense of the Ladies " stated that the empire which men exercised over the opposite sex was usurped, whereas woman's power over man came through nature, leaving her in truth man's ruler. The article gallantly proclaimed that the soul had no sex, leaving the ladies in a most favorable position.[68] An attempt on the part of editors to appeal to feminine readers, actuated in part by a moderate belief in woman's ability, was found in the general remarks on love and the historical instances of learned women which appeared in all the magazines.[69]

Feminine education was the theme of some papers in the *Royal American Magazine* in Boston just before the Revolution. These articles, which were signed Cleo, Leander, and

---

[67] Vol. i, 435. Compare the reflections of Calista in *The Fair Penitent* where she complains of woman's fate. *The Works of Nicholas Rowe* (London, 1756), i, 266.

[68] *American Magazine and Historical Chronicle*, ii, 117-18.

[69] *American Magazine and Historical Chronicle*, ii (1745), 230, 244-48, 344-47, 400-03, 449.

Mira, dealt with women's education from several angles, particularly the neglect of their minds and their consequent failure to realize their capacities.   Wise training of women in youth, these writers thought, would bring about marked improvement in human nature and render the sex more useful to those under its care.[70]   Leander, who apparently preferred his women naive and unspoiled, opposed a school for women as likely by making them pedants to cause loss of feminine qualities;[71] but a satirical answer, signed Sylvia, implied that Leander's opposition arose from the desire of men to keep studies exclusively for themselves.[72]   These papers, though not intrinsically important, are significant as showing increased interest in feminine education.

Miss Stearns, in her study of ladies' magazines, notes that after the Revolution editors openly admitted the importance of the feminine reader by issuing periodicals which catered primarily to her tastes.[73]   In the years between 1784 and 1800 there were four magazines which illustrated this tendency.   *The Gentleman and Lady's Town and Country Magazine,* begun in Boston in 1784, was one of these which scarcely revealed a high literary standard.[74]   Another was *The Ladies' Magazine and Repository of Interesting Knowledge,* published in Philadelphia, which drew heavily on English sources especially in the field of women's interests.   The other two magazines were *The Gentlemen and Ladies' Town and Country Magazine,* a Bostonian publication of the years 1789-91, and *The Lady and Gentleman's*

---

[70] *Royal American Magazine,* i (1774-75), 9-10, 188.

[71] *Ibid.,* i, 131-32.

[72] *Ibid.,* i, 178-79.

[73] Bertha Monica Stearns, "Before Godey's," *American Literature,* ii, 248-49.

[74] Lyon N. Richardson, *A History of Early American Magazines* (New York, 1931), pp. 228-29.

Pocket Magazine of Literature and Polite Amusement which appeared in New York in 1796. The first decade of the new century saw nine more periodicals addressed to women, thus establishing beyond question the demand for such literature.[75]

The contents of the first number of *The Ladies' Magazine* [76] may be of some interest as an example of the type of thing which these periodicals presented. An introductory address bespoke the aid and attention of the ladies of the country. The opening article was an account of the inhabitants of Japan; next was the " Essayist " followed by a brief sketch, " On the Ladies Feet," recommending the adoption of the French heel and of dainty shoes by the women of America. A story, " The Infant Rambler," preceded a " Letter from a Brother to a Sister at Boarding School," reprinted from an English source. This paper which dealt with civility was the first of a series. Then Observer contributed a scheme for increasing the " Power of the FAIR Sex " by discouraging licentious manners and by having the ladies refuse to receive men who associated with licentious women. An account of the Salmon leap in Ireland and a description of Killarney preceded two stories of no great importance which were followed ,by an essay on love. The " Matrimonial Creed " which came next was facetious. There were selections from letters including some by Lady Mary Wortley Montagu, anecdotes, reflections, and poetical efforts of a sentimental sort. Foreign and domestic news, rounded out the first issue of the periodical.[77] An article of peculiar interest in a later number of this volume was a review of Mary Wollstonecraft's *A Vindication of the Rights*

---

[75] For a detailed account of these consult Miss Stearns's article in *New England Quarterly*, ii, 420-57, " Early New England Magazines for Ladies," and the article cited in note 73 *supra*.

[76] The title page had the form, *Lady's Magazine*, but elsewhere *Ladies'* was used.

[77] Issue of June, 1792.

of Woman, then a new publication, which pleased the reviewer although he did not altogether agree with the author's tenets.[78]

Much of the most interesting material dealing with women came not from the ladies' magazines but from the pages of the *American Museum,* Webster's *American Magazine,* the *Columbian Magazine* later the *Universal Asylum,* the *Weekly Magazine* of Philadelphia, and others designed for general circulation. The theories, both English and American, which they published regarding women, have for the most part already been discussed in some detail. Periodical literature, like other forms of writing, clearly reflected English views. Much of the content of the average periodical was the work of English authors, sometimes acknowledged as such, but more often inserted without any indication of its source. A detailed comparison with contemporary English periodicals would probably reveal the latter as the origin of many of the shorter essays and " characters " with which American periodicals abounded. The work of many well-known authors was used in this way.[79] The long extracts from the writings of Gregory, Bennett, and Mrs. Griffith tempt the modern reader to wonder whether they were not chosen as conservative " filler " to impress readers with the moral tone of the publication rather than for their inherent interest. In so far as these selections served to set the tone of the American periodical in relation to women the effect was conservative, but this was offset by the work of some Americans. The principal American articles dealing with women which appeared in periodicals were Witherspoon's *Letters on Marriage* and *Letters on Education,*[80] Webster's *Essays,*[81] several

---

[78] *Ladies' Magazine,* i, 189-98.　　　[79] See p. 93, *supra.*

[80] First published in *Pennsylvania Magazine,* March, May, June, September and December, 1775, and March, 1776, "Letters on Education." The " Letters on Marriage " were in *American Museum,* iv, 21-24, 105-08, 213-7.

[81] *American Magazine* (March and May, 1788), pp. 241-46, 367.

addresses delivered at Andrew Brown's Philadelphia academy,[82] the speech of James Wilson at the opening of the University of Pennsylvania law course,[83] the work of Judith Sargent Murray,[84] Charles Brockden Brown's dialogue on the rights of women,[85] and Governor Livingston's plea for a return to the simpler life of " Our Grandmothers." [86] These ranged from conservative to liberal but were on the whole favorable to educational opportunities for women.

The development of ladies' magazines should have spurred feminine literary production, though the large number of anonymous articles makes this point difficult to ascertain. Except in verse women were probably not frequent contributors until after 1800. Judith Sargent Murray who wrote much for periodicals in the course of her literary career began her long series of essays in the guise of a male commentator. Later she admitted her sex though she continued to employ a pseudonym.[87] It was in the magazines that her writings first found literary outlet though *The Gleaner* was later reprinted in book form. Some of the articles which purported to be the work of women were in reality by men. Francis Hopkinson was among those who often adopted

[82] John Swanwick in *Universal Asylum* (September, 1790), v, 151, 225; Samuel Magaw, *American Museum* (January, 1788), iii, 25-28. Possibly an unsigned article, " Original Thoughts on Education," *Columbian Magazine* (September, 1787), pp. 642-46.

[83] The portion of the speech addressed to the ladies is in *American Museum* (January, 1791), ix, 21-24.

[84] *The Gentleman and Lady's Town and Country Magazine* (October, 1784), pp. 251-53 and numerous essays in *Massachusetts Magazine*, particularly " The Gleaner," series.

[85] *Weekly Magazine* (Philadelphia, 1798), i, 198, 231, 271, 298.

[86] Essay of that title in *American Museum* (1791), ix, 143.

[87] *Constantia* (*University of Maine Studies*, ser. 2, no. 17), and *The Gleaner*, Introduction.

a feminine mask as did Governor Livingston in his political propaganda.[88]

Most periodicals and some newspapers had their poetical departments with both original and selected verse, in which a sentimental tone predominated. For instance in 1784 the *Centinel* of Boston undertook to have a page at regular intervals in which the verse should be either for or about young ladies.[89] Many poems addressed to women were descriptive of their charms. Others were the work of ladies themselves though the writer usually shrank from subscribing her own name. Among the poets whose contributions have been identified were Elizabeth Graeme Fergusson,[90] Phillis Wheatley, the Negro poet,[91] Sarah Apthorp Morton,[92] Judith Sargent Murray,[93] and Ann Eliza Bleecker.[94] Mrs. Morton was described in the *Massachusetts Magazine* as the "Sappho of America."[95]

Stories, of which periodicals printed a fair number, were chosen in large part for the feminine audience and were not of high literary quality. They were likely to deal either

[88] Richardson, *Early American Magazines*, p. 186, note 103; p. 266, note 142; p. 280, note 35. "Nitidia's Defence of Whitewashing," *Columbian Magazine* (April, 1787). "Consolation for the old Bachelor," *Pennsylvania Magazine* (June, 1775). Probably "Arabella's Complaint to the Congress," *Pennsylvania Magazine* (September, 1775). For Livingston *vide*, Philip G. Davidson, "Whig Propagandists of the American Revolution," *American Historical Review*, xxxix, 449.

[89] *Centinel*, March 31, June 9, 1784. Cited by Miss Stearns in *New England Quarterly*, ii, 421.

[90] Richardson, *op. cit.*, p. 193, note 157; p. 292, note 112.

[91] *Ibid.*, p. 193.

[92] *Philenia* (*University of Maine Studies*, ser. 2, no. 20).

[93] "Constantia."

[94] *The Posthumous Works of Ann Eliza Bleecker* (New York, 1793). In the "Address to the Public" it is stated that her verses appeared in the *New York Magazine*.

[95] *Philenia*, p. 52.

with the romantic adventures of a beautiful heroine or to present sentimental accounts of family misfortunes, domestic tragedies, and often the seduction of unfortunate young ladies. The latter group of tales which pointed obvious morals leave the reader almost stifled by the atmosphere of sentimentality and false pathos which pervades them. Naturally the women presented in such works were either vague images of perfection, as in popular romances, or spineless, though possibly pious, victims of misfortune.[96] Brown's *Arthur Mervyn* was a notable exception to the usual run of periodical fiction in literary quality and in the calibre and individuality of the women presented.[97]

After eliminating the periodical contributors mentioned in the preceding paragraphs, few names remain which would be recognized as those of authorities on the position of women. There was, however, an abundance of material dealing with the sex or addressed to women, which, though a bit desultory in character, was sufficient in quantity to afford a basis for certain generalizations on popular ideas about women. This material was composed of essays and brief descriptions, including many series of essays like the " Trifler " or the " Visitant," dealing with a wide range of topics in the manner of the *Spectator* and containing comments on women's character and behavior. Many shorter sketches of perhaps a paragraph, or at most a page or two, also discussed women. Such contributions were rarely signed though the authors have sometimes been identified. Not only was there a tendency to borrow from British sources; it was customary also to make copious extracts from other American publications so that many sketches appeared several times in different cities. These pieces may

[96] *Ladies' Magazine*, i, 33-34, 62; ii, 135-38, for instances of the sentimental type.

[97] *Weekly Magazine* (1798-99), serially in vols. i and ii.

be classified in three general groups. In the decade following 1775 many essays more or less emphasized the patriotic motive. Feminine education was also a topic certain to bring out comment; and finally there were discussions of women's character, particularly as displayed in love and marriage.

Aside from the addresses of Swanwick, Magaw, and Wilson already analyzed under American theory, there were few suggestions as to curriculum, but several articles showing increased interest in popular efforts for education. Thus " A Plan for Establishing Schools in a New Country," suggested vocational training for the lower classes of both sexes.[98] Girls should receive a modicum of literary instruction, learn the duties of farmers' wives, and master the art of brewing. This last, amusingly enough, was offered both as an economic measure and to discourage the use of hard liquor. The efforts of the Massachusetts Charitable Society on behalf of poor female children were described in connection with the raising of a fund for the Society; the moral and economic advantages to the public of educating children of the poor were painted in vivid colors.[99] The improvements possible in women's knowledge through the growth of the Massachusetts public school system received a strong encomium with special emphasis on the benefits which would redound to the next generation.[100] Little was published in opposition to the education of women although one satirical writer described the usual feminine training as leading to pinnacles of refinement above commonplace matters like

[98] *Columbian Magazine* (April, 1787), i, 356. Also in *American Museum* (April, 1787).

[99] *American Museum*, vi (1789), 212-13.

[100] *Nightingale*, p. 300, " The Microcosm," no. 8. This followed the opening of public schools for girls in Boston.

domestic duties and the care of children.[101]   Many articles
on education simply reiterated ideas already familiar.[102]

Just before the Revolution a writer in the *Pennsylvania
Magazine*, probably Francis Hopkinson, published " Arabella's Complaint of the Congress," which represented the
trials of a fashionable lady deprived of her tea and finery.
Seemingly this was meant to arouse women to a sense of
their duty in the existing emergency and to ridicule those
whose patriotic fervor was a transient fad to be dropped
when self-denial became uncomfortable.[103]   Another appeal
to women's patriotic feeling was made in a " Vision of the
Paradise of Female Patriotism," in the form of an allegory.
In this mythical abode posts of distinction were assigned to
ladies of the past like Deborah, Zenobia, the Spartan mother,
and Boadicea.   An American group also, headed by Mrs.
John Adams and Mrs. Samuel Adams, had many followers
and the writer hoped that many others would abandon Tory-
ism and follow these distinguished examples.[104]   The " Economical Plan of the Ladies in Hartford," an agreement
signed by more than one hundred women to avoid extrava-
gance until public affairs were adjusted, told its own story.[105]
The same train of reasoning was used also in purely humorous articles, as in the case of a petition purporting to come
from the young ladies of Portsmouth, Boston, Newcastle,
Charleston, and other cities where Congress had not met.
The petitioners asked that Congress be composed entirely of

[101] *Weekly Magazine*, i, 141-2, " The Ubiquitarian."

[102] *Boston Magazine*, ii, 213; iii, 414; *Weekly Magazine*, ii, 134; iii,
13-14, 37-41.

[103] *Pennsylvania Magazine* (September, 1775), pp. 407-08; Richardson,
Early American Magazines, p. 186, note 103.

[104] *United States Magazine*, i (1779), 122-24, signed " Clarissa a Lady
of this City."

[105] *Worcester Magazine* (1786), p. 393; *American Museum* (1787), ii,
165.

bachelors and meet in rotation in the cities of the country, in order to encourage marriage and increase of population.[106]

Sometimes the patriotic theme was used in attacking current fashions. The high headdress, popular in 1779, was mockingly said to illustrate love for one's enemies since it was an imitation of the British style.[107] A writer protesting against long trains on ladies' gowns argued that the great quantity of money spent for cloth must of necessity go to foreign nations since America was not a manufacturing country.[108] The development of national fashions was especially championed as giving the country more dignity and showing real independence. American ladies were exhorted to cease drawing their styles from a group of coquettes, milliners, and manufacturers who changed the mode constantly from motives of avarice and vanity. Governor Livingston of New Jersey was among the strong advocates of the use of homespun and the development of distinctive American fashions.[109] Writers urged reform in the terminology of dress and it was said that " Washington Blue " might describe a never-fading color as well as " Prince of Wales Buff." [110]

Descriptions, both favorable and unfavorable, of feminine character and of the traits women should cultivate were not new and were found in abundance in " characters," [111] in essays,[112] and in poems exemplifying the true charms of

[106] *American Museum*, i, 308-09.

[107] *United States Magazine* (1779), pp. 268-71.

[108] *American Magazine* (1787), p. 39, signed " Titus Blunt."

[109] *American Museum*, x (July, 1791), 17, " Homespun."

[110] *Ibid.*, ii, 478-82, signed " Frank Amity."

[111] *American Universal Magazine*, i, 283, " The Good Wife "; *American Apollo*, i, 379, " The Coquette "; *Gentleman and Lady's Town and Country Magazine* (1784), p. 27.

[112] *American Museum*, i, 58-59, iv, 118-21, " The Visitant " on female conversation; viii, 280, Rev. Joseph Lathrop " Remarks on Female Honor "; *New York Weekly Magazine*, i, 249, " On Love."

person and mind.[113] Such titles as " Advantage of a Mutual Correspondence between the two Sexes," [114] " On Matrimonial Felicity," [115] "A Complaining Wife," [116] " Way to manage a Husband," [117] " Hints for Young Married Women," [118] show the type of article which was popular. Comparison of the ability of men and women went on as it had always done, in serious and humorous vein.[119] Most writers discussed women's character in relation to that of men, emphasizing marriage as the great goal of women's life. An occasional misogynist urged men not to marry; [120] and there were a few articles of the coarser kind, though these were infrequent.[121] Advice on the choice of husband or wife filled many pages. The future husband was warned that prudes were preferable to coquettes; [122] that he should avoid the celebrated beauty, the high-bred lady, the rich widow, the superannuated virgin, the termagant, and above all the " notable housewife " who might prove mutinous, and the female pedant who felt herself superior to her husband. He might even find the much-desired prudent and affectionate wife in a lady censured by her own sex as lacking

[113] *American Magazine* (July, 1788), p. 594.

[114] *Gentleman and Lady's Town and Country Magazine* (May, 1784), pp. 20-22.

[115] *Ibid.* (September, 1784), p. 193.

[116] *American Magazine* (December, 1787), p. 48.

[117] *Columbian Magazine*, i, 64.

[118] *American Museum* (September, 1789), vi, 198-200.

[119] *Columbia Magazine* (April, 1787), pp. 20-22. "Nitidia on Whitewashing," probably by Francis Hopkinson.

[120] *American Universal Magazine*, i, 302. For a response see i, 406-411.

[121] *American Museum*, i, 140 *et seq.*, "Plan for the Establishment of a Fair of Fairs."

[122] *Gentleman and Lady's Town and Country Magazine* (July, 1784), p. 115.

in good sense.[123]   There was much serious advice to show that, in spite of jests to the contrary, sensible women made good wives.[124]   In this connection a writer in the *American Magazine* charged women with preferring inferior men to those of ability and genius.   An answer to this, ostensibly written by a lady, attributed this preference to the behavior of superior men who either discussed topics entirely beyond feminine comprehension or else treated ladies in very infantile fashion.[125]

Women, as presented in American periodicals, save for some unconvincing fiction, were not idealized figures on pedestals, but more ordinary creatures whose moderate education gave them a taste for the milder forms of literature but did not lead them to deep reasoning or serious study. They formed a part, and a most important one, of the community in their relation to men's pleasures and in their specialized duties as mistresses of families.   Their character was a subject of interest and study rather in social than in intellectual aspects although interest in the latter was increasing.   Despite these signs of change women remained, for most of the men who wrote popular essays and sketches, objects to be smiled at, scolded, loved, perhaps praised, but rarely to be treated as men's equals.

[123] *Columbian Magazine* (June, 1787), i, 473-74, "Qualifications of Wives."

[124] *New York Weekly Magazine*, i, 134.

[125] *American Magazine* (February, 1788), p. 135; (March, 1788), p. 240.

CHAPTER VIII

Women in Law, Politics, and the Church

I

THEORISTS in print and in the pulpit gave expression to the views of only a limited group of persons who had enjoyed special privileges of reading and education. Their opinions, if uncorrected, would leave the reader with a markedly one-sided glimpse of the women of their day. A study of legislation regarding women and of the economic opportunities offered them affords in some ways a more adequate index of their position than the reading of many pages of speculation and moral teaching. At the same time it shows another way in which British influence was felt in America.

The legal status of women tended to lag behind the plans of theorists and even behind the economic usage of the time. For the most part the colonies in dealing with women had adopted the principles of British common law with certain important modifications.[1] This was done early in colonial history, and the laws stood for years with no radical changes so that there was relatively little eighteenth-century legislation concerning women. Even the Revolution brought no startling changes in its wake. Only with the coming of the

---

[1] A brief survey of women's status may be found in A. M. Schlesinger, *New Viewpoints in American History* (New York, 1925), chap. vi. A more detailed account of certain legal phases, especially the civil rights of the married woman, is given in Richard B. Morris, *Studies in the History of American Law* (New York, 1930). G. E. Howard, *A History of Matrimonial Institutions* (3 vols., Chicago, 1904), ii, pt. iii, gives a good survey of the laws on marriage and divorce.

agitation for political rights in the nineteenth century was there real development in the laws regarding property and guardianship.

Women's treatment in the eyes of the law depended much on their marital condition. Unmarried women were far less hampered either by common law or by colonial enactments than were their married sisters. Except for political matters they were comparatively unrestricted. This absence of legal disabilities was not, however, of as great advantage to single women as one might infer; for socially they had no very important place and their other activities suffered in consequence. They were likely to spend their days in a condition of economic dependence in the homes of married relatives where constantly increasing families of children made the unattached sister or niece welcome. Widows, on the other hand, who were also legally *femes soles,* were often in business for themselves or continued the work of their husbands and used to the full the privileges which the law offered.[2] The frequent remarriages of the time led to a series of statutes to adjust property rights.[3]

Apprenticeship laws made little distinction between the sexes except in minor points. Male children were usually bound until they reached the age of twenty-one, females until they were sixteen or eighteen or in some instances until marriage. There were degrees of difference in the education given. If the boys were taught reading and writing the girls were perhaps instructed only in reading. When arithmetic was added to the masculine curriculum, writing was included in the education of girls. In Virginia after 1751 orphan girl apprentices were to be taught reading and writ-

[2] Elisabeth A. Dexter, *Colonial Women of Affairs* (New York, 1924). Most women whose marital status was discussed were widows.

[3] Arthur W. Calhoun, *A Social History of the American Family* (3 vols., Cleveland, 1917-19), discusses this aspect.

ing; in 1769 this clause was extended to the indentures of illegitimate children of both sexes. The inclusion of writing made the standard higher than that for girl apprentices in New England, but despite the law indentures did not always provide for such instruction.[4] Many colonies made no specific provision for education though it might be included in the apprenticeship papers.

Legally male and female indentured servants were treated alike with minor differences in their freedom dues. Women in Virginia and Maryland received a slightly larger sum of money and more Indian corn than men, in place of muskets and axes.[5] Occasionally a woman was given a cow when this had been agreed to in the indenture.[6] In Pennsylvania and the colonies to the south there were special clauses in the laws dealing with bastardy providing for the illegitimate children of women servants. These laws and the advertisements for women servants who had run away do not give a favorable impression of women of this class, but these can hardly be taken as a standard since they present women at their worst. The German, Mittelberger, told several tales of servants who took advantage of these laws to compel prosperous men, not the fathers, to support their children.[7] The question of the position and treatment of women as inden-

[4] Massachusetts, *Acts and Resolves*, 1710-11, 1st sess., chap 6; *Acts and Laws*, 1788, chap. 61. New Hampshire, *Laws*, 1791, chap. 76; *The Public Laws of Rhode Island*, 1798, p. 351, sec. 4. R. F. Seybolt, *Apprenticeship and Apprenticeship Education in Colonial New England and New York* (New York, 1917), pp. 47, 61, 93. Marcus W. Jernegan, *Laboring and Dependent Classes in Colonial America* (Chicago, 1931), pp. 144-70.

[5] Maryland, *Laws*, April, 1715, chap. 44, sec. 10; Hening, *Virginia Statutes*, October, 1705, chap. 49. Freedom dues were payments made to servants at the end of their term of service.

[6] *Gottlieb Mittelberger's Journey to Pennsylvania* (Philadelphia, 1898), p. 28.

[7] *Ibid.*, pp. 52-54, 93.

tured servants is one which merits much fuller attention than has yet been given it.[8]

In the treatment of social offenses women, whether married or single, might be expected to have been the subjects of special legislation; but the pre-Revolutionary laws on adultery and fornication, though establishing some very ignominious punishments, were the same for both sexes.[9] The attempt to restrain vice, especially unchastity and sexual crimes, by legislation was strenuous. Thus Massachusetts had the death penalty for adultery and Plymouth the scarlet letter which Massachusetts later adopted. Rhode Island which was less strict required offenders to sit on the gallows and to undergo a public whipping. Connecticut, which at first had the death penalty, later replaced it by branding and wearing a halter. These severe laws were not often carried into effect though Massachusetts had at least three executions for adultery.[10] The Dutch colonies punished such offenses with fine, whipping, or banishment but not with death or the scarlet letter; New York under English rule did not have

[8] For the laws regarding illegitimate children see, Pennsylvania, *Statutes at Large*, 1700 chap. iii, sec. 3; Hening, *Virginia*, September, 1696, chap. i, 1705, chap. 49, sec. 18, November, 1753, chap. 7, art. 13; *Public Acts of... North Carolina*, 1741, chap. 24, sec. 17. South Carolina, *Statutes at Large*, 1717, no. 383, sec. 20. *Laws of Maryland*, April, 1715, chap. 44, secs. 28-29; October, 1727, chap. 2, secs. 4-6. *Laws of... Delaware*, 1719, chap. 44. For women servants generally see C. A. Herrick, *White Servitude in Pennsylvania* (Philadelphia, 1926), pp. 75, 106, 207, 209, 224-25, 279, which has scattered references to freedom dues, runaways, etc. There is no detailed treatment of women as servants. See also E. I. McCormac, *White Servitude in Maryland* (Johns Hopkins University, *Studies*, ser. 22, nos. 3-4, Baltimore, 1904).

[9] Massachusetts, *Acts and Resolves*, 1692-93, 2nd sess., chap. 18, sec. 5, 1694-95, 1st sess., chap. 5; Connecticut, *Acts and Laws* (1769), pp. 7, 78; New Jersey, *Acts* (Allinson), 1704, sess 1, chap. 2, sec. 3; Pennsylvania, 1700, chap. iii; Maryland, 1715, chap. 27; Delaware, *Laws*, p. 105, chap. 44; Virginia, April, 1691, chap. 11.

[10] Howard, *History of Matrimonial Institutions*, ii, 169-76.

the intense scrutiny of private life found in New England.[11]
The laws of Virginia were also severe.[12] Massachusetts
after the Revolution made a distinction between men and
women offenders. The law of 1785 imposed a fine for
fornication, the maximum penalty being greater for the man
than for the woman, if it was the first offense. If, however,
it was the woman's second conviction she was fined more
than the man. If the man could not pay he was whipped;
if the woman had no money she was imprisoned.[13] Other
states do not seem to have made such a distinction.

Before the Revolution the laws dealing with bastardy
treated the concealment of the death of an illegitimate child
as murder unless it could be proved by a witness that the
child had been born dead. This was still true in Connecticut in 1796 but the law had been altered in Massachusetts,
New Hampshire, Rhode Island, New Jersey, and Pennsylvania.[14] In the southern colonies servant women who bore
illegitimate children were usually required to serve an extra
year's time. There were severer punishments for white
women who bore mulatto children. By the end of the century, if not before, all the colonies, with the possible exception of Georgia, required the reputed father to maintain his
illegitimate child if charges were proved against him.[15]

[11] Howard, *History of Matrimonial Institutions*, ii, 280.

[12] *Ibid.*, ii, 236.

[13] Massachusetts, *Acts and Laws*, 1785, chap. 66.

[14] New Hampshire, *Laws*, 1791, 7th General Court, 2nd sess., chap. 42;
Massachusetts, *Acts and Laws*, 1784, chap. 42; Rhode Island, *Public
Laws*, p. 372; New Jersey (Paterson), March 18, 1796, sec. 12, p. 210;
Pennsylvania, *Statutes at Large*, no. 1241, p. 284; in Pennsylvania the
new law did not apply if there were probable proof that the child had
been born alive. Hening, *Virginia*, i, October, 1710, chap. 12; Martin,
North Carolina, pp. 373, 381; South Carolina, *Statutes*, ii, 513. See also
references on illegitimacy in note 8 above.

[15] See note 8 above.

Suits involving paternity and maintenance were fairly frequent at least in the northern colonies.[16]

Aside from the action taken by the courts, the churches often disciplined social offenders, and the frequency of certain types of offenses in the New England records may perhaps create an impression that social conditions were worse than was really the case. The Puritan church subjected the private conduct of both men and women to an intense scrutiny, ostensibly with the object of preserving the individual soul and of protecting the church from contamination. The preoccupations of New England life led to an undue emphasis on sexual misconduct, the church combining with the state to render such offenses ignominious. This bore heavily on women because of the nature of the offenses involved.[17] Mather and Sewall in their diaries give a number of cases of bastardy and also refer to confessions made to the church, of antenuptial fornication and of other deviations from the social code.[18] From Mather one infers that Boston had its houses of low repute and there were many who frequented them.[19] Howard's work gives more information regarding regulation of sexual morality in New England than in the colonies to the south. All this seems only to mean that New England focussed its attention on certain aspects of conduct, not that its moral standard was exceptionally low. Charles Francis Adams studied this aspect of life in Braintree and some other towns carefully in the church records

[16] Kirby, *Connecticut Cases*, p. 364, 1788; Root, *Connecticut Cases*, i, 107 (1788), 229, 319; ii, 490, 496; Coxe, *New Jersey Cases*, p. 16 (1790); Yeates, *Pennsylvania Cases*, iii, 39.

[17] Charles F. Adams, *Three Episodes of Massachusetts History*, ii, 795-96. "Some Phases of Sexual Morality and Church Discipline in Colonial New England," Mass. Hist. Soc., *Proc.*, ser. 2, vi, 477-516.

[18] Sewall, *Diary*, i, 87, 123, 212-13, 349, 354; ii, 288, 340; Mather, *Diary*, i, 189n, 198n, 261, 276-77, 309-10n, 409n, 518n.

[19] *Ibid.*, ii, 229, 612.

and pointed out several features of the matter. Though the total number of cases found in such records seems large, the church in Braintree had scarcely one case of discipline a year and then handled only exceptional matters. The church oversight of private morals which would be resented today was accepted at that period and was in itself evidence of a high average morality. The absence of a professional criminal class and the fact that the church imposed the same moral code on all classes tended to bring disciplinary cases to the eye of the public more than in other parts of the colonies. This supervision was not confined to sexual conduct but applied also to drunkenness, disorderly behavior, quarrelling and other improper conduct. Adams found two or three possible explanations for the comparatively numerous cases of ante-marital relationships, which were conspicuous because the church refused baptism to children whose parents had not made confession. The New England custom of betrothal or pre-contract left women in an anomalous position between betrothal and marriage. The legal penalty for offenses committed with another man after betrothal was the same as for adultery, but the sentence was comparatively light for misconduct with the man to whom she was contracted. The practice of bundling in rural districts, though it might be carried on in all innocence, increased the opportunity for misconduct. Adams thought also that the emotional stress of the period of the Great Awakening increased misconduct of a sexual nature. His general conclusion was that though New England morality was not on a remarkably high level at this period it was no worse than in other parts of the country.[20] This is borne out by a recent study of court records which shows that the laws

[20] C. F. Adams, *Three Episodes*, ii, 795-99. See also Adams's article in Mass. Hist. Soc., *Proc.*, ser. 2, vi, 477-516; Howard, *History of Matrimonial Institutions*, ii, 180-86.

against sexual immorality were systematically enforced but that the percentage of offenses was not large in proportion to population. There was a distinct increase in cases of bastardy and fornication towards the middle of the eighteenth century.[21]

The laws providing for the treatment of criminals in other than social offenses made little distinction between men and women. In the statutes, punishments for felonies were the same for both sexes; whether this was true of the sentences imposed by courts could only be determined by a detailed study of court records. Virginia had an eighteenth-century provision extending the benefit of clergy to women.[22]

Women prisoners constituted a special problem. Late in the century when long-term imprisonment was replacing earlier methods of punishment some prison laws required the separation of the sexes. In 1785 Massachusetts women could not be sent to the prison at Castle Island because there were no suitable quarters for them; they were given corporal or other infamous punishment as a substitute.[23] In Connecticut a decade later women, liable to be confined at Newgate prison in the mines, were ordered to be put instead at suitable labor in the common workhouse.[24] Maryland in the same period gave women convicted of felony hard labor in prison in place of the road work assigned to men. If men refused to work they were given lashes and solitary confinement. Women who refused had the solitary confinement but not the whipping.[25] Whipping of women was not unknown in colonial days, for a New York vagrancy

[21] Henry Bamford Parkes in *New England Quarterly*, v (July, 1932), 431-52.

[22] Hening, May, 1732, chap. 7, art. 3.

[23] Massachusetts, *Acts and Laws*, 1784, chap. 63.

[24] Connecticut, *Laws* (1796), p. 186.

[25] Maryland, *Laws*, 1793, chap. 57, arts. 10-11.

law of 1721 provided that thirty-one lashes should be the maximum for a man, twenty-five for a woman,[26] but such punishment was going out of use at the close of the century.

After the adoption of the recommendation of the Philadelphia Society for Alleviating the Miseries of Public Prisons, the Philadelphia prison had separate quarters for men and women.[27] The law carrying this into effect was passed in 1790 with the immediate result of keeping women of the lowest class from getting themselves arrested for fictitious debts in order to obtain admission to the quarters of men confined for debt.[28] Women convicts of Philadelphia were employed in spinning, sewing, washing and similar work. Robert Turnbull in 1798 described the treatment of women at the prison. They were given suitable occupations, had a courtyard for exercise, and were kept quite apart from the sight of the men.[29] La Rochefoucauld thought them less strictly guarded and disciplined than the men.[30] In New Jersey there was no segregation of the sexes in prison during the colonial period and no adequate arrangement under the republic before 1830.[31] In New York, though there was always separation in theory, it was of little effect until the opening of the Magdalen Home in 1830 and the erection of a state prison for women at Sing Sing in 1839.[32] The in-

[26] Philip Klein, *Prison Methods in New York State* (New York, 1920), p. 21, quoting *Laws of Colonial New York*, 1721, ii, 58.

[27] Harry E. Barnes, *The Evolution of Penology in Pennsylvania* (Indianapolis, 1927), pp. 86, 88-89.

[28] *Ibid.*, pp. 89, 93.

[29] Robert Turnbull, *A Visit to the Philadelphia Prison* (Philadelphia, 1796), pp. 20-21, 25-26.

[30] *Travels* (London, 1799), iv, 41.

[31] Harry E. Barnes, *A History of the Penal, Reformatory and Correctional Institutions of the State of New Jersey* (Trenton, 1891), pp. 52, 75.

[32] Klein, *Prison Methods in New York State*, p. 57.

creased use of solitary confinement as a punishment, early in the nineteenth century, no doubt somewhat helped the problem of the separation of the sexes.

Turning from the general treatment of women before the law, one finds much legislation which dealt only with married women. Under the common law of England married women were regarded as legally merged in the identity of their husbands during marriage, though this was far from the case in America where wives undertook many activities as the agents of their husbands and had also a considerable degree of contractual freedom. Nevertheless they were still subject to many restrictions.[33]

The legislation on marriage and divorce showed a wide divergence from old English custom though what effect this had on women's position in the community is hard to state. Marriage especially in the New England colonies was viewed as a civil contract and throughout most of the seventeenth century was performed only by magistrates. The custom gradually changed so that by the outbreak of the Revolution ministers usually performed the rite. In the long run the concept of marriage as a civil matter proved to be one step in the separation of church and state. In New England its regulation was a matter for the attention of local governments.[34] The influence of Hebraism, strong in New England affairs, which was one reason for the intense scrutiny of private lives, affected men as well as women. Bachelors

---

[33] An excellent summary of the legal position of the married woman, particularly the disabilities under which she labored in the early nineteenth century, may be found in Tapping Reeve, *The Law of Baron and Femme* (3rd ed., Albany, 1862, first copyright, 1814), pp. 49-343. The conditions were essentially the same as those at the close of the previous century. Morris, *American Law*, pp. 126-200.

[34] Howard, *Matrimonial Institutions*, ii, 127-51. Williston Walker, *A History of the Congregational Churches in the United States* (New York, 1894), pp. 245-6.

were looked on with disfavor, and were required to live in well-ordered families; husbands and wives who did not live together were fined.[35]

The civil forms of marriage in New England and New York perhaps ultimately led to changes in women's condition as property holders. In all the colonies property rights on both sides were safeguarded by elaborate contracts before marriage. The consent of parents was legally required before courting a young woman and parents might be calculating in the use of the power of disposing of a son or daughter in marriage.[36] Because of the formal character of the contracts, breach of promise suits were frequent especially in New England.[37]

Quite as significant in their light on women's position were the divorce laws. Before the Revolution there were few statutes dealing with divorce and cases were rare. When a divorce was granted it was by the legislature.[38] In Connecticut and elsewhere in New England the grounds for granting divorces were the wife's adultery, the adultery and desertion of the husband, fraudulent contract, wilful desertion for three years, or seven years absence of either party.[39] Incestuous marriages were annulled or treated as void *ab initio*. Legislative divorce was also granted in New Jersey and Pennsylvania. Technically there was no divorce in the southern colonies for there were no church courts and where the Anglican Church was established these were necessary

[35] Howard, *History of Matrimonial Institutions*, ii, 152-54, 159.

[36] *Ibid.*, ii, 162-67.

[37] *Ibid.*, ii, 200-03, 246-47, 282.

[38] New Hampshire down to the Revolution had two or three cases, all on grounds of the wife's adultery. New Hampshire, *Laws*, iii, 554. There were two or three cases in Pennsylvania. A legislative divorce given in New Jersey was disallowed in 1773.

[39] Connecticut, *Laws* (1769), p. 43.

for absolute divorce.[40]   After the Revolution legislative divorce became more frequent in New Hampshire.[41]   Massachusetts passed a law naming grounds for divorce like those in Connecticut.[42]   In Rhode Island, gross misbehavior, extreme cruelty, and failure to provide were added to the list of causes.[43]   New York permitted it for adultery only.[44] In New Jersey it could be obtained for wilful and obstinate desertion for seven years, for adultery or polygamy.[45]   In Pennsylvania the grounds for divorce were much the same but the period of desertion was shorter.   These were all absolute divorces with the privilege of remarriage for the innocent party.   In cases of the husband's cruelty Pennsylvania also granted the wife divorce from bed and board.[46] The southern states, in spite of an occasional legislative act to dissolve a marriage, still made no statutory provision for divorce.   The effect of all these laws was to render it difficult for women to free themselves from complicated marital situations but divorce was more easily secured than in Europe, especially in the parts of America where marriage was regarded as a civil affair.   The New England states dealt fairly well with the wife in the matter of property settlements when she was the innocent party.[47]

The bulk of the legislation dealing with married women concerned property rights.   Under the common law the wife's personal property vested absolutely in her husband on

[40] Howard, *op. cit.*, ii, 367.

[41] New Hampshire, *Laws*, 52nd Ass., sess. 4, chap. 15, note.

[42] Massachusetts, *Acts and Laws*, 1785, chap. 69.

[43] Rhode Island, *Public Laws*, p. 479, sec. 3.

[44] New York, *Laws* (Greenleaf ed., 1792), 1787, chap. 79.

[45] New Jersey (Paterson), 1794, Dec. 2, p. 143.

[46] Pennsylvania, *Statutes at Large*, chap. 1187, pp. 94-98.

[47] Massachusetts, *Acts and Laws*, 1785, chap. 69.   Rhode Island, *Public Laws* (1798), p. 479.

marriage. Her real estate passed into his control during the continuance of the marriage. Under some circumstances he had a life interest in her property should he survive her. By British usage the property of married women could be transferred only by the process of fine and recovery. In these and other ways married women virtually lost their legal identity during marriage. The subordinate position of wives was to some extent offset by the husbands' liability for their maintenance and their debts but the loss of personal property might prove embarrassing. As late as 1764 a Massachusetts court held that the apparel and ornaments of a wife became the property of her husband on marriage, and except for necessary wearing apparel, might be taken in payment of his debts.[48] In America when the wife wished to keep her own property the ante-nuptial contract afforded some relief by enabling her to retain control.[49] Such contracts were common although Virginia and South Carolina provided that they must be recorded within a limited space of time to be valid.[50] Richard B. Morris in his *Essays on American Law* suggests that the growth of the Protestant conception of marriage as a civil contract, based on mutual consent and involving certain reciprocal obligations, led to the use of these contracts as a means of controlling property rights. Post-nuptial agreements were also in use between husband and wife although this was contrary to British usage.[51]

The dower rights of wives and widows, an inheritance from common law, persisted in the colonies and afterwards in the states. These gave the widow rights for life in one third of

---

[48] Josiah Quincy, Jr., *Massachusetts Cases* (Boston, 1865), p. 99.

[49] *Virginia Reports*, i, 141 (Wythe).

[50] Morris, pp. 136-37; Hening, xii, 154-55; South Carolina, iv, no. 1257.

[51] Morris, *op. cit.*, pp. 126-27, 136-37, 139, gives several examples of ante-nuptial agreements.

the real estate of her husband and a third share in his personal property. In practically all the colonies she had one half of the personal estate if there were no issue living. Individual colonies and states had minor differences in the laws dealing with dower. In Delaware if there were no issue living the widow had half the real estate for life. If there were no other heirs she held the whole during her life.[52] In Virginia she had dower rights in one third of the slaves, her own slaves becoming the absolute property of her husband on her marriage.[53] Most colonies had a proviso that if the widow was not satisfied with her share under her husband's will she might renounce it and elect to take her dower as she would have done had he died intestate. The widow's right to dower could be barred by jointure. In some colonies, if the jointure had been given before marriage during the wife's minority, or after marriage, she could take dower instead of the jointure since she had not been legally competent to agree to the jointure.[54] It was possible for a wife to lose her right of dower. In Massachusetts and Rhode Island if she committed adultery her husband kept her personal property and had a life interest in her real estate.[55] In New York, New Jersey, and Virginia, elopement with another man barred her from dower rights unless her husband received her back.[56] There was no uniformity in the provisions regarding dower in case of divorce.

[52] Delaware, *Laws*, i, 288-9, chap. 119, sec. 5.

[53] Hening, February, 1727, chap. 11, art. 4. October, 1748, chap. 3.

[54] Yeates, *Pennsylvania Reports*, ii, 302; iii, 79. Harris and McHenry, *Maryland Reports*, iv, 101. The jointure was an estate settled upon the wife instead of dower.

[55] Massachusetts, *Acts and Laws*, 1785, chap. 69; Rhode Island, *Public Laws*, p. 479, sec. 5.

[56] New York (Greenleaf), 1787, 10th sess., chap. 4, art. vii; New Jersey (Paterson), January 31, 1799, sec. 14; Hening, October, 1785, chap. 65.

After the Revolution a number of laws were passed reenacting and sometimes changing the earlier measures, thus insuring the speedy assignment of dower. In the case of an insolvent's estate dower rights were usually saved to the widow. The New York law provided that attainder of the husband should not bar the wife's right of dower.[57] Similar decisions were given in South Carolina.[58] In North Carolina, if there were more than two children, the widow received only a child's share of the personal estate.[59] That state had also a law providing that the widow was not entitled to take dower instead of a legacy if a jury decided that she was equally well off with the legacy.[60] Georgia by a law of February 22, 1785 announced that real and personal estate were to be considered as of the same nature. The widow and children then received equal shares in which they had absolute rights though the widow might elect to take her dower rights in the real estate if she preferred.[61] The same law made the wife's real estate vest absolutely in the husband on marriage.[62] In South Carolina after 1791 the widow was given one half of the real estate if there were no issue living and two thirds if there were no heirs within certain degrees.[63]

Dower cases were frequent in the courts, many of them dealing with semi-technical points some of which evoked special legislation. Thus it was decided that dower could only be given in property of which the husband was seized when he died.[64] In Connecticut the widow's right of dower

[57] William Johnson, *New York Cases* (2nd ed., New York, 1846), i, 28.

[58] *South Carolina Reports,* i (Bay I), 30; (Bay II), 9.

[59] North Carolina, *Public Acts,* 1784, chap. 22, art. 8.

[60] *Ibid.,* 1791, chap. 22.

[61] *Colonial Records of the State of Georgia,* xix, pt. 2, pp. 455-58.

[62] *Ibid.,* xix, pt. 2, p. 457.

[63] South Carolina, *Statutes at Large,* 1791, chap. 1489.

[64] Root, *Connecticut Cases,* i (1772), 50.

was held paramount to the rights of other heirs and their creditors.[65] Many cases hinged on the question of what barred dower, and to what possessions of the husband dower applied.[66] When the will was not clear, a devise to the wife did not bar dower unless the two were obviously incompatible.[67] The problems of dower in slaves led to many complications in the southern states. In New Jersey alienations by a widow, when sole, of her dower could convey the property for her life.[68] On the whole the courts were favorable to dower rights and did what they could to protect women's interests.

One of the more important phases of the legislation dealing with married women, the provision for the conveyance of land, was probably one of America's important contributions to the legal status of women.[69] In this country, in contrast to the English process of fine and recovery, the title was passed by a deed executed jointly by a husband and wife. The deed had to be acknowledged afterwards and the wife examined by a justice in the absence of her husband as to whether her signature had been voluntary. The conveyance was not valid without a certificate of this examination of the wife.[70] All the colonies passed such legislation although the New Jersey provision in a law of 1727-28 was disallowed.[71]

---

[65] Root, i, 227. For other dower cases see Harris and McHenry, *Maryland Cases*, iii, 394. Root, *Connecticut Cases*, ii, 50; Coxe, *New Jersey Cases* (1792), p. 125.

[66] Yeates, *Pennsylvania Reports*, ii, 300.

[67] *Ibid.*, i, 425; ii, 389; iii, 10.

[68] New Jersey, *Acts* (Paterson), March 2, 1798, sec. 9.

[69] On this point see Morris, *American Law*, p. 144.

[70] Coxe, *New Jersey Cases*, p. 242; *Virginia Reports*, i, 36; Yeates, *Pennsylvania Reports*, i, 389; Harris and McHenry, *Maryland Reports*, ii, 19, 38, 422, iii, 430; *Virginia Reports* (Call), i, 79; J. L. Taylor, *North Carolina Cases*, p. 139.

[71] New Jersey, *Laws* (Allinson), chap. 131.

This method of conveyance called forth additional laws to deal with women living in other colonies or in situations which made travel to make the necessary acknowledgments impossible. Conveyance by the husband alone of the lands of his wife did not prejudice her or her heirs.[72] Married women were not allowed to will their lands during marriage even to their husbands, but the right to make wills could be retained at least in part by antenuptial contract. In the case of *Adams* vs. *Kellogg,* Oliver Ellsworth explained the principles of English common law which did not permit wives to make wills. Married women were assumed to be under the power of their husbands, especially when the husbands benefited by the wills. Moreover, wives had no power of separate action since they were legally one with their husbands.[73] The effect of this legislation was to guard women's property rights better here than in Europe, particularly if they and their relations had shown foresight in making arrangements.

The mother had no claim in law to the possession of her children, for the father had the right to delegate their guardianship by will until they were of age. By a law of 1729 Maryland courts might remove the orphan children of a Protestant from his widow and place them where they would be educated as Protestants, if she were a Papist or if she married one.[74] This was repealed in 1798 since it interfered with civil rights on religious grounds.[75] In Connecticut the mother was recognized as the natural guardian of her daughters until they reached an age to choose for themselves. If, however, the court saw fit to remove the

[72] New York, *Laws* (Greenleaf), 1787, chap. 48, sec. 2.

[73] Kirby, *Connecticut Cases*, p. 195 (1786); Yeates, *Pennsylvania Reports*, i, 221.

[74] Kilty, *Laws of Maryland*, July, 1729, chap. 24, art. 12.

[75] *Ibid.*, 1798, chap. 66.

children from her the higher courts would not inquire into the reasons for the decision unless special evidence was brought.[76] Sometimes when parents were separated the courts would refuse to take a child from the mother and give it to the father, but such cases were rare.[77]

Women's business relationships formed another point at which they, whether married or single, might come into close contact with the law. Legally, single women and widows went into business with almost as much freedom as men; but often married women engaged in business and they suffered from distinct disabilities which, in many colonies, could only be removed by special legislation. Women, whose husbands had deserted them or were long away at sea, were in an especially bad position. Virtually every statute of limitations had a saving clause for the benefit of infants, those of unsound mind, and *femes coverts,* which saved their rights until the disability had been removed.[78] It was the classification of women with infants and idiots in these clauses which later aroused the special ire of the leaders of the women's movement. Married women could of course do business if their contracts were made in their husbands' names, but they sometimes had to have special authorization to act alone. The reason for the passage of individual acts was usually the desertion or prolonged absence of the husband. These acts were frequent in New Hampshire in the years from 1776 to 1784, probably because of the disturbed con-

[76] Root, *Connecticut Cases,* ii, 320; Coxe, *New Jersey Cases* (1795), p. 397.

[77] Root, *Connecticut Cases,* ii, 461.

[78] New Hampshire, *Laws,* 1791, chap. 48, v, p. 625; Rhode Island, *Public Laws,* 1798, p. 473; Connecticut, *Laws* (1796), p. 274; New York (Greenleaf), 1787, chap. 47, sec. 5; New Jersey, *Acts* (Paterson), 1799, February 7, sec. 4; Pennsylvania, *Statutes at Large,* iii, chap. 196; Hening, October, 1705, chap. 35, sec. 5.

ditions resulting from the Revolution.[79]   Similar cases were also to be found in the resolves of the Massachusetts legislature.   The system must have been inconvenient, particularly in those cases where individual acts were needed to enable a woman to do business for the support of her family or to settle estates.   Massachusetts in 1787 passed a law which allowed wives of men long absent to do business as *feme sole* traders upon receiving proper authorization.[80]   Pennsylvania had had a statute since 1718 authorizing the wives of mariners to act as *feme sole* traders when they were engaged in shopkeeping, so that the women could sue and be sued without the husband's interposition.   Such mariner husbands were forbidden to alienate any of their property without making provision for their families.[81]   Virginia had a few enabling acts passed to permit individual women who had been deserted by their husbands to dispose of property.[82]   In South Carolina the court decided that carrying on trade by herself over a period of years constituted a woman a *feme sole* trader.[83]

It used to be thought that women in colonial times entered few activities outside the home, that they scarcely knew how to transact business when the occasion arose.   This idea has been ably refuted, first by a chapter in Alice Morse Earle's *Colonial Dames and Good Wives,* and in greater detail by Elisabeth A. Dexter in her study, *Colonial Women of Affairs,* in which she gives an account of the wide range of occupations in which women engaged during the colonial

[79] New Hampshire, *Laws,* iv (Revolutionary period) has many instances.

[80] Massachusetts, *Acts and Laws,* 1787, chap. 32.

[81] Pennsylvania, *Statutes at Large,* chap. 226, iii.

[82] Hening, May, 1742, chap. 33; September, 1744, chap. 41; February, 1772, chap. 60.

[83] *South Carolina Reports* i (Bay, II), 66.

era. Most of her material is drawn from newspapers of the time, family and town records and other varied sources which make it evident that many women engaged in business and that their doing so aroused no particular opposition or comment. This should not be construed as meaning that it was the normal or expected thing for women to do. It was probably rare for girls to grow up with the idea of going into any sort of business or of handling affairs for themselves, particularly if they belonged to the upper classes. There was however no stigma attached to such activities if the need for entering upon them arose, and occasionally women were prepared for such work.

Few European authors, except Mary Wollstonecraft, suggested business education for women although Fénelon wished them to have a considerable knowledge of the management of property. There were several causes for this neglect of practical matters. Men like Dr. Gregory and A. L. Thomas wrote primarily of and for the women of the upper classes, ignoring the groups from which shopkeepers and servants were drawn.[84] Moreover in England the economic order was sufficiently fixed to make certain occupations impossible for persons of the better classes. The greater fluidity of American society, especially in the towns, gave women an opportunity to enter many fields without loss of caste.

As American theory on feminine education developed it was favorable to women's participation in business, but chiefly as a help to their husbands. The letters of John Adams, Joseph Hawley, and others show how completely the running of the farm might be left to the wife. Franklin urged his daughter to study accounting that she might be

---

[84] There were a few books written expressly for such groups like Mrs. Eliza Haywood's *A Present for a Servant Maid* (London, 1743).

able to assist her husband in his business.[85] He believed such training was more practical for young girls than music or dancing since it might prove a means of support in widowhood, and he cited the efficient career of the widow of a partner of his who had had business education in her girlhood in Holland.[86] James Murray's letters showed his sister as active in business on her own account in Boston.[87] Some letters of Eliza Farmar of Pennsylvania, shortly before the Revolution, show the wife managing part of the foreign business correspondence of the family.[88]

The occupations in which Mrs. Dexter found women chiefly engaged were those of tavern hostess, shopkeeper, artificer, nurse, and teacher. All these occupations could be and often were carried on in the home itself, some of them being merely expansion of the duties usually allotted to women. Where the work was of a less common sort it was often a continuation of the trade of husband, father or brother. Many of the women so engaged were widows. The accounts of literary women, religious leaders, and actresses must be regarded as apart from the usual run of things. Such women had special abilities and did not fit into the customary classifications. Mrs. Dexter herself concluded that, though most women had husbands to support them, the social and economic code permitted activity for self-support or aid of the family when necessary, and there were many ways of doing this.[89]

[85] Franklin, Sparks ed., *Works*, vii, 563; Adams, *Familiar Letters*, many scattered references. Hawley Correspondence (manuscript) New York Public Library.

[86] Franklin, *Writings*, Smyth ed., i, 345.

[87] *Letters of James Murray Loyalist* (Printed not published, New York, 1901).

[88] *Pennsylvania Magazine of History and Biography*, xl, 199-207.

[89] Dexter, *Colonial Women of Affairs*, pp. 181-82.

Women's legal status showed a fair degree of respect and protection for the sex with some improvements on English usage. In regard to property rights unmarried women and widows, who were nearly on a par with men, were treated as competent to transact business, engaging in a surprisingly wide range of occupations. If there were sex distinctions made in the punishment of crime they arose in practice rather than from the statutes. It was in the laws which defined the rights of married women tnat the concept of masculine superiority survived. Married women had little freedom of legal action and few property rights although there were hopeful developments like the American method of land conveyance. Since marriage was the expected condition for women it would seem that the laws reflected popular belief that women's sphere was domestic and the their legal and business relationship should be left to the direction of their husbands.

II.

In 1776 and for many years thereafter, women may be said to have had no political rights in the eyes of the law and were as a rule left out of account in any provision for political action. McKinley in his study of the suffrage franchise found only two instances in which the question of women's voting arose, both of which were in the seventeenth century. Margaret Brent, the executrix of Governor Leonard Calvert, in January 1647-48, demanded the right to vote in the Maryland assembly and, when this was refused her, protested against all the proceedings of that body.[90] In 1655 at Gravesend, Long Island, Lady Deborah Moody as one of the patentees of the town took part in the nomination of officers made to the governor.[91] McKinley found also that

[90] A. E. McKinley, *The Suffrage Franchise in the Thirteen English Colonies in America* (Philadelphia, 1905), pp. 53-54, quoting *Maryland Archives* (Assembly, 1637-64), p. 215.

[91] McKinley, *op. cit.*, pp. 192-93.

in Rhode Island the widows of proprietors occasionally gave their consent to civil proceedings which he regarded as an exercise of the political rights of landholders but not strictly speaking an exercise of the suffrage franchise.[92] It is possible that a similar practice prevailed in Massachusetts.[93]

The Virginia law of 1699 explicitly barred any woman, infant, or " recusant convict " from the suffrage, even though a freeholder.[94] South Carolina, Delaware, and Georgia restricted the suffrage to men.[95] In the other colonies exclusion was taken as a matter of course and the laws did not explicitly bar women until after the Revolution. Poll taxes were laid on men, sometimes on female slaves, and occasionally on free Negro women. Massachusetts for one term at the close of the seventeenth century had a two-shilling tax on all single women " that live at their own hand, " which was but half the amount paid by men.[96]

For the most part women accepted this situation passively though during the war there was at least one complaint by a woman who felt herself unrepresented. In 1778 Richard Henry Lee wrote to his sister, Hannah Corbin, apparently in answer to a letter in which she had protested that widows who were not represented were obliged to pay taxes.[97] Her objection was based on economic grounds and referred not to the rights of women as a sex but to the numerous Virginia widows with property who were legally *femes soles* with no man to represent them. Lee answered that he saw nothing in wisdom or policy which would prevent such widows from

[92] McKinley, p. 434n.

[93] *Commonwealth History of Massachusetts*, ii, 366 where reference is made to voting by women property holders. Also iii, 334.

[94] McKinley, *op. cit.*, p. 35, quoting Hening, iii, 172-75.

[95] *Ibid.*, pp. 146, 153, 155, 157, 172, 270, 474.

[96] Massachusetts, *Acts and Resolves*, 1695, chap. 6.

[97] Her letter is apparently not extant.

voting though he admitted that it was not customary. He suggested that the practice of not including women arose from the tumultous nature of the assemblies where men voted, in which feminine attendance would be out of character. He was ready to give the vote at any time to property-holding widows or spinsters but did not think that this was necessary for their security. Since the tax must fall as heavily on the representatives themselves as on others they would not make it unduly burdensome. Complaints against individual assessors could be met by appealing to the tax commissioners who were chosen annually by freeholders and housekeepers of the district, and in this election, Lee said, his sister had as good a right to vote as any one.[98] His letter did not imply that women exercised this right.

Thomas Jefferson reasoned much as Lee did on keeping women from the polls. In 1816, in a letter discussing equal representation, he named among other classes who must be excluded from the suffrage, " Women, who, to prevent depravation of morals and ambiguity of issue, could not mix promiscuously in the public meetings of men." [99] When the federal constitution was under discussion he wrote to a daughter of General Schuyler that the matter need not agitate her for—" the tender breasts of ladies were not formed for political convulsion." [100]

The plea made by Abigail Adams to her husband for better security of women's rights under the new government has

[98] James C. Ballagh, *The Letters of Richard Henry Lee* (2 vols., New York, 1911-14), i, 392-94; *Historical Magazine*, i, 360-61 quoting *National Intelligencer*, October 13, 1857, probably the first publication of the letter.

[99] Jefferson, *Writings*, vii, 36, to Samuel Kercheval.

[100] *Thomas Jefferson Correspondence, from William K. Bixby Collection* (Boston, 1916), p. 35. Compare the appeal to women to support the constitution from *Pennsylvania Gazette*, June 6, 1787, quoted p. 168, *supra*.

often been quoted. It is sometimes assumed to refer to political rights but on examination will be seen to apply particularly to the status of married women. Mrs. Adams said, " Do not put such unlimited power into the hands of the Husbands." She then spoke jestingly of fomenting a rebellion among the ladies against a government in which they had no representation. The phraseology of rebellion fitted in with popular conversation of the day but the whole tone of Mrs. Adams's letter, with her comments on the natural tyranny of men, suggests that the property and personal rights of wives and not the suffrage were what she had in mind.[101] In a letter to Mercy Otis Warren she wrote that their sex was rather hardly dealt with by the laws of England which gave the husband unlimited power to use his wife ill. This difficulty could be met by establishing laws in women's favor upon just and liberal principles. It was evidently the lack of adequate protection for those women, whose husbands took advantage of the laws as they stood, which distressed her.[102] John Adams's response to his wife expressed surprise that the British ministry after stirring up " Tories, land-jobbers, trimmers, bigots, Canadians, Indians, negroes, Hanoverians, Hessians, Russians, Irish, Roman Catholics, Scotch renegadoes," had also stimulated women to demand new privileges.[103] His letter to James Sullivan on this subject treated the question of qualifications for voting. He thought women should be barred from politics on the grounds of physical delicacy and preoccupation with home life, though he said that women and children had as good minds and independent judgments as men destitute of property; if such men were given the ballot he thought women

[101] *Letters of Mrs. Adams*, i, 100; *Familiar Letters*, pp. 149-50.
[102] *Warren Adams Letters*, i, 235-36.
[103] *Familiar Letters*, p. 155.

would demand a vote also.[104]   Adams felt keenly the value
of feminine influence in furnishing the moral element in
public life.   In 1807 he wrote to Benjamin Rush—

I say then that national Morality never was and never can be
preserved without the utmost purity and chastity in women: and
without national Morality a Republican Government cannot be
maintained.   Therefore my dear Fellow Citizens of America,
you must ask leave of your wives and daughters to preserve
your Republick.[105]

Women voted in New Jersey for a time after the Revolution although this was rather the result of political maneu-
vering than of any fixed principle and probably did not occur
frequently.   Tradition was against women's voting but
the letter of the law left the franchise open to either sex.   It
is said that the election law of 1790 used the words "he or
she" out of respect to a Quaker member of the committee
which framed it, since women had equal rights among the
Quakers.   The state constitution read merely that all inhabitants with certain qualifications were entitled to vote;
sex was not mentioned among the requirements.   The admission or rejection of women who possessed the necessary
qualifications depended entirely on the desires of the local
election officers with resulting diversity of practice and in
some instances chicanery.   This gave towns an advantage
over the country since it was easier for town women to come
to the polls.[106]   In 1807 there was an election at Elizabethtown in which there was great local excitement.   Women
were consequently permitted to vote with little regard to any

[104] Adams, *Works* (10 vols., Boston, 1850-56), ix, 375-78.

[105] *Old Family Letters, copied from the originals for Alexander Biddle*
(Philadelphia, 1892), Series A, pp. 127-28.

[106] [William Griffith], *Eumenes* (Trenton, 1799), pp. 33-34.   A
pamphlet on the New Jersey constitution.   The author was opposed to
women's voting.   See also *Historical Magazine*, i, 362.

legal qualifications; but the frauds in this election were so obvious that the next session of the legislature set the returns aside. Later in the year an act was passed which confined the suffrage to free white male citizens.[107]

It was shortly after the close of the American Revolution that Condorcet in France made his plea for the political rights of women. He maintained that women ought to have the same rights as men though they had never yet been permitted to exercise them under any constitution. He denied that women were adequately represented by men for he felt that the interests of the two sexes were different; he even advocated electing women to public office though he thought that those women who were " in the state of domesticity " should be temporarily excluded. His argument though ably developed seems to have been quite unnoticed in America.[108]

In rare instances women performed public duties of a semi-political nature. In two cases juries of matrons were called to determine the fact of pregnancy which had been offered as a bar to sentence. One case occurred in Pennsylvania in 1689 and the other approximately a century later in South Carolina. Another such jury in Virginia examined a woman for witch marks as late as 1705.[109] Such activity by women may have occurred elsewhere.

During the Revolutionary era much feminine activity verged closely on the political though it was not concerned

---

[107] Letter of W. A. Whitehead in *Historical Magazine*, i, 362; F. B. Lee, *New Jersey* (New York, 1902), iii, 266-67 has a synopsis of *Eumenes*; Frank Leslie's *Popular Monthly* (February, 1877), iii, 242, "Women and Voting in New Jersey."

[108] *Oeuvres complètes de Condorcet* (Brunswick and Paris, 1804), xii, 19-27, "Lettres d'un bourgeois de New-Haven." See also A. D. Vickery, *The First Essay on the Political Rights of Women* (Letchworth, n. d.).

[109] George Smith, *History of Delaware County, Pennsylvania* (Philadelphia, 1862), p. 174; *South Carolina Reports* (Bay I), 196; *William and Mary College Quarterly*, ser. I, i, 128, ii, 192.

with legal rights. Women acted as individuals and in organized groups to further the American cause. Such efforts dated from the time of the Stamp Act and took two forms, the boycotting of British goods and the encouragement of American manufactures. Large numbers of women pledged themselves to refrain from the use of tea until the tax was repealed, and signed agreements not to use any articles of British manufacture.[110] Throughout New England, and perhaps elsewhere, groups of women known as Daughters of Liberty met together to spin, their numbers sometimes reaching sixty or seventy at a meeting.[111] These gatherings were particularly encouraged by the clergy.[112] Appeals for the manufacture of homespun as a patriotic duty were common, some of them even antedating the Stamp Act difficulties. A New Jersey writer in 1758 begged women to produce linen and woolen homespun and thus secure economic independence for the colony. He assured the girls that skill in spinning, by demonstrating the lady's domestic ability, would attract young men.[113]

The outbreak of the war affected women in other ways. Mrs. John Adams wrote to her husband that she, with Mrs. Winthrop and Mrs. Warren, had been selected by the gentlemen at Cambridge to examine the Tory women.[114] Adams was quite pleased with this appointment and wrote back—

As you are a politician and now elected into an important office that of judgess of the Tory ladies, which will give you, naturally,

[110] *Boston Evening Post*, February 12, 1770.

[111] See accounts in town histories, newspapers, and in such works as R. M. Tryon, *Household Manufactures in the United States* (Chicago, 1917), and William Bagnall, *Textile Industries* (Cambridge, 1893).

[112] Alice M. Baldwin, *The New England Clergy and the American Revolution* (Duke University Press, 1928), pp. 154-155.

[113] *New Jersey Archives*, ser. I, xx, 256-61. Signed " B. C. Caesaria."

[114] *Familiar Letters*, p. 163 (April 21, 1776).

an influence with your sex, I hope you will be instant, in season and out of season, in exhorting them to use their influence with the gentlemen to fortify upon George's Island, Lovell's, Pettick's, Long, or wherever else it is proper.[115]

In Mecklenburg and Rowan counties in North Carolina young ladies took an extreme step and agreed not to marry anyone who had not entered the army. They presented their resolutions to the Committee of Public Safety who signified their approbation of the decision but there is nothing to show how far this plan or the examination of the Tory ladies in Massachusetts was carried into effect.[116]

As the war went on some propaganda was issued under feminine pseudonyms. A letter in the *Pennsylvania Evening Post*, ostensibly the work of a woman but actually by Governor Livingston, shows the attitude which Revolutionary leaders wished women to adopt.[117]

I do not remember whether your Gazette has hitherto given us the production of any woman correspondent.—Indeed nothing but the most pressing call of my country could have induced me to appear in Print. But rather than suffer your sex to be caught by the bait of that archfoe to American Liberty, Lord North, I think ours ought, to a woman to draw their pens, and enter our solemn protest against it. Nay, the fair ones in our neighborhood have already entered into a resolve for every mother to disown her son, and refuse the caresses of her husband, and for every maiden to reject the addresses of her gallant, where such husband, son or gallant, shews the least symptoms

---

[115] *Familiar Letters*, p. 172.

[116] Jethro Rumple, *History of Rowan County, North Carolina* (Salisbury, 1881), pp. 163-64; J. H. Wheeler, *Historical Sketches of North Carolina* (2 vols., Philadelphia, 1851), ii, 377.

[117] Philip G. Davidson, "Whig Propagandists of the American Revolution," *American Historical Review*, xxxix (April, 1934), 449; Theodore Sedgwick, *A Memoir of the Life of William Livingston* (New York, 1833), p. 282.

of being imposed upon by this flimsy subterfuge, which I call the dying speech, and last refuge of Great Britain, pronounced and grunted out by her great oracle, and little politician, who now appears ready to hang himself, for having brought the nation to the brink of that ruin from which he cannot deliver her—You will be kind enough to correct my spelling, a part of my education in which I have been much neglected *I am your sincere friend.* BELINDA.[118]

During the war there was one large organization of women both charitable and patriotic in its object.   This was an association strongest in and about Philadelphia with branches in New Jersey and Maryland.   It was under the leadership of Esther De Berdt Reed, wife of President Joseph Reed of the Pennsylvania provincial congress.   After her death in September 1780 it was directed by Franklin's daughter, Mrs. Bache, and other prominent Philadelphia women.   Gifts of varying amounts, received and recorded by feminine treasurers, were brought to the leaders in Philadelphia.   By July 1780, according to Ezra Stiles, the amount given by the ladies was $300,766.   The original plan had called for the use of the money in small donations made directly to the soldiers, but after some rather forcible suggestions made by Washington it was spent in the purchase of linen which the women made into shirts for the soldiers.[119]   The French officer Chastellux who saw the finished work was much impressed by the handiwork which these shirts represented.[120]   The

[118] *New Jersey Archives*, ser. 2, ii, 195-96.   From *Pennsylvania Evening Post*, May 8, 1778.

[119] W. B. Reed, *Life of Esther De Berdt Reed* (Philadelphia, 1853), *Life and Correspondence of Joseph Reed* (2 vols., Philadelphia, 1847). Letters of Washington, *Writings*, Ford ed., viii, 322, 324. The constitution of the society is printed in *Daughters of the American Revolution Magazine*, xlvii, 365-6. See also Ezra Stiles, *Literary Diary*, ii, 456. For New Jersey work see *New Jersey Archives*, ser. 2, iv, 502-05, 640-42.

[120] Chastellux, *Travels*, i, 197-98.

organization apparently did not extend to the South but
Richard Henry Lee wrote that the ladies of Virginia, who
were quite equal to those of Pennsylvania, had taken charge
of the meat house during the crisis of 1780.[121]

The lower class of women had other methods of entering
the affairs of the day. In July 1777 a group of a hundred
or more women of Boston became enraged at a merchant,
possibly Thomas Boylston, who had a hogshead of coffee in
his store which he refused to sell at any reasonable price.
They took matters into their own hands, secured a cart and
trucks and drove down to his warehouse demanding the keys.
When he refused to deliver them one of the women seized
him by the neck and tossed him into the cart. He then
delivered the key, the cart was tipped up, he was discharged
and the women entered the warehouse, removed the coffee
and drove off.[122]

America had many friends in England even during the
Revolution. Before discussing the small circle of American
women who were active politically, it is appropriate to say
something of an Englishwoman much interested in American
developments who perhaps afforded an example to this group
of American matrons. She was Catharine Sawbridge
Macaulay, later Mrs. Graham (1731-1791), who published a
History of England, the first volume of which appeared in
1763. Her enthusiasm for liberty made her follow closely
the struggles of the colonies for their rights. In 1769 she
sent James Otis a copy of her history with a note of praise
for his patriotic conduct.[123] When Henry Marchant of
Rhode Island was in London as agent of that colony, in 1772,
she talked with him and was delighted to know that two such

[121] Ballagh, *Letters of Richard Henry Lee*, ii, 190-91.
[122] *Letters of Mrs. Adams*, i, 111-12.
[123] *Warren Adams Letters*, i, 7.

free states as Connecticut and Rhode Island still existed.[124] On Marchant's return, she entrusted to him a fine edition of her works for Ezra Stiles with whom she had some subsequent correspondence.[125] Josiah Quincy, when he was in England in 1774, had two long conversations with her at Bath and was impressed with her good sense and liberal turn of mind.[126] In 1775 she published "An Address to the People of England, Scotland, and Ireland, on the present Important Crisis of Affairs," in which she defended the American position and attacked the closing of the Port of Boston.[127] In 1784 she visited North America where she was well received in Boston, spent ten days at Mount Vernon, and met many well-known Americans.[128] She evidently entertained exalted standards of simplicity for America, when in 1787 she told Mercy Warren she had heard that prices were lower and hoped that this was an indication that our taste for European luxuries had declined.[129] She was pleased with our proposed federal constitution believing that its principles might stand for ages, if the people of America devoted themselves to their land and necessary industries, and did not engage in commerce or consume foreign goods.[130] How far she influenced the work of Mercy Warren is uncertain but she was known to many men in America and her work was favorably received.

New England had a small circle of women, profoundly interested in matters political, and not without influence over

[124] Letter of Marchant in Stiles, *Literary Diary*, i, 251.

[125] Stiles, *Literary Diary*, i, 293, 411.

[126] Quincy's "London Journal" in Mass. Hist. Soc., *Proc.*, l, 451-52.

[127] Reprinted in *Magazine of History*, extra no. 114, vol. xxix, 78-90.

[128] Stiles, *op. cit.*, iii, 171, 172; *Warren Adams Letters*, ii, 241, 254, 257. Account of Mrs. Macaulay in *Dictionary of National Biography*.

[129] *Warren Adams Letters*, ii, 283.

[130] *Ibid.*, ii, 298-99, 303.

the men of their own families and other leaders of the nation. Chief among them were Abigail Adams, Mercy Otis Warren and Hannah Winthrop, wife of Professor John Winthrop of Harvard College. From their own statements, notably those of Mrs. Adams, one would suppose them women of limited education, but the frequent historical and poetical allusions in their letters belie this.[131] Mrs. Adams quoted from at least three of Shakespeare's plays and from the verses of Collins, Dryden, Pope, Goldsmith, and Thomson. In her discussion of current happenings, she made historical reference in her letters to the Spartans, Polybius, Caesar Borgia, Charles XII of Sweden, Nero, Caligula, Cicero, Aurelian, and others. She read Paine's *Common Sense* and other political writings of her day and knew French.[132] Among the many books which she and Mrs. Warren mentioned in their letters there were no novels; to them reading must have been primarily a means of improvement. In spite of her wide reading, Mrs. Adams's advice to her daughter savored strongly of the domestic character. She believed that the order and regulation of the household and assistance to her husband were the wife's first duties, and that in educating girls, one must always remember that no man had ever prospered without the cooperation of his wife. After one had trained girls for these duties one might add any accomplishments, remembering that after all they were mere embellishments.[133]

Mrs. Adams enjoyed writing political news to Mrs. Warren and indulging in discussions of the country's needs. Her letters to her husband abounded in little political maxims

[131] *Familiar Letters*, p. 213; *Letters of Mrs. Adams*, i, 131.

[132] *Familiar Letters*, pp. 25, 136, 139, 141, 161-2; *Letters of Mrs. Adams*, i, 13, 30, 41, 52, 62, 72, 73, 89, 93, 96, 101, 127, 148, 164, 165; Alice Brown, *Mercy Warren* (New York, 1896), pp. 234-38.

[133] *Letters of Mrs. Adams*, ii, 265.

of a sage nature.   As early as December 1773, she suggested
civil war as the probable outcome of American difficulties.[184]
In November 1775 she was urging separation from England
and two months later was speculating on the type of government to be adopted in case of separation; she herself
favored a republic.[185]   Her remarks on the legal status of
women were another indication of her political interests.
These last were no doubt intensified by the part which her
husband and friends were taking in the affairs of government, but they showed a clear view of what was happening.
Her daughter was also a close observer of political events
after her marriage, though as a young girl she remarked that
she never thought or talked of them.[186]

Mercy Otis Warren, sister of James Otis, wrote verses,
including poetical drama of a ponderous nature,[187] and later
a *History of the American Revolution*.[188]   Some of her early
work, which appeared anonymously, dealt with political
figures of the war.   Her literary efforts and even her correspondence had an attempted grandeur of manner which is
irksome to the modern reader.   Conscious of her own ability
she yet feared or professed to fear that she was exceeding
the bounds of female decorum.   She discussed with John
Adams whether she was wise as a Christian author to hold
individuals up to public derision when it was the crime, and
not the criminal, with which she was concerned.   If the
nature of the times permitted such acrimony, might not the
female character suffer and the writer be suspected of lack-

[184] *Warren Adams Letters*, i, 18.

[185] *Familiar Letters*, p. 170; *Letters of Mrs. Adams*, i, 80, 82, 89.

[186] *Journal and Correspondence of Miss Adams*, ii, 94.   Letter written
at the time of the adoption of the federal constitution.   Root, *Colonel
William Smith and Lady*, p. 113, letter written December, 1785, pp. 202-
04, 231.

[187] *Poems, Dramatic and Miscellaneous* (Boston, 1790).

[188] 3 vols., Boston, 1805.

ing the candor and charity necessary in a woman?[139]   In
this letter to Adams she was referring to her political satires,
such as *The Group*, which treated certain Tory figures in no
favorable light.   In her correspondence one can trace the
same theory of women's sphere as that presented by the older
British writers and can see that it affected her work.   Mrs.
Warren suffered much distress because she took one of
Adams's letter as a hint that she had gone beyond a woman's
proper place in discussing politics, which he protested had
not been at all his meaning.[140]   When he first wrote to ascertain her views on the form of government to be adopted in
America, she thought he was perhaps ridiculing her sex.
After she learned that this was not the case she expressed
herself as strongly in favor of a republic, which she thought
developed many qualities in human nature not otherwise to
be obtained.   She did not want a monarchy, whatever might
be demanded by European ideas of fashion; she was not
sure, however, that America had reached the stage of development necessary for a republic.[141]   In her reaction to her
own husband's political vicissitudes she showed a good deal
of personal feeling.[142]

Whether or not politics was a proper subject of conversation for women was always a question for discussion.[143]
In 1778 John Quincy Adams wrote of meeting more than one
woman who thought politics indelicate and unfeminine.   He
sarcastically observed that perhaps it would be as well if all
women thought so; but added that he wished even females
to feel some interest in the welfare of their country.[144]   Reg-

[139] *Warren Adams Letters*, i, 37-39.

[140] *Ibid.*, i, 106-07, 115; Brown, *Mercy Warren*, pp. 241-43.

[141] *Mercy Warren*, p. 90.

[142] *Warren Adams Letters*, ii, 17-18, 147, 180.

[143] Compare Stiles's topics for debate at Yale, p. 154, *supra*.

[144] *Life in a New England Town* (Boston, 1903), pp. 69, 82.

ulaf participation in politics by women was a thing not contemplated save in rare instances. At the same time intelligent thought favored women's knowledge of political events and some activity within their proper sphere to forward the movements of the day. The cooperation of women in the economic measures of the Revolutionary era was of great importance. For the exceptional and gifted woman there was an opportunity to exert real influence on the men of her immediate group and if she were skilled in the use of her pen she might reach others. Such participation in public affairs depended on individual ability and its effect can hardly be measured. In general one may safely say that politics was still considered a field outside the range of the normal woman.

III

Although the religious activities of women do not in themselves represent popular opinion, yet a knowledge of them throws much light on the prevalent ideas of proper and improper feminine conduct, and is essential to an adequate portrayal of any period. Even the occasional appearances of women as leaders of religious sects have their place in the picture. If one turns back for a moment to New England in the seventeenth century it will be remembered that one of Anne Hutchinson's first activities in Boston was her assumption of the leadership of a group of women who met for religious purposes. These gatherings were not looked upon with disfavor until Mrs. Hutchinson expounded her own views and reached a wider circle of hearers than the women of the neighborhood.[145] If Mrs. Hutchinson's banishment put such meetings under a ban they were later revived. In December 1706 Cotton Mather recorded in his diary that he had visited a society of devout women who were keeping the

[145] C. F. Adams, *Three Episodes of Massachusetts History*, i, 397-401.

day together as one of private thanksgiving. He prayed and preached for them but did not say what was the immediate occasion of their assembling.[146]   Such intimate groups may have been common but were seldom mentioned until the time of the Great Awakening when the preaching of Whitefield and Tennent aroused women as well as men to a high pitch of religious excitement.   One manifestation of this was the formation of small circles of women for prayer.   Whitefield spoke of such a society in Philadelphia whose meetings were marked by what a modern observer would consider religious hysteria.[147]   Jonathan Edwards and his wife lent their approbation to similar groups, and Edwards advised membership in one of them for a young lady who was seeking directions for a religious life.   Dwight, in his life of Edwards, observed that some persons disapproved the formation of such groups; he did not make it clear whether this disapproval was due to theories about women's sphere, or dread of " enthusiasm." [148]

Two of these societies survived the period of the revival, and presented remarkable exceptions to the rule of inactivity for women outside the home.   One, at the Old South Church in Boston, was described by Thomas Prince in the funeral sermon of his daughter Deborah, as " the Female *Society* to which she joined for the most indearing Exercise of social Piety."   Deborah Prince had been much influenced by the preaching of Whitefield and Tennent,[149] as had Abigail Dawes, later Mrs. Waters, who took the initiative in the formation of the society.   This group, which gave one afternoon a week to prayer, continued uninterruptedly until the siege of Boston in 1775 and resumed its meetings after

[146] *Diary*, i, 579.

[147] Whitefield, *Journals*, pp. 418, 421.

[148] Edwards, *Works* (1828 ed.), i, 131, 149-52.

[149] Sermon (1744), pp. 22, 24, 25.

the evacuation of the city. It was still in existence in the middle of the nineteenth century. The members shunned publicity and left no record of any activity other than prayer.[150] At Newport a society which attained larger proportions was formed in 1741 soon after Whitefield's preaching there. It was composed of young women under the particular direction of Sarah Osborn, then about twenty-seven years of age.[151] A year or two later she aided in forming a society of women at Little Compton.[152] The Newport group met first two evenings a week and later one afternoon weekly. The weekly meetings were continued for nearly half a century, Mrs. Osborn being considered as the head until her death in 1796. It was customary to keep four quarterly days for confessing sins and asking God for spiritual blessings on the church and all nations. The first meeting of the month was usually spent in prayer, as was the Saturday before the administration of the Lord's Supper. A regular meeting was opened with reading from some profitable book; after all had assembled there was prayer, Bible reading, and religious conversation. A box for contributions, placed in the meeting room, was opened once or twice a year, the contents being used for the support of the gospel. In 1774 the ladies made a substantial donation to Samuel Hopkins's African Mission.[153] The society had a set of rules signed by the members, providing for membership, for payment for wood used, and for the procedure at the meetings. New members were proposed at one meeting and, if no objection was offered, were admitted at the next

[150] Joshua Huntington, *Memoirs of Mrs. Abigail Waters* (Boston, 1817), pp. 56-61.

[151] Samuel Hopkins, *Life of Sarah Osborn* (2nd ed., Catskill, N. Y., 1814), p. 50.

[152] *Ibid.*, p. 53.

[153] Hopkins, *Works*, i, 132.

after signing the articles.[154] A life-long member of this group was Susanna Anthony of whose religious career Samuel Hopkins left a record, as he did of Mrs. Osborn.

Religious meetings of women took other forms. During the revivals of 1766 and 1767, Mrs. Osborn had a group of young women from nine to twenty years of age who met with her for prayers and instruction.[155] There were from forty to fifty young ladies in this group. She also instructed groups of children, of heads of families, and even of Negroes. In her old age, Esther Stoddard Edwards, the mother of Jonathan Edwards, held meetings for the ladies of her neighborhood at which she expounded religious books, always closing the meeting with prayer. These gatherings were approved by the pastor at East Windsor, Connecticut where she made her home.[156] When Ezra Stiles was pastor in Newport he had meetings of the young women of his congregation though perhaps not at stated intervals. They came to his house in numbers ranging from fifty to seventy, for what he called a " religious exercise." These meetings were held from 1770 to 1774.[157] Samuel Hopkins, also of Newport, had meetings of the young men and young women of his congregation on alternate weeks, to whom he discoursed on religious topics. For a time there were seventy young ladies who attended regularly. Later these separate meetings were replaced by a Sunday evening lecture on the catechism for all the young people.[158] Gatherings such as these were not likely to promote other than conservative thought since they were in close touch with the clergy who,

[154] Hopkins, *Life of Sarah Osborn*, pp. 70-73.

[155] *Ibid.*, p. 81.

[156] Edwards, *Works* (1829), i, 18. From Dwight's life.

[157] *Literary Diary*, i, 36, 88, and elsewhere.

[158] Hopkins, *Works*, i, 84; John Ferguson, *Memoir of the Life and Character of Rev. Samuel Hopkins* (Boston, 1830), pp. 80-81.

as in the charitable societies of the early nineteenth century, were inclined to view women's careers in a restricted sense. If there were such groups in any numbers outside of New England they left no record. The town and village life of New England no doubt facilitated attendance by the women.

Women like men were expected to attend church regularly and the sexes were usually seated separately in church, especially in the early part of the century. In Hadley there were even separate stairs for the galleries occupied by young men and women.[159] Many references in Samuel Sewall's diary show that the places occupied by women served to denote rank as much as those of the men.[160] In the Congregational churches of New England, though women were often present at business meetings, it was not customary according to the statement of Ezra Stiles for them to speak or vote.[161] A covenant signed by members of the church at Shirley about 1762 bore the names of men only.[162] On the other hand, the first Baptist church of Grafton, Massachusetts organized about 1774 or 1775 had its articles of faith and its covenant signed by men and women in nearly equal numbers.[163] Women also seem to have signed the covenant in many Congregational churches. They had indirect methods of mixing in church politics, for Stiles, in 1777, observed that Mrs. Osborn's society had exerted themselves vigorously and to effect in the controversy over the calling of Samuel Hopkins to the First Congregational Church at Newport.[164] Stiles reported a dispute which had arisen in the Baptist church at Newport,

[159] Judd, *History of Hadley*, pp. 51, 320, 414; Felt, *Annals of Salem*, ii, 620.

[160] *Diary*, iii, 116, 163, 234, 306, etc.

[161] *Literary Diary*, i, 147.

[162] Seth Chandler, *History of the Town of Shirley* (Shirley, 1883), p. 215.

[163] F. C. Pierce, *History of Grafton* (Worcester, 1879), pp. 219-20.

[164] *Literary Diary*, i, 44.

in which two thirds of the members were women. The church was much concerned as to whether a majority of members was required for transaction of business and if so whether the majority should include women. There was precedent for the latter course since women had voted on the dismissal of an elder as early as 1747. The Baptist Association of Rhode Island declined to give an opinion, regarding the matter as the business of the individual church. Stiles remarked that it was usually the older women who voted and that the practice might entirely disappear with the growing up of another generation.[165]

The sect whose women were most prominent in religious expression was the Society of Friends. The Quaker attitude towards women differed somewhat from that of the Puritans and put the sexes more nearly on an equal basis. Since the Quakers believed that religion rested on inner light and inspiration, not on education or the acceptance of explicit tenets, there was no reason why women as well as men should not take an active part in the ministry and many of them did so, especially in the early days of Quakerism. They found scriptural warrant for the calling of women to preach.[166] Some of the early women preachers endured imprisonment, torture and death, though these punishments had disappeared by the period of this study.[167] Such educational provisions as the Quakers made were for both sexes.[168] Women had a share in the management of affairs through the women's meeting which was instituted about 1658.[169] Men's and

[165] Stiles, *Literary Diary*, i, 145-46.

[166] A. Jorns, *The Quakers as Pioneers in Social Work* (New York, 1931), p. 25 note 17; G. P. Gooch, *Democratic Ideas in the Seventeenth Century* (2nd ed., Cambridge, 192-), p. 230, note 5.

[167] See Sewall, *Diary*, i, 43, for account of a disturbance of a meeting by a Quaker woman.

[168] Jorns, *Quakers as Pioneers*, pp. 109-111.

[169] *Ibid.*, pp. 67-68.

women's meetings for the transaction of business were held separately as a matter of convenience; but the work supervised by women was fully as important as that under the care of men.[170]   The women's meeting for business at Nansemond, Virginia, dated back to 1672 and that in Pennsylvania to 1681.[171]   Maryland had a regular women's meeting before 1700 and in that year there was established a private meeting of the " solidest women friends " to meet three times a year and discuss problems of dress, marriage, and the like.[172]   In 1788 Brissot de Warville who was much interested in the Quaker system mentioned the women's meetings as an excellent substitute for the confessional system of the Roman Catholic church.   He described them as chiefly for discipline with no power to make regulations.[173]   Actually these groups, both in England and America, had many responsibilities, whether they drew up rules or not.   Proposed marriages were always referred first to the women's meeting for discussion.   The very form of the Quaker marriage ceremony, an agreement made by both parties together and not a pronouncement by a minister, tended to place the sexes on a more equal basis.

A particularly interesting feature of Quaker life as compared with other denominations was the part which women took in the services.[174]   Though at first Quaker women had met with severe usage, during most of the eighteenth century

[170] Mabel R. Brailsford, *Quaker Women* (London, 1915), pp. 3-9.   A discussion very sympathetic to the Quaker viewpoint.   Rufus M. Jones, *Quakers in the American Colonies* (London, 1911), pp. 283, 305, 309, 312, 314, 387, etc.

[171] Jones, *op. cit.*, 283, 305.

[172] *Ibid.*, pp. 312, 309.

[173] *New Travels* (1792), p. 407.

[174] *Pennsylvania Magazine of History and Biography*, xvii, 452, the " Journal of Ann Warder " gives an instance.   There are many scattered references in the pages of the *Friends' Library*.

they preached in the colonies with no more serious obstacles than ridicule and criticism. In a list of ministers and elders at Burlington, New Jersey, in 1767, twenty-five of the sixty names were those of women. In the records of the Philadelphia Yearly Meeting, showing for nearly a century (1684-1773) the ministers from abroad who attended, there were one hundred and eleven listed of whom thirty-two were women.[175] In their work as " public Friends " women made trips about the country and even across the ocean. As the century wore on, however, the call to undertake protracted " religious visits " became less frequent among women with family responsibilities. In the *Friends' Library* and elsewhere are the records of at least four women of American birth who engaged in such work, as well as of two from England and Ireland who became permanent residents of the new world. There are also accounts of British women who travelled here but returned to their native land.

The biographical sketches of these women ministers are as a rule disappointing to the social historian because the writers dealt almost exclusively with the religious experiences of the travellers and told little of other events. In the diary of Hannah Callender there is an account of the experiences which led Rebecca Jones of Philadelphia to become a Quaker and minister.[176] Patience Brayton of Rhode Island, another " public Friend," was drawn to leave her family and visit the middle and southern colonies. She left a family of young children, one of whom died during her absence and another shortly after her return. Her trip left her with such a profound distaste for slavery that she and her husband later freed their own slaves.[177] Other American women ministers were Sarah Morris of Philadelphia and Elizabeth Collins of

[175] R. M. Jones, *Quakers in the American Colonies*, pp. 409, 540-43.
[176] *Pennsylvania Magazine of History and Biography*, xii, 434-35.
[177] *Friends' Library*, x, 441-80.

New Jersey.   The former when she was approaching seventy went on a religious visit to Great Britain.[178]   Catherine Phillips, an English Quakeress, who visited in America, referred in her narrative to Grace Fisher of Philadelphia and Grace Crosdale of Bucks County, Pennsylvania, as women gifted in the ministry.[179]   Elizabeth Ashbridge, who afterwards became a Quaker and a "public Friend," came to this country as an indentured servant.   Her first glimpse of women taking part in Quaker meetings startled her but in time she was herself converted.   She and her husband were school teachers with separate schools a mile or so apart in New Jersey.   She died while on a religious visit to Ireland.[180] Jane Hoskens, "that faithful servant of Christ," as her biographer described her, came to Pennsylvania under a religious conviction and was indentured as a teacher for three years to a group of Quaker families in Plymouth.   Next she was housekeeper for David Lloyd, a prominent Quaker. During this period the Friends treated her kindly and encouraged her religious activities.   After she became convinced of women's authority to preach, she went on religious visits to the southern colonies and Barbadoes, to New England, and Ireland, visiting the American colonies more than once.   Such trips were undertaken in company with other women Friends, the ministers usually travelling in pairs.[181]

Of the visiting women from Great Britain few left accounts of themselves.   One Irish woman preacher, who journeyed through the Carolinas, recorded her queer reception in the districts where, as she said, the lawfulness of women's preaching was not known.[182]   Catherine Phillips, who travelled

[178] *Friends' Library*, vi, 478-80; xi, 450-73.

[179] *Ibid.*, xi, 226.

[180] *Ibid.*, iv, 10-24.

[181] *Ibid.*, i, 460-73.

[182] *Ibid.*, xi, 73-119, account of Mary Neale. See especially p. 107.

over 8750 miles on a religious trip to America and back in the years, 1753-1756, left in her journal some cautions to be observed towards unmarried members of the other sex, by young women in a single state who travelled in the service of the ministry. She advised them to guard themselves against imagination lest it be mistaken for revelation and so lead them into a freedom of behavior which might engage the affection of the young men with whom they were travelling. At the same time they must avoid hurting anyone's spirit by austere conduct.[183] Both John Rowe, Boston merchant, and Ezra Stiles spoke well of Mrs. Rachel Wilson, an English Quakeress, who preached in Boston and Newport in 1769. Stiles called her a pious sensible sort of a woman and Rowe reported that she had an audience of over twelve hundred people in Boston.[184] To judge from the list of the Philadelphia Yearly Meeting there must have been many other English Quaker women who visited the country.

Those Quaker women who did not act as "public Friends" were busy, energetic housewives like other women in the colonies. Many letters and diaries written by them are in existence which reveal no particular intellectual interests but afford interesting descriptions of society and Revolutionary events.[185] The part which Quaker women took in religious activities was apparently without effect upon the women of other denominations.[186] This was perhaps because they formed only a small part of the population and were often held in disfavor.

[183] *Friends' Library*, xi, 188-287, especially pp. 220-21.

[184] Stiles, *Literary Diary*, i, 14; *Letters and Diary of John Rowe* (Boston, 1903), p. 189.

[185] For the Revolution see journal of Hannah Drinker in *Pennsylvania Magazine of History and Biography*, xiii, 298-308 and diary of Margaret Morris in *Bulletin of Friends' Historical Society*, ix, 2, 65, 103.

[186] Much information about Quaker women may be found scattered through Jones, *The Quakers in the American Colonies* and Brailsford, *Quaker Women*.

The Moravian seminary for young ladies at Bethlehem has already been mentioned; but the whole treatment of women by the Moravians was enough out of the ordinary to evoke comment, especially from foreign travellers. A modified community life was practiced in which women, while leading a sheltered existence, were able to provide for their own support. Unmarried women, whose families had sent them, and others who wished to do so, lived in the Single Women's house at Bethlehem, which had something less than one hundred residents. Some Moravian women worked as domestics in the village but by a payment of four or five dollars a year retained the right to remove to the house when they chose. The women who were regular residents of the house followed an orderly schedule, giving their time to knitting, weaving and kindred occupations, and they were paid for this work by the matron, who sold the articles for the benefit of the house. They were reputed particularly skilful in making ruffles, working pocketbooks, pincushions and other little niceties.[187] The sisters, as they were called, paid board and the house was thus self-supporting.

This Moravian house was run in many ways like a school. The inhabitants all shared one large bedroom, which covered the whole of the second floor, and were under the supervision of an inspectress who in the 1780's was a former woman of fashion born in Saxony. John Eliot, the Boston clergyman, who compared the matron to the abbess of a nunnery, thought the girls were kept too much confined and did not enjoy life.[188] Eliza Southgate also remarked on the convent-like atmosphere of the place.[189] The inmates were

---

[187] Southgate, *A Girl's Life*, pp. 174-75.

[188] *Belknap Papers*, iii, 235-36. A description in the diary of Hannah Callender (1761) in *Pennsylvania Magazine of History and Biography*, xii, 451-53; Schoepf, *Travels in the Confederation* (2 vols., Philadelphia, 1911), i, 137; Chastellux, *Travels*, ii, 324-327.

[189] *A Girl's Life*, p. 175.

allowed to go out but could not have any communication with men. Marriages were arranged by the society, the women having the right to refuse an unwelcome suitor. The traveller, Anburey, stated that such a refusal placed a girl at the bottom of the list and made it impossible for the man to marry anyone else, but this statement is not confirmed by other observers.[190] Franklin wrote that when several candidates seemed equally available the marriage was sometimes decided by lot.[191] In the young ladies' school all the teachers were members of the society who had received their own education there; La Rochefoucauld expressed the fear that they might offer provincial or inadequate instruction.[192]

There was also a house where widows were cared for at the expense of the society—those who were able to work doing what they could toward their own support. An additional feature of this plan was a voluntary insurance company to which the male members of the society contributed. The interest on such contributions was later given to the widows, either to add to their comfort in the widows' home or to meet part of their housekeeping expenses elsewhere.[193] The Moravians thus combined economic security for their women with a moderate degree of activity on the part of the women themselves. Their daily life emphasized religious devotion more than intellectual pursuits. That the Moravians attracted general respect was evidenced by the number of girls of good family who were sent to their seminary.

Women of the Ephrata Community had, like the Moravians, a communal life. They lived apart from the men and

---

[190] Thomas Anburey, *Travels through the Interior Parts of North America* (2 vols., London, 1791), ii, 452, 455-56.

[191] Franklin, *Writings*, Smyth ed., i, 413-14.

[192] La Rochefoucauld, *Travels through the United States of North America* (4 vols., London, 1799), iv, 141-43.

[193] *Ibid.*, iv, 142.

the sexes seldom met except for worship.   The women wore
a distinctive white gown as did the men.   Marriage though
infrequent was not entirely forbidden.[194]

Towards the close of the century two new religious groups
arose which provoked unfavorable comment and in which
women played a large part.   One of these sects was the little
band of followers who gathered about Jemima Wilkinson,
or the " Universal Friend " as she called herself; the others
were the Shakers under Ann Lee.   Ezra Stiles observed that
it was remarkable that there should be two women at once
with such different " monstrous & sacrilegious Systems." [195]

Jemima Wilkinson was born in Rhode Island of a Quaker
family.   According to La Rochefoucauld, she took part at
an early age in Quaker meetings for the handling of discipline; but this was doubtless his interpretation of the customary duties of the women's meeting in any Quaker group.
Jemima was much moved by a sermon of Whitefield's in 1770
and attended " New Light " Baptist meetings, though not a
member of that church.   During a severe illness in 1776 she
was in a trance for thirty-six hours and on her recovery announced that Jemima Wilkinson had died and a new soul
had entered into her body.   Later she described herself to
her nearest followers as the embodiment of Christ at his
second coming. She was personally attractive and affected a
mannish dress, which excited the ire of some hearers, though
others thought it striking and helpful in accomplishing her
work.   She went about the country preaching and attracted
a number of followers, including some quite respectable persons.   Ezra Stiles, who gave many details of her life, cited
instances of insanity in the Potter family who were among
her ardent supporters.   He regarded Jemima's own illness
and subsequent behavior as a form of insanity.   Of her

[194] Anburey, *Travels*, ii, 256-59; Schoepf, *Travels*, ii, 16-17.
[195] *Literary Diary*, ii, 510.

theology, Stiles recorded that she used the plain language of the Quakers but allowed water baptism. She wished to bring all sects together under her own teaching;[196] and preached extensively in Rhode Island, Worcester and Philadelphia. In the Quaker city her presence and teachings aroused violent controversy, possibly because of her former relations with the Quakers. At this time the question of her claims to divinity was broached publicly and her followers were accused of plotting to kill a woman who had derided these claims. The plot was designed to make it appear that the scoffer had been providentially struck down as a punishment for her sins; so the alleged victim and her friends reported.[197] Some of Jemima's teachings were vigorously attacked, notably in a tract published by Abner Brownell in 1783, as a menace to domestic morality. In 1788 she founded a colony, New Jerusalem, in the Genessee country in New York, which lived on good terms with the Indians, but as it became more prosperous suffered from internal dissensions. In spite of the unfavorable account given in David Hudson's monograph, Jemima Wilkinson appears to have been a genuine enthusiast, not an adventuress.[198] Ezra Stiles was impressed with her piety if not her sanity. La Rochefoucauld who visited the colony in 1795 gave a long but not very favorable account of her career. He accused her of pretended sanctity, of manipulating chance events, and persecutions to

196 *Literary Diary*, ii, 380-82; iii, 289-90.

197 The intended victim of the plot was Abigail Dayton. See letters in *Pennsylvania Gazette*, February 28, 1787, cited as from the *Freeman's Journal* of February 14, and the *Gazette*, March 28, April 4, 1787. The first letter is also reprinted in *American Museum*, February, 1787, with a counter attack and reply in March, April, and May, i, 150, 218, 297, 389.

198 For biography consult, Rev. John Quincy Adams, " Jemima Wilkinson, the Universal Friend," *Journal of American History*, ix (1915, no. 2), 249-63; Robert P. St. John, " Jemima Wilkinson," *New York State Historical Association Quarterly*, xi (April, 1930), 158-75; David Hudson, *History of Jemima Wilkinson* (Geneva, N. Y., 1821).

her own end; but he believed that she succeeded in imposing only on simple minds and on religious enthusiasts. Her preaching he described as facile but repetitious.[199] Barbé-Marbois who also heard her preach thought the preacher beautiful but the sermon commonplace; her personal conduct seemed to him irreproachable.[200]

Stiles's other "monstrous sacrilegious system," it will be remembered, was that of Ann Lee.[201] She was born in England, the daughter of a blacksmith; and in early life she worked in a cotton factory and as a cook. In 1758 she joined the English Shakers, an offshoot of the Quakers, who believed in open confession of sins. Her personal reactions to her marital experience convinced her of the value of a celibate life.[202] In 1774 she came to America with a small group of followers, and after some delay established a religious community in New York state. She was head of the central community at what is now Watervliet near Albany, with branches elsewhere.[203] The American Shakers believed that the second coming of Christ must be as a woman since he had come first as a man. Ann Lee, who was regarded as their "Mother in Christ," was also called the "Elect Lady." Through her they believed female character was restored to the plane from which it had been degraded by Eve's fall.[204] Shaker religious services were marked by ceremonial dancing and according to popular report by most un-

[199] *Travels*, i, 201-16.

[200] *Our Revolutionary Forefathers* (New York, 1929), pp. 162-66.

[201] *Literary Diary*, ii, 510-11; Stiles delivered a lecture on these two women in 1781.

[202] F. W. Evans, *Shakers, Compendium* (New York, 1859), pp. 120-155.

[203] *Literary Diary*, ii, 510. Stiles thought her coming was perhaps a plot of the British ministry to cause religious confusion in America.

[204] Calvin Green and S. Y. Wells, *A Summary View of the Millennial Church* (2nd ed., Albany, 1848), p. 45, and the chapter on "The Manifestation of Christ in the Female," pp. 258-71.

desirable practices.[205] In 1784, when Ann Lee died, a note in the *Connecticut Journal* suggested that her death might be due to the violence of "gymnastic religion,"[206] and warned others against the sect on this ground. Women had important parts in this organization, but the number of members was so small and the popular disapproval so strong as to prevent any effect on the social customs of other sects. The Shakers in the nineteenth century claimed that they had been the first group to free woman from the vassalage to which all other religious societies subjected her.[207]

[205] For a description see Madame de La Tour du Pin, *Recollections of the Revolution and the Empire* (Walter Geer trans., London, 1921), pp. 217-18.

[206] September 29, 1784 under Hartford news. See also Barbé-Marbois, *Our Revolutionary Forefathers*, p. 181.

[207] Shakers, *Compendium*, p. 34; Dwight, *Travels*, iii, 137-57 has an unfavorable treatment. Article on "Ann Lee" in *Dictionary of American Biography*.

CHAPTER IX

INDIVIDUAL OBSERVATIONS AND EXPERIENCES

FOREIGN visitors during the eighteenth century commented freely on American women and their manners. Frenchmen were numerous among these commentators, perhaps because of their native gallantry or, in the case of enthusiasts like Brissot de Warville, from a desire to prove their own social theories. Strangers from other countries were not silent. Diaries of American women themselves and journals of Americans who travelled from one part of the country to another were also numerous. From these sources it is possible to reconstruct something of the actual life and attainments of American women, as distinguished from a mere study of theory. Such information may lack the clarity and compactness of the theorist's work but is the only means of checking the effectiveness of his ideas. The opinions of travellers, especially of Europeans, must often be taken with the proverbial grain of salt, but they do serve to show how American women appeared to unacademic observers.

Many critics were favorable; in his published travels the Duc de la Rochefoucauld delivered a long panegyric on the women of America.

The women every where possess, in the highest degree, the domestic virtues, and all others; they have more sweetness, more goodness, at least as much courage, but more sensibility, than the men. Good wives, and good mothers, their husbands and their children engage their whole attention; and their household affairs occupy all their time and all their cares; destined by the manners of their country to this domestic life, their education

274

in other respects is too much neglected. They are amiable by their qualities and their natural disposition, but there are very few among them who are so by any acquired accomplishments. What they esteem to be virtue in wives is the virtue of the whole sex; and if in the United States malice may throw out her suspicion upon twenty, there are certainly not above ten of them who can be accused justly, and all the rest treat these with great rigour. I have heard some husbands complain, that the urgency of their wives makes this irreproachable virtue cost them dear. But where in the world is there a place where evil is not found by the side of good?

The young women here enjoy a liberty, which to French manners would appear disorderly; they go out alone, walk with young men, and depart with them from the rest of the company in large assemblies; in short, they enjoy the same degree of liberty which married women do in France, and which married women here do not take. But they are far from abusing it; they endeavour to please, and the unmarried women desire to obtain husbands, and they know that they shall not succeed if their conduct becomes suspected. Sometimes they are abused by the men who deceive them, but then they add not to the misfortune of having engaged their hearts to a cruel man the regret of deserving it, which might give them remorse. When they have obtained a husband, they love him, because he is their husband, and because they have not an idea that they can do otherwise; they revere custom by a kind of state religion, which never varies.[1]

This description, though overdrawn, was not altogether inaccurate; but there was another side to the story as the German physician, Schoepf, had already observed. Schoepf spoke of the general praise accorded American women by foreigners and though he did not object to this he noted certain less desirable practices. " Thus, a traditional practice of bundling, the vogue in certain parts of America, especially New England, might well give our European fair

---

[1] La Rochefoucauld, *Travels through the United States*, iv, 591-92.

another idea of western restraint."[2] Bundling demands
some notice although it seems to have attracted the attention
of foreign visitors in undue proportion to its real significance.
It took two forms, one the accommodation of strangers over-
night in a crowded household, and the other courtship under
similar conditions. According to the custom, persons of
opposite sexes shared the same bed remaining more or less
fully clad and with the proviso that they should not go beyond
innocent endearments. Explained in part by the lack of fuel
and the limited sleeping space of the more primitive settlements, it was probably never common in the larger towns or
among the better classes. H. R. Stiles who made a careful
study of the subject found Dutch, Scotch, and Welsh precedents for the usage. It was fairly widespread in New England where the long winters made economy of fuel and light
most necessary but appeared also in New York and Pennsylvania.[3] It was as a form of courtship that it was peculiarly liable to abuse. In the early days of New England
settlement there were comparatively few evil results, but during the years from 1750 to 1780 when public morals had
been undermined by the French and Indian War and the
Revolution, there were many confessions in church of pre-
marital relations between husband and wife, probably trace-
able in part to bundling.[4] Jonathan Edwards while at Northampton attacked it as an evil custom peculiar to New England
which had encouraged uncleanness in the land. He also condemned frolics in which young people of both sexes were
together until late at night.[5] After 1785 bundling went out

[2] Schoepf, *Travels in the Confederation*, i, 100-01.

[3] Stiles, *Bundling; its Origin, Progress and Decline in America*
(Albany, 1869), pp. 66-71.

[4] *Ibid.*, pp. 74-82, 107.

[5] Edwards, *Works* (1808), vii, 150-51, "Joseph's Great Temptation
and Gracious Deliverance."

of use following a campaign of ridicule, though occasional traces were to be found even in the nineteenth century.[6]

Although bundling called out so much comment from foreigners most of them derived their knowledge from hearsay. Andrew Burnaby, one of the first travellers to mention it, thought it due to the innocence and simplicity of the people.[7] La Rochefoucauld many years later attributed it to the same cause. His reports were obviously secondhand, for he referred to it only as a form of hospitality and wrote that it had ceased long before he visited America.[8] Thomas Anburey, a British officer, professed to have had an opportunity of bundling, which he had declined, with a young lady in Massachusetts. He thought that Americans must be lacking in feeling, or have a high standard of virtue, to countenance such a practice. As he borrowed Burnaby's description of bundling word for word one cannot trust too far his account of his own experience.[9] Schoepf who gave a detailed account believed that the object of the practice was regular betrothal and that it seldom led to evil results.[10] Barbé-Marbois was puzzled by the delicacy of women who objected to hearing the words, " knees," " shirt," or " legs," but regarded bundling as a courtesy. In this he probably confused women of different classes; a contemptuous use of " bundlers " in a letter of Abigail Adams showed that it was not countenanced by persons in her circle.[11] Marbois wrote that the New England cities had recently abandoned bundling

[6] Stiles, *Bundling*, pp. 80-93, 110-12.

[7] Burnaby, *Travels through the Middle Settlements in North America* (3rd ed., London, 1798), p. 110.

[8] La Rochefoucauld, *Travels*, iv, 593-95.

[9] Anburey, *Travels through the Interior Parts of North America* (2 vols., London, 1791), ii, 38-39, 87-88.

[10] Schoepf, *Travels in the Confederation*, i, 101.

[11] *Letters of Mrs. Adams* (2 vols., Boston, 1841), ii, 9.

though it was still common in Connecticut. Possibly some light is shed on the interest of foreigners in the matter by his statement that the practice was suspended during the presence of the French army because of the behavior of the officers.[12]

Along with tales of bundling came also accounts of great familiarity in the manners of American women, the approval or disapproval of such familiarity depending on the bias of the writer. The Marquis de Chastellux told of a girl who, " like all American women," had, despite her serious demeanor, no objection to being looked at by strangers or even receiving caresses if they were not offered with too much freedom. Elsewhere in his book he remarked that Americans thought it no crime for a girl to embrace a young man but that such freedom ceased at once after marriage. The difference between French and American practice he attributed to the purity of American manners, " licentious manners, in fact, are so foreign in America, that the communication with young women, leads to nothing bad, and that freedom itself there bears a character of modesty far beyond our affected bashfulness and false reserve." [13]   Brissot de Warville wrote in similar strain,

The young women here enjoy the liberty they do in England, that they did in Geneva when morals were there, and the republic existed; and they do not abuse it. Their frank and tender hearts have nothing to fear from the perfidy of men. Examples of this perfidy are rare; the vows of love are believed; and love always respects them, or shame follows the guilty.[14]

Some spectators judged more harshly. A French officer, telling of a flirtation with the young wife of an American

[12] Barbé-Marbois, *Our Revolutionary Forefathers*, pp. 103-04.
[13] Chastellux, *Travels*, i, 15. See also, i, 153-55.
[14] Brissot de Warville, *New Travels* (London, 1792), pp. 95-6.

officer, suggested that the free manners of the women did not always change instantly after their marriage. He believed, from his experiences, that American women thought lightly of a thousand little things which French women considered as great favors. Among these were kissing, pinching, and other little endearments which, far from being seriously intended, often ended in the woman's laughing at the man.[15] Another Frenchman, Claude Blanchard, was perplexed by the air of entire propriety with which a young woman aged twenty had a French officer as a lodger at her house.[16] At the beginning of the nineteenth century, Janson who was not fond of Americans remarked that a stranger could soon discover " the pertness of republican principles " among the females of the country. He applied this term to their manners, expressly stating that he was not calling their morals in question.[17]

Testimony on manners varied from section to section. Of peculiar interest in this connection are the accounts left by women themselves. One of these, a journal kept by Madam Sarah Knight on a journey from Boston to New York, was penned at the beginning of the century. This trip, taken more or less alone, was an unusual feat for a woman. A shrewd observer with the pen of a ready writer, she left a vivid picture of her adventures and of people whom she met. She encountered a number of tavern hostesses to whom her pen did full justice, indicating marked differences between women of the upper and lower classes. Madam Knight possessed some degree of education and was evidently on terms of social equality with clergymen in the towns she

[15] " Letters of a French Officer," *Pennsylvania Magazine of History and Biography*, xxxv, 91, 95, 96.

[16] Claude Blanchard, *Journal* (Albany, 1776), p. 50. See also pp. 178-79.

[17] C. W. Janson, *The Stranger in America* (London, 1807), p. 87.

visited, in itself a sign of good social standing. The women she met were not merely poor but ignorant and uncouth to a degree, even judged by the standards of their own day. Not more than two of the seven women described would merit the title of a passable housewife, let alone an accomplished one. Most of them were equal in slovenliness to the woman whom Madam Knight suspected of boiling the cabbage in the dye pot, an interesting sidelight on an age when excellence in household arts was among women's first virtues.[18]

In 1744 Dr. Alexander Hamilton remarked that the women of Boston appeared in public more than those of New York and were as a rule free and affable in manner, as well as pretty, but that he had seen no prudes among them.[19] Burnaby fifteen years later found Boston women stiffer and more reserved than those of other colonies; Brissot de Warville after the Revolution spoke of this, as well as of their devotion to their husbands and families.[20] Lambert, early in the nineteenth century, found their reserved and sedate manners more English than those of their New York sisters.[21] New England women generally, he thought, had easy and affable manners free from uncouth rusticity; they were as well bred as city ladies despite the lack of polished education.[22] Barbé-Marbois on the other hand described the young ladies whom he met as having no hesitation in offering the names of men of their choice as toasts at dinner.[23] It is interesting to ·compare comments like these with descriptions of bundling

[18] *The Journals of Madam Knight and Rev. Mr. Buckingham* (New York, 1825).

[19] *Hamilton's Itinerarium; being a Narrative of a Journey*, Albert B. Hart, ed. (privately printed, St. Louis, 1907), p. 179.

[20] Burnaby, *Travels*, p. 109; Brissot de Warville, *New Travels*, p. 96.

[21] John Lambert, *Travels through Canada and the United States* (2 vols., 3rd ed., London, 1816), ii, 341-42.

[22] Lambert, *Travels*, ii, 323-24.

[23] *Our Revolutionary Forefathers*, p. 68.

and other indications already mentioned of primitive social customs. A German officer who regarded the manners of American women as naturally good, though unconstrained and bold, remarked, perhaps for the benefit of a feminine correspondent, that the gentle languishing delicate manner which gave his own countrywomen so much charm was rarely found in the beauties of America.[24]

In New York during the early part of the century Dutch women, especially in the vicinity of Albany, formed a group by themselves which Dr. Hamilton did not find agreeable. It was customary for a stranger on being introduced to kiss the women, a practice which in Hamilton's opinion might well have passed for penance, so ugly were most of them. Not only were they the " hardest-favoured " he had ever seen but the older women stared like witches.[25] Peter Kalm, the Swedish traveller, who in general did not like Albany Dutchmen, nevertheless praised the women for their industry; they rose early, retired late, and were almost over-cleanly with their floors which they scoured several times a week.[26] The more attractive Dutch women were mistresses of the manorial estates, where they lived simply but very comfortably. Mrs. Anne MacVicar Grant, in her *Memoirs of an American Lady*, gave an idyllic picture of this life. The American lady of the book was Madam Margaretta Schuyler, wife of Philip Schuyler.[27] Mrs. Grant, the daughter of a British army officer, spent some years of her childhood near Albany where she became intimate with the Schuylers. Many years

[24] Ray W. Pettengill, *Letters from America* (Boston and New York, 1924), pp. 116-18.

[25] Hamilton, *Itinerarium*, pp. 75, 89, 90.

[26] Kalm, *Travels into North America* (3 vols., London, 1771, J. R. Forster, translator), ii, 264, 267.

[27] Her Christian name was erroneously given by Mrs. Grant as " Catalina ". See edition of the book published at Albany 1876 by Joel Munsell, pp. 42, 97.

later she wrote an account of life on this vast estate as she recalled it. Her impressions were perhaps a bit too favorable but she furnished much information not to be found elsewhere. The women of New York City were not, according to William Smith, addicted to extravagant gaming, as was said to be the case elsewhere, but modest, temperate, and charitable, managing their families with economy and neatness.[28]

In the 1740's, Philadelphia women were reputed to be attractive but quiet. William Black, who visited Philadelphia in 1744 as one of the commissioners sent from Virginia to treat with the Iroquois, went to market at seven in the morning and was delighted at seeing the pretty young ladies who came there followed by their maids with baskets. Some ladies who merely wanted fresh butter or green peas acted as their own porters.[29] At church Black noticed more fine women than he had ever seen at one time and place in America; this surprised him for he had not heard that Philadelphia was noted for its women.[30] Dr. Alexander Hamilton in the same year reported that the ladies of Philadelphia seldom appeared in the streets and never in public assemblies except at church. Hence he had had but little opportunity of seeing them but thought them as handsome as their neighbors.[31] Hamilton attributed their retiring life to the influence of Whitefield and reported that when the commissioners to the Iroquois were there they wished to have a ball but could not find enough ladies to take part.[32]

[28] *History of New York* (Albany, 1814), p. 324.

[29] "Journal of William Black," *Pennsylvania Magazine of History and Biography*, i, 406.

[30] *Ibid.*, i, 411.

[31] *Itinerarium*, p. 33.

[32] *Ibid.*, p. 25.

Something of daily life as seen by one of these Philadelphia ladies may be learned from the diary of Miss Sarah Eve, kept in 1772 and 1773 when she was in her early twenties. Teas, walks, visits, and reading occupied her time, in company with the circle of young people who were her close friends. Her scattered remarks give occasional glimpses of manners, as when she noted the disorder in her headdress after one of Dr. Shippen's kisses, deciding that on the whole she preferred more formal salutes; or when she reflected doubtfully on the propriety of walking on the common during a general review without a masculine escort. Her conclusion in this matter was that it was more from custom than from real service that gentlemen were so necessary to ladies.[33]

During the Revolution, Rebecca Franks, a brilliant Jewess, who visited in Flatbush, wrote her sister an animated comparison of the women of New York and Philadelphia. New York women, she thought, had nicer hair and better figures, but their teeth decayed early. She had much to say of the manners of New York ladies, remarking that few of them knew how to entertain company without the introduction of the card table. Their ability at making conversation was limited to discourses on fashion. Philadelphia ladies had more cleverness in the turn of an eye than New York girls did in their whole composition. Only in love-making she found the latter very forward and fancied that it was always leap year in New York. In London, after the Revolution, Abigail Adams Smith found the manners and education of the Philadelphia women who visited there superior to those of her Boston acquaintance.[34]

[33] "Extracts from the Journal of Miss Sarah Eve," *Pennsylvania Magazine of History and Biography*, v, 19-36; 191-205.

[34] "Letter of Miss Rebecca Franks," *Pennsylvania Mag. of Hist. and Biog.*, xxiii, 304-05; Root, *Colonel William Smith and Lady*, pp. 151-2.

The life of Southern women ranged from the aristocratic and gay society of Charlestown and Baltimore and the more prosperous plantations to a frontier crudity which formed a startling contrast. This diversity of living conditions and opportunities must be taken into account in judging any description by travellers. Less is known of the women of the frontier than of those on wealthier plantations, though there is a description of one such in Philip Ludwell's journal in 1710.

It is said of this Mrs. Jones from whose house we came that she is a very civil woman and shews nothing of ruggedness or Immodesty in her carriage, yett she will carry a gunn in the woods and kill deer, turkeys, &c., shoot down wild cattle, catch and tye hoggs, knock down beeves with an ax and perform the most manfull Exercises as well as most men in those parts.[35]

When Colonel William Byrd journeyed inland in 1728 he met several women living in remote districts and was very frank in his descriptions of them. Byrd, however, disliked this region so much that he was hardly an impartial observer. Women as well as men of doubtful character sometimes sought refuge along the boundary or were sent from England to conceal earlier errors.[36] Near the North Carolina line Byrd encountered oddly enough a woman who had in her earlier days been a laundress at the Temple in London and who delighted in telling endless tales of her experiences there.[37] In general the picture he drew of the women of the Dismal Swamp country was far from inviting though he credited them with more resourcefulness and energy than the men. The women at least spun, wove and produced some sort of clothing for themselves and their families. The men were

---

[35] "Boundary Line Proceedings, 1710," *Virginia Magazine*, v, 10.
[36] Byrd, *The Westover Manuscripts* (Petersburg, 1841), pp. 13, 128.
[37] *Ibid.*, p. 14.

lazy and those who did attain any success owed it to the efforts of their wives.[38]

During the Revolution Nicholas Cresswell, a young Englishman, found in the remoter parts of Virginia the same crudity of manners which Byrd had seen earlier. Cresswell was on the extreme frontier long enough to have actual experience of the custom of white men taking temporary Indian " wives ".[39] In the white settlements he told of a notable housewife whose skill did not extend to cleanliness. Other frontier types were a committee man's daughter who was offended at Cresswell's failure to kiss her when they were introduced and consequently made political trouble for him; an energetic but unattractive landlady; and another woman who was unfortunately too inebriated to attend to necessary business.[40] These experiences suggested that rural manners left something to be desired. Nevertheless Cresswell thought America a paradise on earth for women because of the rarity of old maids.[41] He referred occasionally, as Byrd had done, to persons of good family who were not crude but made the best of frontier conditions.[42] The general features of the active life of frontier women may be found in Kercheval's *History of the Valley of Virginia.*

Byrd's own social circle was quite different and had well defined social distinctions, as indicated, for instance, by his condemnation of a girl who had the bad taste to marry her uncle's overseer.[43] Byrd's somewhat Rabelaisian letter to his sister-in-law suggests a gay social life with little glimpses

[38] Byrd, pp. 15, 20, 27, 31, 87, 119.

[39] *The Journal of Nicholas Cresswell* (New York, 1924), pp. 105-122.

[40] *Journal of Nicholas Cresswell*, pp. 186, 204. At Leesburg, Virginia.

[41] *Ibid.*, p. 271.

[42] *Ibid.*, cf. Byrd, *Westover Manuscripts*, pp. 132, 134, 141.

[43] *The Writings of Colonel William Byrd*, John S. Bassett, ed. (New York, 1901), p. 338.

of the interests of educated women.[44]   Detained at a plantation by the rain he discussed physic with the mistress but after a time fearing the conversation might become too grave he offered to read aloud and they whiled away some time with the second part of *The Beggar's Opera.* He gave an amusing account of a tea table upset by a tame deer at the Spotswood plantation.[45]   Andrew Burnaby, travelling through Virginia, compared the women unfavorably with those of England both as to looks and accomplishments.[46] Philip Fithian's remark that to refrain from swearing was a distinguished virtue in a Virginia lady suggests that informality of manners had not entirely disappeared.[47]

Probably manners were more formal in the cities than on the plantations.   William Eddis thought that Annapolis exceeded any town of its size in England in the number of fashionable and handsome women who gave the impression of familiarity with the manners and habits of London; they were accomplished and possessed cultivated minds.[48]   At Wilmington, North Carolina, Miss Schaw observed that although their clothes were not fashionable the women would make a good figure in any part of the world.   For the men she had less to say.   This difference puzzled her but was partly explained by an observer, who said that many of the original settlers were people of education.   After their arrival in this country the men were much occupied with duties out-of-doors and trained their sons to such activities at an early age.   This left men little time for formal education. On the other hand, " The mothers took the care of the girls,

---

[44] Byrd, *Writings*, pp. 394-96.

[45] *Westover Manuscripts*, pp. 126, 132.

[46] Burnaby, *Travels*, pp. 28-29.

[47] Philip Vickers Fithian, *Journal and Letters 1767-1774* (Princeton, 1900), p. 85.

[48] *Letters from America* (London, 1792), pp. 31-32, 113.

they were train'd up under them and not 6nly instructed in the family duties necessary to the sex, but in these accomplishments and genteel manners that are still so visible amongst them, and this descended from mother to daughter." [49]

Josiah Quincy, who visited Charleston in 1773 with many letters of introduction so that he met the best society of the town, attended the St. Cecilia ball at which there were over two hundred and fifty ladies. His comment was not wholly favorable—

In loftiness of head-dress these ladies stoop to the daughters of the North: in richness of dress surpass them: in health and floridity of countenance veil to them: in taciturnity during the performances greatly before our ladies: in noise and flirtations after the music is over pretty much on a par. If our Women have any advantage it is in white and red, vivacity and fire.[50]

He observed that Charleston ladies took part in the first round of toasts at dinner and then withdrew. Two toasts offered by ladies were, " Delicate pleasures to susceptable minds," and " When passions rise may reason be the guide." [51] It seemed to him that the ladies of Charleston lacked the liveliness of their northern contemporaries.[52]

Another topic which appealed to the more enthusiastic travellers was their impression of American customs in regard to marriage. Bayard was delighted with the absence of dowry which seemed to him to make marriage an affair of morals and family happiness, rather than of wealth. He believed that love in America was slower and graver than in

[49] *The Journal of a Lady of Quality* (New Haven, 1921), pp. 154-55.

[50] " Journal of Josiah Quincy, Jr.," Massachusetts Historical Society, *Proceedings*, xlix, 442.

[51] *Ibid.*, xlix, 448.

[52] *Ibid.*, xlix, 456.

France; lovers spent the period of their engagement in careful observation of one another's character. American girls, he thought, showed great independence and enjoyed receiving praise for those qualities which would render them good wives and good mothers rather than for their beauty.[53] Among the benefits which Brissot de Warville attributed to marriage without dower was the entire absence of adultery in Philadelphia.[54]

Travellers in the North had usually praise for the wives and mothers whom they met, but in the South the presence of slavery led some visitors to draw erroneous conclusions. For instance the Marquis de Chastellux wrote—

We see that the women have little share in the amusements of the men; beauty here serves only to procure them husbands; for the most wealthy planters, giving but a small fortune with their daughters, their fate is usually decided by their figure. The consequence of this is, that they are often pert and coquettish before, and sorrowful helpmates after marriage. The luxury of being served by slaves still farther augments their natural indolence; they are always surrounded by a great number of them, for their own service, and that of their children, whom they content themselves with suckling only. They, as well as their husbands, pay attention to them when young, and neglect them when grown up.[55]

There was little or nothing to justify these charges. Women on the wealthier plantations were capable superintendents of affairs; others participated in the work them-

[53] Ferdinand Bayard, *Voyage dans l'intérieur des États-Unis* (Paris, 2nd ed., 1791), pp. 99-104. He was speaking particularly of Maryland but made observations on the whole country.

[54] Brissot de Warville, *New Travels*, p. 319.

[55] Chastellux, *Travels*, ii, 203. The actual suckling of babies was often done by slaves. See Fithian, *Journal*, p. 70 and Ravenel, *Eliza Pinckney*, pp. 151-52.

selves. William Byrd told of one housewife who blushed when detected at her industry in the meat house.[56] The papers of Eliza Lucas Pinckney reveal the life and problems of an energetic woman on a plantation. From an early age she had responsibilities of plantation management as well as the usual duties of the mistress of a family. She was noted for her interest in agriculture and her biographer thought her by no means unique among the women of her time.[57]

Janet Schaw who visited North Carolina at the outbreak of the Revolution left a manuscript journal which affords glimpses of plantation details and supervision. The American sister-in-law of the diarist took great delight in the pursuit of an alligator by the negro boys, being fired with a desire of revenge for the many geese it had stolen.[58] The same lady was averse to English and Scottish methods of gardening, especially objecting to the use of manure as fertilizer. She resented anything British, even demonstrations of washing by Miss Schaw's maid who followed the British practice of bleaching.[59] Miss Schaw gave other details of American customs such as the gathering of moss from the trees at the proper seasons for use in mattresses.[60] At Wilmington she heard of a woman who supported her household by her own industry. She supplied from her own garden much of the vegetables, melons, and other fruit used in Wilmington, sent poultry, eggs, and butter to market as well as mince pies and cheese cakes, and managed to have a supply of milk when her less thrifty neighbors had none.[61]

[56] Byrd, *Westover Manuscripts*, p. 141.
[57] Ravenel, *Eliza Pinckney* (New York, 1896).
[58] *Journal of a Lady of Quality*, p. 149.
[59] *Ibid.*, 160-61, 204.
[60] *Ibid.*, p. 152.
[61] *Ibid.*, p. 178.

Wealthy women often attended to domestic details.   When Philip Fithian was tutor for the Carter children at Nomini Hall in Virginia their mother often took him to walk, showing him her asparagus bed, and her apricot grafts, finding in such occupations some of the pleasures of country life.[62]

In the 1790's Richard Parkinson pictured the life of a planter's wife as far from cheerful.   The constant presence of negro children in the kitchen was expensive and had a bad effect on the manners and morals of the planter's own children.[63]   Joseph Hadfield who was in Virginia in 1785 spoke admiringly of the way in which ladies on the plantations managed provisions and clothes for the negroes as well as their own domestic duties.   He thought they displayed remarkable efficiency and skill and carried the work through well and without confusion.[64]   Climate perhaps lessened the physical activity of Southern women but the responsibilities of the mistresses were heavy throughout the slavery era.[65] The account which Harriet Martineau gave fifty years after the Revolution might well serve for this earlier period also and leaves the reader little reason to suppose the life of a plantation mistress either carefree or indolent.[66]

Most travellers said nothing of women of the lowest class. La Rochefoucauld wrote that opportunities for libertinism in American towns were perhaps greater than in Europe; but this does not quite accord with his description of women of

[62] Fithian, *Journal and Letters*, pp. 61, 77, 126.

[63] Parkinson, *A Tour in America* (2 vols., London, 1805), ii, 435-36.

[64] *An Englishman in America 1785*, edited Douglas S. Robertson (Toronto, 1933), p. 8.

[65] Lambert, *Travels*, ii, 156; *Lady of Quality*, pp. 182-83; U. B. Phillips, *Life and Labor in the Old South* (Boston, 1929), p. 302 and scattered references.

[66] *Retrospect of Western Travel* (2 vols., London, 1838), i, 214-16, 220-21; Emily James Putnam, *The Lady* (New York, 1910), chapter on "The Lady of the Slave States."

the country as a whole. He stated that prostitution was regarded simply as a trade which women left to become servants or to marry—and made good wives or domestics.[67] These remarks, however, can scarcely be taken as presenting an accurate picture.

The treatment of women by men called forth occasional notice. Barbé-Marbois, whose interest in the women of Boston extended to more than mere polite social usage, stated that men in that city might beat their wives if they paid a fine of ten pounds. The same penalty applied to wives who were aggressors, but if they had no money and their husbands refused to pay the fine they ran the risk of being whipped.[68] The German Mittelberger during his stay in Pennsylvania was naively amazed at the attention and good treatment which Englishwomen in that colony received from men. He thought them beautiful as a result of their superior food. They were handsome, clever, and friendly; but his attitude was not approving. Women did not, he reported in surprise, expect to work except of their own free will; they even attended parties and received callers without their husbands' permission. Public opinion did not permit the husband to box his wife's ears. It was also remarkable, observed Mittelberger, that the evidence of one woman should be accepted by the courts as worth that of three men, a privilege said to have been granted the women by Queen Elizabeth.[69] There is nothing to show from what source Mittelberger derived this extraordinary impression but it is of a piece with other odd notions of his, as for instance that a charge of bigamy could be evaded by marrying a third wife since the law prohibited two, but not three wives.[70]

[67] La Rochefoucauld, *Travels*, iv, 596-7.
[68] *Our Revolutionary Forefathers*, p. 74.
[69] Mittelberger, *Journey to Pennsylvania*, pp. 98-99.
[70] *Ibid.*, pp. 93-96.

In this connection Brissot de Warville made a curious comment on the women of Philadelphia and indeed of all the United States. They were, he thought, peculiarly liable to consumption, and he attributed this fact partly to excessive dancing and unwise diet but also to women's " want of civil existence." He believed that the submission, to which women were habituated, enfeebled their bodies by depressing their minds. This observation apparently applied to European women as well as to those of America.[71]

For American women of the better classes life, especially in cities, had its share of social gaiety. In the vicinity of Boston there was much formality, with amusements of various sorts. In 1768 Ann Hulton, sister of Henry Hulton, Commissioner of Customs in Boston, came out from England with her brother's family. During much of her stay political complications kept them in a state of anxiety and sometimes of actual danger but the letters which she sent to an old friend at home revealed the life of the official group, some of whom were native Bostonians. The circle of the Hultons' acquaintance was large. Miss Hulton spoke of having twenty people for dinner on more than one occasion; her sister-in-law had more than fifty ladies making calls of congratulation after the birth of a son.[72] There was a good dancing assembly in Boston with about sixty couples, members of the social circle in which the Hultons moved; there was also an opposition " Liberty Assembly " set up in 1769.[73] Gay assemblies in Boston were common as early as 1744, when Hamilton wrote that ladies and gentlemen met almost every week at concerts and balls, where the ladies, music, and dancing were equal to any he had ever seen.[74] One

[71] Brissot de Warville, *New Travels*, pp. 347-48.

[72] Hulton, *Letters of a Loyalist Lady* (Cambridge, 1927), pp. 15, 21, 30, 33.

[73] *Ibid.*, p. 19.

[74] Hamilton, *Itinerarium*, p. 178.

assembly of which Miss Hulton wrote was probably that at the Concert Hall mentioned by Anna Green Winslow as attended by " Mrs. Barrett dress'd in a white brocade, & cousin Betsey dress'd in a red lutestring, both adorn'd with past, perls, marquesett &c." [75] Cambridge had its assembly of twenty couples, patronized by the families of gentlemen with estates near by, who danced once a fortnight throughout the winter.[76] Another form of entertainment was going into the country for a dinner and dance; such parties often lasted until daybreak. Miss Hulton spoke also of fishing parties.[77] Entertaining in the home was carried on in elaborate style with great feasts prepared by " Professed Cooks " imported from London who were hired for particular occasions.[78] The Hultons had all told six servants white and black but found one of the housewife's problems the obtaining of reliable help.[79] Miss Hulton was careful to explain that all this luxury and elegance was confined to a radius of twenty miles from Boston. Life in the smaller towns was simple even after the Revolution.[80]

In the diary of Anna Green Winslow, the Boston schoolgirl previously mentioned, there are glimpses of the social life which she and her elders enjoyed as members of the more prosperous group in Boston. She tells of an assembly of young ladies, who made several couples at country dancing, and did minuets " mighty cleverly " to the tune of a flute; they also played games and enjoyed refreshments of nuts, raisins, cakes, wine and punch.[81] She spoke of New

[75] *Diary of Anna Green Winslow*, p. 20.

[76] Hulton, *Letters of a Loyalist Lady*, p. 43.

[77] *Ibid.*, p. 45.

[78] *Ibid.*, pp. 36, 37.

[79] *Ibid.*, pp. 42, 49.

[80] *Ibid.*, p. 45. Compare S. G. Goodrich, *Recollections of a Lifetime*, i, 71-75, 85-88.

[81] *Diary of Anna Green Winslow*, pp. 7, 17, 18.

Year's calls and of visits and dinners at the home of friends and relatives.[82]

New York City had much social life throughout the century. At first the English and Dutch groups were quite separate, but by the time of the Revolution this was no longer true. Women attended concerts and assemblies in the time of William Smith.[83] In 1758 Hannah Callender, a young Quakeress from Philadelphia, told of shopping, sight-seeing, trips to Flushing and to points of interest in Manhattan which were enjoyed by groups of young people.[84] Hannah Thomson, wife of the Secretary of Congress, who lived in New York from 1785 to 1788, noted details of social affairs, in her letters to a gentleman in Philadelphia. New York ladies of fashion she found gay and agreeable, though rather too numerous. They were said to outnumber the gentlemen ten to one. The chief social events were calls, plays which were given three times a week, concerts and fortnightly assemblies. With these records it is interesting to compare the fashionable way of spending time as suggested in contemporary plays, and especially in the speeches of Maria Airy in Samuel Low's *The Politician Out-Witted*. Her mornings were devoted to shopping, with visits later in the day. In winter, cards, assemblies, and occasional plays filled her social calendar. In spring or summer there were excursions to Long Island, sails on the East River, walks on Broadway, and strolls on the Battery.[86]

[82] *Diary*, pp. 9, 10, 11, 13, 18, 49.

[83] Smith, *History of New York*, p. 324.

[84] "Extracts from the diary of Hannah Callender," *Pennsylvania Magazine of History and Biography*, xii, 432-56.

[85] "Letters of Hannah Thomson," *Pennsylvania Magazine of History and Biography*, xiv, 28-40. Other letters dealing with social life in New York at this time may be found in Margaret Armstrong's *Five Generations* (New York and London, 1930), pp. 39-44, 48-57, 66-68, 128-29.

[86] New York, 1789. Moses, *Representative Plays*, i, 351-429.

The Europeans who were in America during and immediately after the Revolution found Philadelphia a most interesting city. Chastellux who enjoyed social life made many scattered comments on usage and on individuals. He followed the local custom of paying calls during the morning hours and met Franklin's daughter, Mrs. Bache; a Mrs. P————, who wished to introduce a revolution in the manners as well as the politics of her country; and Mrs. Bingham, who at seventeen had all her later charm.[87] He described the dances, which were managed methodically, each feature being pre-arranged and each dance having its own name.[88]

The social life of the Quaker women differed somewhat from that of the women of other sects in the middle colonies though it was not lacking in pleasures. Their social activities were for the most part limited to members of their own society since association with outsiders was frowned upon. Brissot de Warville, who was a good deal of a theorist, thought that the tendency to consumption, which in women of other sects he had attributed to a dissipated life, resulted among the Quakers from their excessive gravity and immobility; but the letters and journals of Quaker women themselves hardly bear this out.[89] Hannah Callender's diary was filled with her trips to New York and Bethlehem and told in no grave fashion of pleasure jaunts about Philadelphia.[90] One of the most illuminating accounts of Quaker customs was the journal kept by Ann Head Warder, an English Quaker, who came to Philadelphia with her American husband soon after the Revo-

[87] Chastellux, *Travels*, i, 197-99, 224. See also, Armstrong, *Five Generations*, pp. 7-20, 24-33, 58-59.

[88] Chastellux, *Travels*, i, 277-78, 315-16.

[89] Brissot de Warville, *New Travels*, p. 347.

[90] *Pennsylvania Magazine of History and Biography*, xii, 432-56.

lution.[91]   She spoke much of the differences between American and English Quakers in manners and dress.   Among the Americans she noticed particularly the frill worn at the neck by young girls and the absence of caps on young women, modes which savored of worldliness.   She found other peculiarities due merely to custom.   Certain features of American usage seemed unusual to her and sometimes undesirable, as for instance the free way in which women rode about the country.[92]   It was usual in summer for families to sit on the porches after dark, a custom which, Mrs. Warder believed, exposed young girls too early to the acquaintance of men.[93] Among Quakers she observed many marriages of young girls to older men, which she regarded as an unnecessary sacrifice.[94]   On the whole, the visits, calls, dinners including some elaborate ones with turtles as the *piece de resistance,* and the occasional trips into the country which she records, suggest a pleasant and well filled life.

Andrew Burnaby thought that on the Southern plantations women's lack of advantages made them unequal to refined or interesting conversation, so that their amusements were limited to dancing and an occasional barbecue in the woods. This made them unreasonably fond of dancing, though their performance lacked the elegance shown by his countrywomen.[95]   Despite these remarks, Southern women of the upper classes did not lack pleasures and diversions, though the mistress of the household had little time for frivolity.   Dancing, as Burnaby said, was the great amusement.   Girls learned early and enjoyed their dancing lessons; Anne Blair in Virginia described her little niece as giving them " her

[91] In *Pennsylvania Magazine of Hist. and Biog.,* xvii, xviii.
[92] *Ibid.,* xvii, 457.
[93] *Ibid.,* xvii, 448.
[94] *Ibid.,* xviii, 51 and elsewhere.
[95] Burnaby, *Travels,* pp. 28-29.

thoughts by Day & dreams by night." [96] The routine of Fithian's school in the Carter household was disturbed at frequent intervals by the dancing school which met in rotation at the homes of members, usually for a two-day session.[97] During the Revolution there were girls at Shenandoah who went seven miles three times a week to a French dancing master.[98] With so much dancing music was a popular accomplishment though it was often badly performed. In the Carter household several instruments were played.[99] Card playing was general; other games, including kissing games, were popular with young people.[100] Needlework was always a resource for women and one of Philip Fithian's afternoons was spent in drawing flowers for a counterpane which Priscilla Carter was about to embroider.[101] Women rode much, especially in Virginia, though this was as much from necessity as for pleasure; many women were adepts at handling horses. Fithian amusingly described the effect of their red riding cloaks and the red kerchiefs tied about their heads in a manner which led him to suppose that every lady he saw was suffering from toothache.[102] The rougher amusements of men were barred to women though Lucinda Lee wrote that many women attended the races. She herself decided not to go any more as there was no lasting happiness to be found in such amusements.[103] One traveller thought that the milder

[96] Letter in *William and Mary College Quarterly*, xvi, 177.

[97] Fithian, *Journal and Letters*, pp. 50, 54, 62, *et passim*.

[98] Chastellux, *Travels*, ii, 115-6, translator's note.

[99] Fithian, *op. cit.*, pp. 51, 56, 57, 184; Mason, *Young Lady of Virginia*, pp. 33-34, 38.

[100] Fithian, *op. cit.*, p. 65; Mason, *op. cit.*, pp. 10, 15, 36.

[101] Fithian, *op. cit.*, p. 75.

[102] Fithian, *Journal and Letters*, p. 58; Bayard, *Voyage*, p. 74; Mason, *Young Lady of Virginia*, p. 20.

[103] Mason, *op. cit.*, pp. 11, 20, 43; Chastellux, *Travels*, ii, 203.

amusements and more temperate regimen of the women of South Carolina actually lengthened their lives in comparison with those of the men.[104]

One detail which visitors, especially foreigners, were quick to note about American women, was their dress and personal appearance. These descriptions, interesting in themselves, formed the basis for frequent comments on manners and customs. The clergyman, Andrew Burnaby, who visited Boston about 1760, was impressed by the charming appearance of the women in every particular except their teeth.[105] Lord Adam Gordon soon afterwards reported that women of Boston and Rhode Island were considered the most beautiful on the continent. His explanation of the proportion of beautiful women at balls as due to the absence of class distinctions, which made it possible for every girl with a pretty face and good clothes to attend, was perhaps more of a tribute than American democracy deserved.[106] Twenty years later Brissot de Warville found the brilliant complexions and elegant simplicity of dress of Connecticut girls particularly charming.[107]

In Boston, visiting Frenchmen thought the women simply dressed as compared with Parisian ladies, though Ann Hulton noted that the young ladies followed English fashions closely and were as smart as those she had known at home.[108] Barbé-Marbois was surprised at the plainly dressed unpowdered hair of the Boston women and at their lack of rouge. When he mentioned his astonishment to an American lady

[104] J. D. A. Smythe, *Tour in the United States of America* (2 vols., London, 1784), ii, 53-54.

[105] Burnaby, *Travels*, p. 109.

[106] Journal in N. D. Mereness, *Travels in the American Colonies* (New York, 1916), p. 451.

[107] *New Travels*, pp. 134-35.

[108] *Letters of a Loyalist Lady*, p. 45.

she asked whether his countrywomen powdered their eye-brows as well as their hair.[109] Brissot de Warville's praise of calico and chintz gowns without the " gewgaws " of French custom was at variance with Marbois's remarks on the unreasonableness of satin and damask in hot weather.[110]

Country women, and those of the lower classes, attracted much attention, particularly from the Germans sent to Cambridge after Burgoyne's defeat. Their picture of slender straight women, with pretty feet and healthy complexions unmarred by paint, was an attractive one. New England women understood the little arts of dress, so one German wrote,

Generally they go bareheaded and at most put a tiny heart-shaped cap or other such trifle on their heads; now and then a rustic nymph lets her hair fall free and ties it with a ribbon. If they go out, they put on a silk wrap and pull on gloves, no matter how miserable the hut in which they live. They know how to drape themselves very neatly in their wraps so that one little white elbow peeks out. Then they put on their heads a Corsican or other well-made sun-hat, from beneath which they peep out very roguishly with their mischievous eyes. In the English colonies the beauties have fallen in love with red silk and woolen wraps.[111]

Inoculation had been so long in use that pockmarks were rare. Women paid much attention to cleanliness, curled their hair daily, and liked good footwear.[112] They had an elegant air as they rode freely about the country in calico gowns, white aprons, and fashionable hats.[113] Their appear-

[109] *Our Revolutionary Forefathers*, pp. 69-70.
[110] *Ibid.*, 69-70 and Brissot de Warville, *New Travels*, p. 96.
[111] Pettengill, *Letters from America*, p. 117.
[112] *Ibid.*, pp. 116-17.
[113] Brissot de Warville, *New Travels*, pp. 134-35.

ance was indeed so far superior to that of their husbands and gallants that the men appeared to be stealing the girls.[114]

Such observations led one German officer to draw some far-fetched conclusions as to manners. He was sure that the style of dress indicated either city women or those of the middle class, until he saw the fathers whom he characterized somewhat unjustly as poor peasants. He then concluded that the display made by wives and daughters was beyond the incomes of most men and was maintained only by the wife's insistence. Thus " petticoat rule " was spread throughout America and unlike similar domination in Canada was calculated to ruin the men. Mothers on their death beds ordered their daughters to retain the mastery of the house and control of the father's purse-strings. This officer was not quite sure how women gained their point, for they did not stamp their feet, bite or scratch their husbands, fall in a faint or feign illness, but gain it they did. The war had raised the prices of finery so high that most ladies were wearing their Sunday best for every day. When that was worn out, he thought the men would have to make peace with the crown in order to replace it.[115]

America had few examples of special costume though the older women near Albany retained the typical Dutch dress.[116] Quaker women were supposed to dress simply and the Moravians and other German sects regulated attire. Both Brissot and La Rochefoucauld, however, noted the luxurious and sometimes gay dress of many of the younger Quaker women. As early as 1732, the women of New York City had the reputation of being comely and well dressed.[117] A decade

[114] Pettengill, *Letters from America*, pp. 123-24.

[115] Pettengill, *op. cit.*, pp. 118-19.

[116] Hamilton, *Itinerarium*, pp. 89.

[117] Smith, *History of New York*, p. 324; La Rochefoucauld, iv, 108; Brissot, p. 381.

later Dr. Alexander Hamilton wrote that they dressed more gaily than the women of Philadelphia and appeared more often in public. He particularly noticed the number of elaborately clad ladies at church. Sometimes they rode through the streets in light chairs; but when walking they carried umbrellas, painted and adorned with feathers.[118] Mittelberger wrote that Pennsylvania women dressed in English fashion, " very fine, neat and costly " with white aprons and silver buckles for everyday wear. English servant women in Philadelphia he thought as well dressed as aristocratic ladies in Germany.[119]

The Revolutionary era brought an unprecedented wave of luxury in dress which affected all classes. Ann Hulton noted a distinct increase in expenditures for clothes in Boston after 1768.[120] Abbé Robin commented on the extensive use of silk by Bostonian ladies who, it seemed to him, attended church as much from a desire of self-display as from motives of piety.[121] In Rhode Island the wives of cobblers, tailors, and day-laborers were said to wear chintz, muslin, and silk trains for every day.[122] Brissot de Warville regarded the dress of the non-Quaker women of Philadelphia as far too extravagant for a republic.[123] La Rochefoucauld thought the luxury displayed by the wealthier women of America was comparable with that of Europe.[124] This increasing luxury among American women was noted in the South as well as in the North. Chastellux found the change very obvious during his three years residence in America though

[118] *Itinerarium*, pp. 52-53, 108.

[119] Mittelberger, *Journey to Pennsylvania*, pp. 116-17.

[120] *Letters of a Loyalist Lady*, p. 45.

[121] Robin, *Nouveau Voyage*, pp. 14-15.

[122] Pettengill, *Letters from America*, p. 166.

[123] *New Travels*, p. 318.

[124] *Travels*, iv, 107.

he admitted that proper dress might have value in developing self-esteem.[125] The translator of his book noted the rage for dress, at the height of the war in remote regions where elaborate costumes could have had few witnesses.[126] Schoepf also found in a lonely cabin ladies dressed in silk and decked with plumes, and Bayard told of Governor Livingston's protests against foreign luxury. This attention to dress in America may have been responsible for Abigail Adams's surprise at the simple dress of London ladies on festive occasions and at the plain gown of the Marquise de Lafayette.[127]

Barring emergencies New England women, even in the poorer classes, did not do field work. President Dwight of Yale, writing of a trip in 1799 when he had seen German women so employed in New York, remarked: " Women in New England are employed only in and about the house and in the proper business of the sex." [128] It was, however, thought suitable for them to look after the dairy, poultry, and kitchen garden.[129] During the Revolution there was some talk of women performing farm work as a patriotic necessity but this did not have extensive results.[130]

The women of Nantucket, according to Crèvecoeur's idyllic description, formed a possible exception to those who attended only to "the proper business of the sex." Marriage there, Crèvecoeur wrote, took place early and without marriage portions, the bride's only dowry being her educa-

[125] *Travels*, ii, 358-59.

[126] *Ibid.*, ii, 115 note.

[127] Schoepf, *Travels*, ii, 33; Bayard, *Voyage*, p. 253; Root, *Colonel William Smith and Lady*, pp. 53, 58.

[128] Dwight, *Travels*, iii, 192.

[129] Bidwell and Falconer, *History of Agriculture in the Northern Colonies* (Washington, 1925), p. 116.

[130] Adams, *Familiar Letters*, pp. 48, 150.

tion, health, and the customary outfit. Her fortune consisted of her future economy, modesty, and skilful management. Since the men were much away at sea, it became customary for the women to transact business and settle accounts; this, according to Crèvecoeur, "ripens their judgment and justly entitles them to a rank superior to that of other wives." The women were industrious, spinning wool and flax enough for the household's use. Some of them went into business; one of the wealthiest men on the island owed his fortune largely to his wife who began by trading in pins and needles and teaching school while he was away on his early cruises. She turned her profits to good advantage and soon had London connections. The social customs of the young people on the island appeared delightful to the Frenchman who enjoyed their simplicity. There was much simple social life among the women also. When their husbands were away they visited one another for "a social chat, a dish of tea, and an hearty supper." Many women on the island were said to take opium every morning apparently without damage.[131]

German women of Pennsylvania and upstate New York did some field work, a practice not generally followed by American women. Germans and Swedes who visited in the colonies were surprised at the absence of women from the fields and from heavy labor. Kalm in speaking of the Canadian women called them industrious as a rule though there were some who "like the English women in the Colonies did nothing but prattle all the day."[132] Ann Eliza Bleecker who lived beyond Albany during the 1770's had laboring women for neighbors of whom she wrote—

[131] Michel-Guillaume Jean de Crèvecoeur, *Letters from an American Farmer* (Philadelphia, 1793), pp. 137-59.

[132] Kalm, *Travels*, iii, 81.

304 WOMEN IN EIGHTEENTH CENTURY AMERICA

We live perfectly retired, and see very little company at present, as the ladies in our vicinage are busy hoeing their corn and planting potatoes. As we are not quite so well calculated for this rural employment, we left the sun-burnt daughters of Labour yesterday, and went on pilgrimage to the *Half-Moon,* to visit Mrs. P———s." [133]

These neighbors of Mrs. Bleecker may have been German but in any case were living under semi-frontier conditions. Acrelius, the Swedish pastor, spoke scornfully of women who sat in the house by the fire while men did the milking.[134] The German women of America must have relieved the minds of Kalm and Acrelius for they worked in the fields at harvest time and were expected to take care of the gardens.[135] In 1799 President Dwight noticed with surprise German women breaking flax near Canajoharie, New York.[136] When Rush wrote his account of the Germans in Pennsylvania he found scarcely a German of either sex who could not read, but many women of farming families who were unable to write, a matter which in their state of society seemed to him of little importance.[137] In the South there was outdoor activity by frontier women and by servants which has already been discussed. It was not expected of women of the upper classes.

Travellers had less to say of the intellectual life of women than of their appearance and social habits.[138] Women may have lacked formal schooling but many of them had certainly read widely and were able to keep up interesting conversations. Madam Knight, the traveller, had literary interest

[133] *Posthumous Works of Ann Eliza Bleecker*, p. 123.
[134] Pennsylvania Historical Society, *Memoirs*, xi, 155.
[135] Rush, *Essays*, pp. 219, 232.
[136] Dwight, *Travels*, iii, 192.
[137] *Proceedings of the Pennsylvania German Society*, xix, 105.
[138] See chapter v *supra* for New England schools.

enough to beguile the tedious portions of her journey by composing poetry.[139] Dr. Alexander Hamilton in Boston in 1744 was much taken with the tea-table conversation of ladies there. He spoke of it as—

Lively, entertaining and solid; neither tainted with false nor trifling wit nor ill-natured satire or reflexion,—of late so much the topic of tea-tables. I was glad to find that in most of the politer cabals of ladies in this town, the odious theme of scandal and detraction over their tea had become quite unfashionable and unpolite, and was banished entirely to assemblies of the meaner sort, where it may dwell forever quite disregarded and forgotten, retiring to that obscure place Billingsgate, where the monster first took to its origin.[140]

Reading in New England included a great variety of books. Little Anna Winslow read *Gulliver's Travels,* and received the *History of Joseph Andrews* as a New Year's gift. Among her other reading she mentioned *Pilgrim's Progress,* the *Puzzling-Cap* (a collection of riddles), the *Female Orator,* the *Generous Inconstant, Sir Charles Grandison,* and the *History of Gaffer too-shoes.*[141] With all this, the question of the degree of education possessed by the average woman remains doubtful. The intellectual group to which Mrs. Adams and Mrs. Warren belonged was small, and literary women like Hannah Adams and Judith Sargent Murray were few and far between.

Madam Schuyler of Albany, according to Mrs. Grant's description, was a well-read woman and mistress of five languages but in this respect she was far from a typical Dutch woman.[142] Mrs. Grant wrote that girls of wealthy

[139] Knight, *Journal,* pp. 20, 24, 27.

[140] Hamilton, *Itinerarium,* 172.

[141] *Diary of Anna Green Winslow,* pp. 13, 60, 64, 70.

[142] The languages were English, French, Dutch, German and Mohawk.

Dutch families usually learned to read the Bible and perhaps some devotional tracts in Dutch; but writing was for them a somewhat rare accomplishment. English was spoken by the women, though not much read, and, if a woman wished to read extensively or to study, there was nothing to prevent her from doing so.[143] The women of a later generation in the Schuyler family spoke French well and had a decided interest in public affairs both in America and abroad. They read newspapers eagerly when these could be had.[144] Mrs. Grant concluded that the Dutch settlers were indifferent, rather than antagonistic, to the academic side of their daughters' education but regarded domestic training as essential. Her opinion on this point is substantiated by William Smith, historian of New York, who described the ladies of New York City as " tinctured with a Dutch education," which made them accomplished in every direction except the intellectual. The " help of a more elevated education " would, he thought, have made them quite perfect.[145] On the other hand, Samuel Loudon in 1774, in an advertisement for his circulating library, refuted the charge which he said the *American Gazetteer* had made a dozen years earlier that there was nothing the ladies neglected so much as reading. If the statement had ever been true Loudon was sure it had changed at the time he wrote; ladies were his best customers and showed a becoming delicacy in the choice of books.[146]

The middle colonies had apparently no considerable groups of intellectual women though there were a few of them who were serious readers and students. Jane Colden,

[143] *Memoirs of an American Lady* (2 vols., London, 1808), i, 33, 64, 118.

[144] Marquise de la Tour du Pin, *Recollections*, pp. 194-95.

[145] *History of New York*, p. 324.

[146] *New York Gazette and Weekly Mercury*, November 7, 14, 21, 28, 1774.

whose distinguished father had taught her the Linnaean system of botany to fill her leisure moments, gave much time to this study before her marriage and made sketches of American plants not previously classified which were sent to her father's correspondents.[147]   Ann Eliza Bleecker (1752-1783,), who spent most of her life near Albany, produced a few verses and some tales, which during her lifetime were read only by her immediate circle; some of them however later appeared in the *New York Magazine*.   Her daughter, Margaretta V. Faugeres (1771-1801) also wrote poetry occasionally and in 1793 published her mother's *Posthumous Works* with some poems and essays of her own.[148]   Their work was highly sentimental and in imitation of European models.   Elizabeth Graeme Fergusson of Philadelphia was somewhat of the learned lady.   She wrote verses and translated *Télémaque* into heroic couplets.[149]   A reader of serious books, her letters often mentioned the works of Addison and Pope, and she made inquiries concerning Paine's *Age of Reason*.[150]   She carefully supervised the reading of her niece as an essential part of a girl's education.[151]

There are many records of the reading done by other women of this region.   Colden's daughter, Elizabeth De-Lancey, in her letters to her father spoke of reading some-one's *Dialogues on Education,* of which she remarked, " Reading such things will I hope be of service to me," and she asked for the *Economy of Human Life* which her sister

[147] *Colden Papers*, iv, 475, v, 5, 10, 29, 139, 203; William Darlington, *Memorials of John Bartram and Humphrey Marshall* (Philadelphia, 1849), pp. 400-01.

[148] See articles on Mrs. Bleecker in *Dictionary of American Biography* (Ernest S. Bates), and *National Cyclopedia of American Biography*, viii, 457. For Mrs. Faugeres, *ibid.*, ix, 366.

[149] *Pennsylvania Magazine of History and Biography*, xxxix, 260.

[150] *Ibid.*, xxxix, 270, 318, 408.

[151] *Ibid.*, xxxix, 387.

Jane had recommended.[152]   Chastellux told of seeing the
works of Milton, Addison, Richardson, and others of the
same sort on the table of two New Jersey sisters.[153]
Bayard met a widow who had read Swedenborg.[154]   Mrs.
Bleecker spoke of reading Theocritus, Tasso, and Virgil,
those "pastoral enthusiasts."   One of her poems, "On
Reading Dryden's Virgil" drew a parallel between the experiences of Aeneas after the destruction of Troy and her
own during the Revolution.   One young friend of hers who
was leading a gay life in Albany was also reading Homer's
Odyssey which Mrs Bleecker thought would soon bring her
to emulate Penelope.[155]   These works were apparently read
in translation.   Long after the Revolution Rachel Huntington in New York wrote to her sister in New England who
had finished Hume's *England* that she wanted to send her a
novel "for dessert."   Among the popular works in the
winter of 1797 which she thought of sending were *Camilla*
and Miss Burney's other books, *The Mysteries of Udolpho,*
Mrs. Radcliffe's *Castles of Athlin and Dunbayne,* some other
romances in the same vein, and *Caleb Williams.*[156]   The
books read by Sarah Eve and Sally Wister in Pennsylvania
were not serious in character.   They included Cumberland's
Fashionable Lover, Don Quixote, Joseph Andrews, and *The
Lady's Magazine.*[157]

The young ladies whom William Black met at Philadelphia discussed with their callers the works of Addison, Prior,
Otway, Congreve, Dryden, Pope, and Shakespeare, and

[152] *Colden Papers,* iv, 221, 302.

[153] *Travels,* i, 343.

[154] *Voyage,* pp. 82-83.

[155] *Posthumous Works,* pp. 128, 162, 230.

[156] *Huntington Letters,* pp. 143-45 (New York, 1897, privately printed).

[157] Journals in *Pennsylvania Magazine of History and Biography,* v, ix.

attempted to analyze poetry, style and wit.[158]   At one tea party a young lady expended much energy in defending the constancy of women as opposed to that of men and when that topic was exhausted turned to literary criticism of a superficial kind.   Black observed that such young ladies, having no minds of their own, had no idea of other people's sensations.   " They cannot I think be well liable to the Curse attending Eve's Transgression, as they do not Enjoy the Benefit propos'd by it of knowing Good from Evil." [159] Hamilton, like Black, was a little troubled by a loquacious lady in Philadelphia, but her theme was religion.   She pretended to some knowledge of the religious history of Maryland and discoursed disapprovingly on the character of the clergy.   She also felt constrained to remind Hamilton of his duties as a Presbyterian.[160]

Education of individual Southern women perhaps varied more than in other parts of the country though it would be erroneous to suppose that there were not general standards for women of the upper classes.   Girls rarely had the opportunity, which was common for their brothers, of studying abroad though there were a few who did so.   Among this favored group were Martha Laurens, later the wife of Dr. David Ramsay, the daughters of Thomas Jefferson and the daughter of Eliza Lucas Pinckney.[161]   Girls' schools in the South were rare though there were a few at the close of the century.   La Rochefoucauld remarked that girls in the vicinity of Norfolk were sent to Williamsburg or Baltimore if their parents wished them to attend school.[162]

[158] Journal in *Pennsylvania Mag. of Hist. and Biog.*, ii, 46-47.

[159] *Ibid.*, ii, 47.

[160] *Itinerarium*, p. 31.

[161] *Memoir of Mrs. Ramsay*, S. N. Randolph, *The Domestic Life of Thomas Jefferson* (New York, 1871), pp. 113-14; Ravenel, *Eliza Pinckney.*

[162] *Travels*, iii, 26.

Jefferson had his older daughter in school at Philadelphia for a time.[163]   In 1808 Edward Hooker wrote that there were academies for young ladies in Salem, Raleigh, Warrenton and elsewhere in North Carolina, though some Southern girls were sent to Bethlehem.[164]   After 1770 Charleston had a number of schools for girls, some with women teachers who came from England.[165]

The usual thing was instruction at home, perhaps by mother or aunt, sometimes by the brothers' tutor, as at Nomini Hall, or by a governess.   Anne Blair gave a lively description of the studies of a young niece whom she was teaching to read and giving instructions on behavior.   The child had improved, so her teacher wrote to the mother; she was no longer fond of the company of negroes and did not use bad words, but she still ate green apples and had to be whipped for fighting with her cousin.[166]   In well-to-do families, home instruction was supplemented by visits of the music teacher and the dancing master.   The diary of Philip Fithian describes his little school at Nomini Hall on the Carter estate.   Five of the eight pupils were girls, the daughters of the household.   The youngest, still little more than a baby, was learning her letters while her oldest sister, almost a young lady, was reading the *Spectator,* writing and beginning to cipher.   For the older girls, school was rather a desultory affair.   Once or twice a month they went to dancing school which occupied them for two days.   Tuesdays and Thursdays their father allowed for practice on the guitar and piano-forte.   Then there were interruptions for the visits of the music master and other holidays for the eldest daughter

---

[163] Randolph, *op. cit.,* pp. 69-70.

[164] Diary in American Historical Association *Report* (1896), i, 916.

[165] Edward McCrady, *The History of South Carolina under the Royal Government 1719-1796* (New York, 1901), p. 491.

[166] Letter in *William and Mary College Quarterly,* xvi, 177.

who went visiting with her mother or rode to county court with her parents.[167] The girls on a neighboring plantation had an English governess who taught them to read and write English and to speak French.[168]

Southern libraries were likely to have even more books of interest to women than those in New England because of the larger proportion of *belles-lettres*.[169] Fithian's older pupils read the *Spectator* and the *Compleat Letter Writer*.[170] Wilson Cary ordered for his granddaughter the *Spectator*, *Clarissa Harlowe*, *Sir Charles Grandison*, and *Pamela*, all handsomely bound in calf.[171] Mary Jefferson read *Don Quixote*, Robertson's *America*, *Anacharsis*, and Gibbon's *Roman Empire*. It is a relief to know that the *Magasin des Modes* and *Tales of the Castle* were also at Monticello.[172] Lucinda Lee read *Lady Julia Mandeville*, *Victoria*, *Malvern Dale* and *Evelina*, but admitted in a letter to her bosom friend that she spent too much time in novel reading.[173] She found *Télémaque* delightful and improving.[174] Eliza Pinckney in her girlhood gave an amusing description of how she alarmed an elderly lady of the neighborhood by her devotion to Plutarch and Virgil.[175] She knew a little law, read Locke and endeavoured to train her small son by his theories.[176] She sent to England for books on music and also studied

---

[167] Fithian, *Journal*, pp. 50, 51, 53, 54, 76, *et passim*.

[168] Fithian, *Journal*, p. 142.

[169] Mary N. Stanard, *Colonial Virginia, its People and Customs* (Philadelphia and London, 1917), pp. 299-307 gives partial lists.

[170] Fithian, *op. cit.*, pp. 50, 66.

[171] Stanard, *op. cit.*, p. 299.

[172] Randolph, *Domestic Life of Jefferson*, pp. 182, 186, 190, 193.

[173] Mason, *Young Lady of Virginia*, pp. 12, 17, 25.

[174] *Ibid.*, p. 45.

[175] Ravenel, *Pinckney*, pp. 28, 50.

[176] *Ibid.*, pp. 29, 49, 51-52, 113.

shorthand and French. Like all girls of her time she read Richardson.[177] Martha Laurens Ramsay prepared herself for the education of her children by reading both French and English works, but she preferred Locke and Witherspoon to other authors.[178] Her reading also included Young's *Night Thoughts,* Greek and Latin classics in translation, botanical works, some medical books to assist her husband, and a number of writers in divinity.[179] To her daughter she recommended Robertson's and Rollin's histories, Plutarch, and Priestley's lectures on history, with the reminder that Priestley was a Socinian.[180] There were few other Southern ladies who could aspire to the title of learned, though one or two are known as serious students of agriculture. Martha Logan of South Carolina corresponded with John Bartram and his family on botanical topics and wrote a treatise on gardening after she was seventy.[181] Even more noted for her botanical and agricultural experiments was Eliza Pinckney who was much interested in developing the indigo industry and after decided efforts established it on her father's plantation. She also experimented with silk culture but this did not go beyond the stage of a curiosity.[182]

The Revolution and the years which followed were a period of increasing accomplishments for young ladies in every part of the country. President Dwight attacked fashionable education in the 1790's as designed to make children, especially girls, objects of admiration. Accomplishments, perhaps harmless in themselves, were used to a wrong end.

[177] *Pinckney*, pp. 27, 29, 136.

[178] Ramsay, *Memoirs of Mrs. Ramsay*, p. 25.

[179] *Ibid.,* 33-35.

[180] *Ibid.,* p. 193.

[181] Darlington, *Memorials of John Bartram,* pp. 414-15 and note.

[182] Ravenel, *Eliza Pinckney,* chaps. i, ii, and pp. 102-07, 239, 254.

Embroidery was done only to show visitors or for framing, music for the performance of a few pieces before guests and so on.[183]   Brissot de Warville attacked one particular accomplishment as dangerous to the women of America.   Piano playing was then in its infancy, but from its popularity he feared an increasing amount of time would be given to it. " God grant," he wrote, " that the Bostonian women may never, like those of France, acquire the malady of perfection in this art!   It is never attained but at the expense of the domestic virtues." [184]

[183] Dwight, *Travels*, i, 471-74; *Belknap Papers*, iii, 223-24.
[184] *New Travels*, p. 95.

CONCLUSION

GENERALIZATIONS about the treatment of women and about contemporary estimates of their abilities and duties during an entire century, are obviously subject to numerous exceptions, but the outlines of the picture are clear. Perhaps the outstanding feature of eighteenth-century American ideas, in this as in many cultural fields, is the close relationship to European thought, a dependence more marked in theory than in practice since American economic conditions, especially after the Revolution, made some changes in the latter. Among European theorists, and among Americans after the early part of the century, there were two schools of thought, the liberal and the conservative. In 1700 women were taught little except domestic duties and religion—any education given was designed to further these ends. As religious beings, however, women held positions of dignity and respect. It was this side of feminine life on which the Mathers and Samuel Sewall laid stress, and it was this aspect alone which interested American writers before Franklin. The English liberals of the day, especially Mary Astell and Daniel Defoe, believed that wider education would render women better wives and mothers and that it was wrong to deny them its privileges, but Americans generally offered only a limited training to their women. Though individual women here and abroad read widely and were interested in study for its own sake, this did not change the general standard.

By the middle of the century literary influences became stronger. Richardson's work was much read; the *Spectator* and *Tatler,* as well as many less important books, circulated throughout America. Franklin's writings also helped to spread more liberal ideas on marriage and feminine training. Women in the cities enjoyed greater opportunities for study. The Revolutionary period, particularly the years succeeding the conflict, brought an increased interest in women's education and a new recognition of its importance. This was shown in the extension of town and village school facilities, in the opening of female academies and in the publication of books and addresses on the subject. Americans liked to claim independence of Europe in thought and action; but this claim was hardly justified in the writings dealing with women, which ran the whole gamut of European ideas from Lord Halifax to Rousseau. Both here and in England there was more instruction in " accomplishments " which had little of practical or intellectual value, though they served to fill women's leisure time. By 1790 even the conservatives had adopted views which would have been thought liberal in 1700. Richardson's books, when first published, probably widened the horizon of most feminine readers through their accounts of the study and conversation of the heroines. As education for women became more general the insistence of Richardson, Dr. Gregory, Mrs. More and their American imitators on women's strict observance of convention served to retard rather than promote the cause of feminine independence.

The testimony of travellers shows that American usage somewhat modified the European tradition, especially in regard to manners and marriage. Economic activity for women of the upper classes was greater here than in England, partly because wartime and frontier conditions, by taking men from home, left women with added responsibilities. Mistresses of plantations had probably heavier duties than women of corresponding status elsewhere. In the poorer classes, on the other hand, women received better treatment, did less outdoor work and dressed better than in Europe.

American manners generally were less formal than European, and this was reflected in the greater freedom given women, especially young girls. Whether this liberty was regarded favorably or otherwise depended largely on the standpoint of the commentator.

American law towards the close of the century showed some changes in the provisions for conveyance of land by women, in more liberal regulation of dower, and in greater ease in obtaining divorce. Women were still in a legally subordinate position, but perhaps less so than in most European countries. Despite some Revolutionary appeals, political activity was reserved for a select group which wielded only indirect influence. Opportunities for religious leadership and participation in church government were confined to a few denominations. By 1800 the work of new liberals, especially Mary Wollstonecraft, was well known; these writers advocated greater economic and educational opportunities for women. Condorcet even suggested feminine participation in government. At the same time Hannah More and others, who feared religious and social innovations, limited sharply the fields open to women, though they did not object to work and education along approved lines. A few Americans like Charles Brockden Brown were sympathetic with the liberal views, but most, including the clergy, were conservative and bitterly attacked the new ideas. Viewing the period as a whole one can see distinct gains in the education provided for women, though it was far from being equal for the two sexes. European ideals and methods still predominated, somewhat modified by American conditions. In legal and economic affairs women's position had improved but fear of radicalism was restricting new developments. Despite occasional suggestions of the fuller life which the next century and a quarter were to open to them American women were still in a state of dependence.

BIBLIOGRAPHICAL ESSAY

I. Source Material

A. European Background

European material dealing with women's position falls into two classes, that addressed directly to women, their guardians and instructors, and that which reveals feminine status indirectly in novels, essays, and plays. Sometimes the distinction between these groups is difficult to draw as in some of the work of Mrs. Haywood and of Richardson. The circumstances under which these books appeared have been discussed in the first three chapters.

1. Works dealing primarily with the position of women

a. English

William Alexander, *The History of Women from the Earliest Antiquity to the Present Time* (2 vols., 3rd ed., London, 1782).

[Richard Allestree?], *The Ladies Calling* (Oxford, 1677).

[Mary Astell?], *An Essay in Defence of the Female Sex*, Written by a Lady (4th ed., London, 1721).

[Mary Astell], *Some Reflections upon Marriage* (4th ed., London, 1730).

John Bennett, *Letters to a Young Lady* (2 vols., Hartford, 1798).

[John Bennett], *Strictures on Female Education* (London, 1788).

Hester Mulso Chapone, *Letters on the Improvement of the Mind* (2 vols., Hagers-town, 1815).

Daniel Defoe, *The Earlier Life and the Chief Earlier Works of Daniel Defoe*, Henry Morley ed. (London, 1889).

James Fordyce, *Sermons to Young Women* (14th ed., 2 vols., London, 1814).

Thomas Gisborne, *An Enquiry into the Duties of the Female Sex* (4th ed., London, 1799).

John Gregory, *A Father's Legacy to his Daughters* (New York, 1775).

Elizabeth Griffith Griffith, *Letters Addressed to Young Married Women* (Philadelphia, 1796).

George Savile, Marquis of Halifax, *Miscellanies* (London, 1700).

[Eliza Haywood], *Epistles for the Ladies* (2 vols., London, 1749-50).

[Eliza Haywood], *The Female Spectator* (3rd ed., 4 vols., Dublin, 1747).

Henry Home, Lord Kames, *Loose Hints upon Education* (Edinburgh, 1781).

Elizabeth Joceline, *The Mother's Legacy to her Unborn Child* (First printed 1624, London, 1894).

[William Kenrick], *The Whole Duty of Woman.* By a Lady (London, 1753).

Gervase Markham, *The English House-Wife* (9th ed., London, 1683).

Hannah More, *Works* (1st complete American ed., 2 vols., New York, 1835).

The Works of Hannah More (19 vols., London, 1819).

William Seymar, *Conjugium Conjurgium: or, Some Serious Considerations on Marriage* (London, 1675).

[Richard Steele], *The Ladies' Library,* Written by a Lady (4th ed., 3 vols., London, 1732).

Thomas Tusser, *The Points of Huswifery United to the Comfort of Husbandry,* In *Five Hundred Points of Good Husbandry,* William Mavor, ed. (London, 1812).

Edward Ward, *Female Policy Detected: or, the Arts of a Designing Woman Laid Open* (London, 1695).

William Whately, *A Bride-bush; or, A Direction for Married Persons* (London, 1619).

John Wing, *The Crowne Coniugall or, the Spouse Royall* (Middleburgh, Holland, 1620).

Mary Wollstonecraft, *A Vindication of the Rights of Woman* (London, 1792).

b. French

Abbé d'Ancourt, *The Lady's Preceptor, Or, a Letter to a Young Lady of Distinction upon Politeness* (3rd ed., London, 1745).

Marie Jean Antoine Nicolas Caritat, Marquis de Condorcet, *Oeuvres Complètes de Condorcet* (Brunswick and Paris, 1804).

A. D. Vickery, *The First Essay on the Political Rights of Women. A Translation of Condorcet's Essay " Sur l'admission des femmes au droit de cité "* (Letchworth, n. d.).

François de Salignac de la Mothe Fénelon, *Adventures of Telemachus,* Dr. Hawkesworth, trans. (Boston, 1881).

——, *The Education of Girls,* Kate Lupton, trans. (Boston, 1891).

——, *Oeuvres de Fénelon* (3 vols., Paris, 1835).

Stéphanie-Félicité du Crest de Saint-Aubin, Comtesse de Genlis, *Adelaide and Theodore; or Letters on Education,* translated from the French (3rd ed., 3 vols., London, 1788).

——, *Le Petit La Bruyère, ou caractères et moeurs des enfans de ce siècle* (Paris, 1825).

Marie de Gournay. Mario Schiff, *La fille d'alliance de Montaigne* (Paris, 1910). Contains the texts of Mademoiselle de Gournay's essays.

Anne Thérèse, Marquise de Lambert, *A Mother's Advice to her Son and Daughter* (1st American ed.? Boston, 1814).

Jean Jacques Rousseau, *Emilius and Sophia; or, A New System of Education*, Translated from the French of Mr. J. J. Rousseau, Citizen of Geneva (4 vols., London, 1783).

Antoine Leonard Thomas, *An Account of the Character, the Manners, and the Understanding of Women, in Different Ages, and Different Parts of the World*, Translated from the French by Mrs. Kindersley (London, 1800).

2. General Literature

Joseph Addison, *The Works of the Right Honourable Joseph Addison*, Tickell ed. (6 vols., London, 1804).

Joseph Addison and others, *The Spectator* (8 vols., Boston, 1872).

——, *The Athenian Oracle* (3 vols., London, 1703-06).

John Bunyan, *The Pilgrim's Progress*, Notes by John Bradford (London, 1792).

Frances Burney, *Evelina; or, the History of a Young Lady's Entrance Into the World*, Annie Raine Ellis ed. (London, 1907).

Elizabeth Carter, *A Series of Letters between Mrs. Elizabeth Carter and Miss Catherine Talbot, from the year 1741 to 1770* (3rd ed., 4 vols., printed in 3, London, 1819).

——, *Letters from Mrs. Elizabeth Carter to Mrs. Montagu, between the Years 1755 and 1800* (3 vols., London, 1817).

Philip Dormer Stanhope, Earl of Chesterfield, *Letters written by the Earl of Chesterfield to his Son* (New York, 1857).

——, *The Economy of Human Life* (London, Wm. Dorton and Son, n. d.).

Henry Fielding, *Works* (12 vols., New York, Jenson Soc., 1911).

——, *The History of Tom Jones, A Foundling* (4 vols., London, 1900).

George Fox, *Journal of George Fox*, Wilson Armistead ed (17th ed., 2 vols., London, 1852).

William Godwin, *Enquiry concerning Political Justice, and its Influence on Morals and Happiness* (4th ed., 2 vols., London, 1842).

Oliver Goldsmith, *The Vicar of Wakefield* (London, The Scholartis Press, 1928).

Eliza Haywood, *The History of Miss Betsey Thoughtless* (4 vols., 4th ed., London, 1768).

Charlotte Ramsay Lennox, *The Female Quixote; or, the Adventures of Arabella* (2 vols., 2nd ed., London, 1752).

John Locke, *Some Thoughts Concerning Education*, Canon Daniel ed. (London, n. d.).

Teresia Constantia Muilman, *A Letter Humbly Address'd to the Right Honourable The Earl of Chesterfield* (London, 1750).

Ann Radcliffe, *The Castles of Athlin and Dunbayne* (3rd ed., London, 1799).

Samuel Richardson, *Works* (12 vols., London, 1883).

——, *Works* (Shakespeare Head ed., Stratford-on-Avon, 1929-1931).

Jonathan Swift, *The Works of Jonathan Swift, D. D.*, Sir Walter Scott, ed. (2nd ed., 19 vols., Edinburgh, 1824).

——, *Works*, Temple Scott ed. (12 vols., London, 1897-1908).

——, *The Poetical Works of Jonathan Swift*, Aldine ed. (3 vols., London, 1833).

The Tatler: The Lucubrations of Isaac Bickerstaff Esq. (4 vols., London, 1711-1713).

[William Wollaston], *The Religion of Nature Delineated* (6th ed., London, 1738).

B. AMERICAN MATERIAL

For theory on the status of women American material is less abundant than European. The same is true of American novels and plays. Eighteenth century periodicals afford many essays dealing with women. The number of personal narratives by Americans and travellers is legion, but in many cases the significant items constitute only a paragraph or two of the entire volume.

1. Works dealing with the position and education of women

a. American Writings

Charles Brockden Brown, *Alcuin; A Dialogue* (New York, 1798).

Thomas Greene Fessenden, *The Ladies Monitor, a Poem* (Bellows Falls, Vt., 1818).

[Hannah Webster Foster], *The Boarding School*, By a Lady of Massachusetts (Boston, 1798).

Benjamin Franklin, *Benjamin Franklin on Marriage* (Larchmont, Peter Pauper Press, 1929).

Enos Hitchcock, *Memoirs of the Bloomsgrove Family...containing Sentiments on a Mode of Domestic Education, Suited to...the United States* (2 vols., Boston, 1790).

Cotton Mather, *Ornaments for the Daughters of Zion Or The Character and Happiness of a Vertuous Woman* (Cambridge, 1692).

James A. Neal, *An Essay on the Education and Genius of the Female Sex* (Philadelphia, 1795).

The Rise and Progress of the Young Ladies' Academy of Philadelphia (Philadelphia, 1794).

Benjamin Rush, *Thoughts upon Female Education* (Philadelphia, 1787).

Charles Stearns, *The Ladies' Philosophy of Love* (Leominster, Mass., 1797).

John Swanwick, *Thoughts on Education* (Philadelphia, 1787).

b. Compilations

The American Spectator, or Matrimonial Preceptor (Boston, 1797).
The Lady's Pocket Library, Mathew Carey ed. (Philadelphia, 1792).
A Series of Letters on Courtship and Marriage (Springfield, 179-?).
The Young Lady's Parental Monitor (printed, London: Hartford reprinted, 1792).

2. American Literature

a. Novels

Henry Hugh Brackenridge, *Modern Chivalry* (4 vols., Richmond, 1815).
The Novels of Charles Brockden Brown (7 vols., Boston, 1827).
Charles Brockden Brown, *Novels* (6 vols., Philadelphia, 1887).
[William Hill Brown?], *The Power of Sympathy* (2 vols., Boston, 1789).
[Hannah Webster Foster], *The Coquette or, the History of Eliza Wharton*. By a Lady of Massachusetts (13th ed., Boston, 1833).
Daniel Jackson, Jr. [Isaac Mitchell?], *Alonzo and Melissa or the Unfeeling Father* (1830).
Susanna Haswell Rowson, *Charlotte Temple A Tale of Truth* (New York, 1905).
Tabitha Gilman Tenney, *Female Quixotism; Or, the Extravagant Adventures of Dorcasina Sheldon* (2 vols., Boston, 1825).
Royall Tyler, *The Algerine Captive; or, the Life and Adventures of Doctor Updike Underhill* (2 vols., Walpole, N. H., 1797).
[Sally Sayward Borrell Keating Wood], *Dorval; or, the Speculator*. By a Lady (Portsmouth, N. H., 1801).
Samuel Woodworth, *Champions of Freedom* (2 vols., New York, 1816).

b. Plays

Several plays of the period may be found in two collections: Montrose J. Moses, *Representative Plays by American Dramatists* (3 vols., New York, 1918), and Arthur H. Quinn, *Representative American Plays* (2nd ed., New York, 1922). References to other plays cited are given in the text.

c. Periodicals

The American Apollo, January 6–September 28, 1792, Boston.
The American Magazine, Noah Webster ed., December 1787–November 1788, New York.
The American Magazine and Historical Chronicle, 1743-1745, Boston.
The American Museum or Repository of Ancient and Modern Fugitive Pieces, 12 vols., Philadelphia, 1787-1792.
American Universal Magazine, 4 vols., January 1797–March 1798, Philadelphia.

The Boston Magazine, Boston, 1783.
Christian's, Scholar's and Farmer's Magazine, 2 vols., Elizabethtown, 1789-1791.
Columbian Magazine or Monthly Miscellany, 3 vols., Philadelphia, 1786-1789.
Columbian Phenix and Boston Review, Boston, 1800.
Gentleman and Lady's Town and Country Magazine, Boston, 1784.
Gentlemen and Ladies' Town and Country Magazine, Boston, 1789-1790.
The Lady's Magazine; and Repository of Entertaining Knowledge, 2 vols., Philadelphia, 1792-1793.
Massachusetts Magazine, Boston, 1789-1796.
New York Weekly Magazine, New York, 1795-1797.
The Nightingale, Boston, 1796.
The Pennsylvania Magazine; or, American Monthly Museum, Philadelphia, 1775-1776.
The Royal American Magazine, Boston, 1774-1775.
The United States Magazine: A Repository of History, Politics and Literature, Philadelphia, 1779.
The Universal Asylum and Columbian Magazine, Philadelphia, 1790-1792.
The Weekly Magazine, 3 vols., Philadelphia, 1798-1799.

3. Personal narratives, letters, accounts of travellers

Only the more important accounts are given here.[1]   Reference is made to others in footnotes in the text.

[1] Some material may be found in *America through Woman's Eyes* (New York, 1933) edited by Mary R. Beard though many of Mrs. Beard's selections are from a later period.

a. Personal records of women

Abigail Adams, *The Letters of Mrs. Adams, the Wife of John Adams*, C. F. Adams ed. (3rd ed., 2 vols., Boston, 1841).
Mary Gould Almy, Diary written during the siege of Newport, 1778. *Newport Historical Magazine*, i (1880).
Susanna Anthony, *vide* Samuel Hopkins, *The Life and Character of Miss Susanna Anthony* (Worcester, 1796).
Ann Eliza Bleecker, *The Posthumous Works of Ann Eliza Bleecker* (New York, 1793).
Esther Burr, "The Journal of Esther Burr," Josephine Fisher, *New England Quarterly*, iii, 297-315.
Hannah Callender, "Diary," *Pennsylvania Magazine of History and Biography*, xii, 432-456.
Sarah Winslow Deming, Letter describing siege of Boston, *Daughters of American Revolution Magazine*, iv, 45-49.

Hannah Drinker, Diary during British occupation of Philadelphia, *Pennsylvania Magazine of History and Biography*, xiii, 298-308.

Sarah Eve, Journal 1772-1773. *Pennsylvania Magazine of History and Biography*, v, 19-36, 191.

Rebecca Franks, Letters 1778 and 1781. *Pennsylvania Magazine of History and Biography*, xvi, 216-17; xxiii, 303-309.

Ann Hulton, *Letters of a Loyalist Lady* (Cambridge, 1927).

The Huntington Letters, William D. McCrackan ed. (Privately printed, New York, 1897).

Sarah Kemble Knight, *The Journals of Madam Knight and Rev. Mr. Buckingham* (New York, 1825).

[Lucinda Lee], *Journal of a Young Lady of Virginia*, Emily V. Mason, ed. (Baltimore, 1871).

Margaret Morris, "Revolutionary. Journal," *Bulletin of Friends' Historical Society*, ix, 2-14, 65-75, 103-114.

[Judith Sargent Murray], *The Gleaner* (3 vols., Boston, 1798).

Sarah Osborn, *vide* Samuel Hopkins, *Memoirs of the Life of Mrs. Sarah Osborn* (2nd ed., Catskill, N. Y., 1814).

Interesting Family Letters of the late Mrs. Ruth Patten of Hartford, Conn. (Hartford, 1845).

William Patten, *Memoirs of Mrs. Ruth Patten of Hartford, Conn.* (Hartford, 1834).

Eliza Lucas Pinckney, *Journal and Letters of Eliza Lucas* (Wormsloe, 1850).

Harriott Horry Ravenel, *Eliza Pinckney* (New York, 1896).

David Ramsay, *Memoirs of the Life of Martha Laurens Ramsay* (3rd ed., Boston, 1827).

Margaretta Schuyler, *vide* Anne MacVicar Grant, *Memoirs of an American Lady* (2 vols., London, 1808).

Abigail Adams Smith, *Journal and Correspondence of Miss Adams, Daughter of John Adams* (2 vols., New York and London, 1841).

Eliza Southgate, *A Girl's Life Eighty Years Ago*, Clarence Cook ed. (New York, 1888). Selections from the letters of Eliza Southgate Bowne.

Hannah Thomson, Letters. *Pennsylvania Magazine of History and Biography*, xiv, 28-40.

Ann Head Warder, Diary. *Pennsylvania Magazine of History and Biography*, xvii, 444-461; xviii, 51-63.

Mercy Warren, *vide* Alice Brown, *Mercy Warren* (New York, 1896).

——, *The History of the Rise, Progress and Termination of the American Revolution* (3 vols., Boston, 1805).

——, *Poems, Dramatic and Miscellaneous* (Boston, 1790).

Warren Adams Letters, Massachusetts Historical Society, *Collections*, 72-73.

Abigail Waters, *vide* Joshua Huntington, *Memoirs of the Life of Mrs. Abigail Waters* (Boston, 1817).

Phillis Wheatley, *vide* Charles Frederick Heartman, *Phillis Wheatley (Phillis Peters) A Critical Attempt and a Bibliography of Her Writings* (New York, 1915).

Anna Green Winslow, *Diary of Anna Green Winslow*, Alice M. Earle, ed. (Boston, 1894).

Hannah Winthrop. Letter after Battle of Lexington. Massachusetts Historical Society, *Proceedings*, xiv (1875), 29-31.

Sally Wister, "Journal of Miss Sally Wister," *Pennsylvania Magazine of History and Biography*, ix, 318-333, 463-478; x, 51-60.

b. Comments of American men

John Adams, *The Works of John Adams*, C. F. Adams ed. (10 vols., Boston, 1850-1856).

——, *Letters of John Adams, addressed to his wife* (2 vols., Boston, 1841).

——, *Familiar Letters of John Adams and His Wife Abigail Adams, during the Revolution*, C. F. Adams ed. (New York, 1876).

Jeremy Belknap, *Belknap Papers* (Massachusetts Historical Society, *Collections*, ser. 5, ii-iii, ser. 6, iv).

William Byrd, *The Westover Manuscripts* (Petersburg, Va., 1841).

——, *The Writings of Col. William Byrd*, John S. Bassett ed. (New York, 1901).

The Letters and Papers of Cadwallader Colden 1711-1775 (Collections of the New York Historical Society, 1918-1923). 7 vols.

Timothy Dwight, *Travels in New England and New York* (London, 1823, 4 vols.).

Jonathan Edwards, *The Works of President Edwards* (8 vols., Worcester, 1808-09).

——, *The Works of President Edwards: with a Memoir of his Life* (10 vols., New York, 1829).

Philip Vickers Fithian, *Journal and Letters 1767-1774*, John Rogers Williams ed. (Princeton, 1900).

Benjamin Franklin, *The Works of Benjamin Franklin*, Jared Sparks ed. (10 vols., Boston, 1844).

The Writings of Benjamin Franklin, Albert H. Smyth ed. (10 vols., New York, 1905-1907).

The Writings of Thomas Jefferson, H. A. Washington ed. (9 vols., New York, 1853-1855).

Cotton Mather, *Diary of Cotton Mather* (Massachusetts Historical Society, *Collections*, ser. 7, vii-viii).

James Murray, *Letters of James Murray Loyalist* (Printed not published, Boston, 1901).

Josiah Quincy, Jr., *Diary* (Massachusetts Historical Society, *Proceedings*, xlix, 424-481).

——, "Josiah Quincy's London Journal 1774-1775" (Massachusetts Historical Society, *Proceedings*, l, 433-470).

Letters and Diary of John Rowe (Boston, 1903).

Benjamin Rush, *Essays, Literary, Moral & Philosophical* (Philadelphia, 1798).

Samuel Sewall, *The Diary of Samuel Sewall* (Massachusetts Historical Society, *Collections*, ser. 5, v-vii).

——, *Letter Book* (Massachusetts Historical Society, *Collections*, ser. 6, i-ii).

William Smith, *History of New-York, from the First Discovery to the Year 1732* (Albany, 1814).

Ezra Stiles, *The Literary Diary of Ezra Stiles*, F. B. Dexter ed. (3 vols., New York, 1901).

John Swanwick, *Poems on Several Occasions* (Philadelphia, 1797).

George Washington, *The Writings of George Washington*, W. C. Ford ed. (New York and London, 14 vols., 1889-1893).

Noah Webster, *Collection of Essays and Fugitiv Writings on Moral, Historical, Political and Literary Subjects* (Boston, 1790).

John Witherspoon, *Works* (2nd ed., 4 vols., Philadelphia, 1802).

c. Travellers

Thomas Anburey, *Travels through the Interior Parts of North America* (2 vols., London, 1791).

François, Marquis de Barbé-Marbois, *Our Revolutionary Forefathers*, Eugene Parker Chase trans. and ed. (New York, 1929).

Ferdinand Bayard, *Voyage dans l'intérieur des États-Unis* (2nd ed., Paris, 1791).

Jacques Pierre Brissot de Warville, *New Travels in the United States of America* (London, 1792).

Andrew Burnaby, *Travels through the Middle Settlements in North America* (3rd ed., London, 1798).

Marquis de Chastellux, *Travels in North-America in the Years 1780, 1781, and 1782* (2 vols., Dublin, 1787).

The Journal of Nicholas Cresswell 1774-1777 (New York, 1924).

John Dunton's Letters from New England (Prince Society, *Publications*, iv, Boston, 1867).

William Eddis, *Letters from America* (London, 1792).

Alexander Hamilton, *Hamilton's Itinerarium; being a Narrative of a Journey...1744*, Albert B. Hart ed. (Privately printed, St. Louis, 1907).

Peter Kalm, *Travels into North America*, John Reinhold Forster trans. (3 vols., London, 1770-71).

John Lambert, *Travels through Canada and the United States* (3rd ed., 2 vols., London, 1816).

François Alexandre, Duc de la Rochefoucauld Liancourt, *Travels through the United States of North America* (4 vols., London, 1799).

Gottlieb Mittelberger, *Journey to Pennsylvania in the Year 1750*, Carl Theo. Eben, trans. (Philadelphia, 1898).

Ray W. Pettengill trans., *Letters from America 1776-1779* (Boston and New York, 1924).

Abbé Robin, *Nouveau voyage dans l'Amérique Septentrionale 1781* (Philadelphia, 1782).

[Janet Schaw], *Journal of a Lady of Quality*, Evangeline Walker Andrews ed. (New Haven, 1921).

Johann David Schoepf, *Travels in the Confederation*, A. J. Morrison, translator (2 vols., Philadelphia, 1911).

4. Laws and Court Reports

Massachusetts.

> *The Acts and Resolves, Public and Private, of the Province of Massachusetts Bay* (21 vols., Boston, 1869-1922).
>
> *Acts and Laws of the Commonwealth of Massachusetts* (13 vols., Boston, 1890-1898).
>
> Josiah Quincy, Jr., *Reports of Cases ... in the Superior Court of Judicature of Massachusetts Bay Between 1761 and 1772* (Boston, 1865)

New Hampshire.

> *Laws of New Hampshire*, Albert S. Batchellor ed. (10 vols., place of publication varies, 1904-1916).

Rhode Island.

> *The Public Laws of the State of Rhode-Island and Providence Plantations* (Providence, 1798).

Connecticut.

> *Acts and Laws of His Majesty's English Colony of Connecticut, in New-England, in America* (New-Haven, 1769).
>
> *Acts and Laws of the State of Connecticut, in America* (Hartford, 1796).
>
> Ephraim Kirby, *Reports of Cases Adjudged in the Superior Court of the State of Connecticut* (Litchfield, 1789).
>
> Jesse Root, *Reports of Cases Adjudged in the Superior Court and Supreme Court of Errors* (2 vols., Hartford, 1798).

New York.

> *Laws of the State of New York* (2 vols., New York, Thomas Greenleaf, 1792).
>
> William Johnson, *Reports of Cases Adjudged in the Supreme Court of New York* (2nd ed., 3 vols., New York, 1846).

New Jersey.
> *Acts of the General Assembly,* Samuel Allinson (Burlington, 1776).
> *Laws of the State of New Jersey,* William Paterson (Newark, 1800).
> Richard Coxe, *Reports of Cases...in the Supreme Court of New Jersey* (Burlington, 1816).

Pennsylvania.
> *The Statutes at Large of Pennsylvania* (18 vols., Harrisburg, 1896-1915).
> Jasper Yeates, *Reports of Cases Adjudged in the Supreme Court of Pennsylvania* (4 vols., Philadelphia, 1817).

Delaware.
> *Laws of the State of Delaware 1700-1797* (2 vols., New-Castle, 1797).

Maryland.
> William Kilty, *The Laws of Maryland* (2 vols., Annapolis, 1799).
> Thomas Harris and John McHenry, *Maryland Reports* (4 vols., New York, 1809).

Virginia.
> William W. Hening, *Virginia Statutes at Large* (13 vols., Richmond and Philadelphia, 1819-1823).
> *Virginia Reports,* I-II.

North Carolina.
> *The Public Acts of the General Assembly of North-Carolina,* James Iredell and F. X. Martin rev. (Newbern, 1804).
> John Lewis Taylor, *Cases determined in the Superior Courts of Law and Equity of the State of North Carolina* (Newbern, 1802).

South Carolina.
> Thomas Cooper, *The Statutes at Large of South Carolina* (13 vols., Columbia, 1836-1866).
> *South Carolina Reports.*

Georgia.
> *The Colonial Records of the State of Georgia,* Allen D. Candler ed. (25 vols., Atlanta, 1907-1916).

5. Sermons

For a list of sermons preached to female charitable societies see Appendix A. Funeral sermons were numerous but only a few of special importance are cited here.

Amos Chase, "On Female Excellence, or A Discourse, in which, Good Character in Women is described." Extracts in *Connecticut Magazine,* x (1906), 81.

Charles Chauncy, *A Funeral Discourse on the Death of Mrs. Lucy Waldo* (Boston, 1741).

Thomas Clap, "Memoirs of a College President, Womanhood in Early America," transcribed by Edwin Stanley Welles, *Connecticut Magazine*, xii, 233.

Benjamin Colman, *Reliquiae Turellae, et Lachrymae Paternae* (Boston, 1735).

Nathaniel Emmons, *A Discourse delivered at the Funeral of Mrs. Bathsheba Sanford* (Wrentham, Mass., 1801).

Thomas Foxcroft, *A Sermon Preach'd at Cambrige* [sic] *After the Funeral of Mrs. Elizabeth Foxcroft* (Boston, 1721).

Thomas Prince, *A Sermon Occasioned by the Decease of Mrs. Deborah Prince* (Boston, 1744).

II. Secondary Material

Secondary treatments of women's status in America have, until recent years, fallen into two classes. On the one hand is the " filio-pietistic " work like Mrs. Elizabeth Ellet's *The Women of the American Revolution* (3 vols., 1848, reprinted in 2 vols., Philadelphia, 1900), presenting individual biographies in which feminine patriotism and industry are lauded with little accuracy or study of social conditions. Mrs. Ellet's work, one of the earliest of its kind, being based partly on personal reminiscences has more interest than others which followed. On the other hand the movement for women's suffrage brought more serious studies, some with useful information, but frequently too biased to give a clear statement of conditions and stressing only certain types of feminine activity. The classic work in this field by Elizabeth Cady Stanton, Susan B. Anthony, and Matilda Joslyn Gage, *History of Woman Suffrage* (4 vols.), gives in the first volume (Rochester, 1881), an historical background which includes the eighteenth century. In the 1890's Mrs. Alice Morse Earle with her *Colonial Dames and Good Wives* (Boston, 1895), *Home Life in Colonial Days* (New York, 1899), and other works threw much light on the living and working conditions of women, and their social activities, especially in New England. Mrs. Earle's work, which marked a new development in the subject, though seldom documented, is usually accurate. For the theoretical aspects of women's position, certain chapters in Emily James Putnam's *The Lady* (New York, 1910) are suggestive.

In the last ten years two scholarly works have supplied much valuable information regarding two phases of women's existence. Elisabeth Anthony Dexter in *Colonial Women of Affairs* (Boston and New York, 1924, 2nd ed., 1931), gives detailed accounts of the many business activities undertaken by women and the ways in which they supported themselves and their families. This work contradicts many older assumptions regarding the bounds of feminine activity. Thomas Woody's *A History of Women's Education in the United States* (2 vols., Science Press, 1929), presents by far the most complete treatment of women's position in

America yet published. His handling of the eighteenth century, however, is merely background for the rest of the book and leaves some gaps. He gives many extracts from Mary Astell, Hannah More, Mary Wollstonecraft, Fénelon and other European writers. In his treatment of American ideas he touches only slightly on the religious influence in New England and the ideas of Mather and Sewall. This is natural since their influence on later educational usage is not large but it does not give an adequate picture of the early part of the century. For the Revolutionary period his treatment is more extensive. The whole is concerned primarily with educational aims and opportunities and only incidentally with general theory.

Women's history in England has been treated more fully than in America. Several books in this field are helpful in furnishing a background for American developments and a basis for comparison. Particularly valuable is Dorothy Gardiner, *English Girlhood at School* (Oxford University Press, 1929), which treats of curriculum and educational theory from Anglo-Saxon times to the days of Mary Wollstonecraft. Myra Reynolds in *The Learned Lady in England 1650-1760* (Boston and New York, 1920), gives much information on the literature dealing with women at that time and has an excellent bibliography. Ida Beatrice O'Malley, *Women in Subjection* (London, 1933), is a study of Englishwomen of the late eighteenth and early nineteenth century with some discussion of earlier ideas. These are presented largely through the lives of individuals, as are the discussions in Ada Wallas, *Before the Bluestockings* (London, 1929). For the history of one group of women, Mabel R. Brailsford's *Quaker Women 1650-1690* (London, 1915), has much significant material.

Many books not dealing primarily with women's position have been helpful. For biographical data the *Dictionary of American Biography*, the *Dictionary of National Biography*, and Franklin B. Dexter's *Biographical Sketches of the Graduates of Yale College* (6 vols., New York, 1885-1912), are particularly useful. The following biographies have supplied much information.

Margaret Armstrong, *Five Generations, Life and Letters of an American Family 1750-1900* (New York and London, 1930).

Florence M. Smith, *Mary Astell* (New York, 1916).

William Dunlap, *The Life of Charles Brockden Brown* (2 vols., Philadelphia, 1815).

George Frisbie Whicher, *The Life and Romances of Mrs. Eliza Haywood* (New York, 1915).

George Everett Hastings, *The Life and Works of Francis Hopkinson* (Chicago, University of Chicago Press, 1926).

Kenneth Ballard Murdock, *Increase Mather, the foremost American Puritan* (Cambridge, Harvard University Press, 1925).

Emily Pendleton and Milton Ellis, *Philenia; The Life and Works of Sarah Wentworth Morton* (University of Maine, *Studies*, ser. 2. no. 20).

Vena Bernadette Field, *Constantia; A Study of the Life and Works of Judith Sargent Murray* (University of Maine, *Studies*, ser. 2, no. 17).

Harry G. Good, *Benjamin Rush and his Services to American Education* (Witness Press, Berne, Ind., 1918).

Katharine Metcalf Root, *Colonel William Smith and Lady* (Boston, 1929). For life of Abigail Adams Smith.

Alice Brown, *Mercy Warren* (New York, 1896).

Marthe Severn Storr, *Mary Wollstonecraft et le mouvement féministe dans la littérature Anglaise* (Paris, 1931).

There is much material in the pages of historical and educational journals, particularly the following.

Henry Barnard, ed., *American Journal of Education* (32 vols., 1855-1882, Hartford and Washington).

The Friends' Library (14 vols., Philadelphia, 1837-1850).

Massachusetts Historical Society, *Collections* (77 vols., Boston, 1792-1927).

Massachusetts Historical Society, *Proceedings* (64 vols., Boston, 1859-1932).

The New England Quarterly (Vols. 1-6, Baltimore, Portland, 1928-1933).

Collections of the New York Historical Society (Vols. 1-66, New York, 1868-1933).

Pennsylvania Magazine of History and Biography (57 vols., Philadelphia, 1877-1933).

Documents relating to the Colonial History of the State of New Jersey (33 vols., Newark, 1880-1928). Cited as *New Jersey Archives.*

Information on schools and local customs is to be gleaned here and there in the pages of state and local histories, which, however, vary greatly in value. The following have been helpful.

Charles Francis Adams, *Three Episodes of Massachusetts History* (2nd ed., 2 vols., Boston and New York, 1892).

Charles Brooks, *History of the Town of Medford*, revised by J. M. Usher (Boston, 1886).

Frances Manwaring Caulkins, *History of Norwich, Connecticut* (2nd ed., Hartford, 1866).

Mellen Chamberlain, *A Documentary History of Chelsea* (Boston, 1908).

Joseph B. Felt, *Annals of Salem* (2nd ed., 2 vols., Salem, 1845, 1849).

History of the Town of Hingham, Massachusetts (3 vols., published by the town, 1893).

Sylvester Judd, *History of Hadley* (Northampton, 1863).

Samuel Kercheval, *A History of the Valley of Virginia* (3rd ed., Woodstock, Virginia, 1902).

Commonwealth History of Massachusetts, Albert B. Hart ed. (5 vols., New York, 1927-1930).

Edward McCrady, *The History of South Carolina under the Royal Government, 1719-1776* (New York, 1901).

Jethro Rumple, *History of Rowan County, North Carolina* (Salisbury, 1881).

William B. Weeden, *Economic and Social History of New England 1620-1789* (2 vols., Boston, 1890).

OTHER SECONDARY WORKS USED

Alice M. Baldwin, *The New England Clergy and the American Revolution* (Duke University Press, 1928).

Arthur W. Calhoun, *A Social History of the American Family* (3 vols., Cleveland, 1917-1919).

The Cambridge History of American Literature (4 vols., New York, 1917-1923).

Charles Evans, *American Bibliography* (11 vols., Chicago, 1903-1931).

Cheesman A. Herrick, *White Servitude in Pennsylvania* (Philadelphia, 1926).

George Elliott Howard, *A History of Matrimonial Institutions* (3 vols., Chicago and London, 1904).

Marcus W. Jernegan, *Laboring and Dependent Classes in Colonial America 1607-1783* (Chicago, 1931).

Rufus M. Jones, *The Quakers in the American Colonies* (London, 1911).

Auguste Jorns, *The Quakers as Pioneers in Social Work*, Thomas Kite Brown, trans. (published in Germany, 1912, New York, 1931).

Eugene Irving McCormac, *White Servitude in Maryland 1634-1820* (Johns Hopkins University, *Studies in History and Political Science,* ser. 22, nos. 3-4), Baltimore, 1904).

Albert E. McKinley, *The Suffrage Franchise in the Thirteen English Colonies in America* (Philadelphia, 1905).

Thomas H. Montgomery, *A History of the University of Pennsylvania, from its foundation to A. D. 1770* (Philadelphia, 1900).

Richard B. Morris, *Studies in the History of American Law* (New York, 1930).

George C. D. Odell, *Annals of the New York Stage*, i (New York, 1927).

William C. Reichel, *A History of the Rise, Progress, and Present Condition of the Moravian Seminary for Young Ladies at Bethlehem* (2nd ed., Philadelphia, 1870).

Lyon N. Richardson, *A History of Early American Magazines, 1741-1789* (New York, 1931).

Arthur M. Schlesinger, *New Viewpoints in American History* (New York, 1925).

Robert Francis Seybolt, *Apprenticeship and Apprenticeship Education in Colonial New England and New York* (New York, 1917).

——, *The Evening School in Colonial America* (University of Illinois, Bureau of Educational Research, Bull. no. 24, Urbana, 1925).

——, *Source Studies in American Colonial Education: The Private School* (University of Illinois, Bureau of Educational Research, Bull. no. 28, Urbana, 1925).

Mary Newton Stanard, *Colonial Virginia, its People and Customs* (Philadelphia and London, 1917).

Henry Reed Stiles, *Bundling; its Origin, Progress and Decline in America* (Albany, Joel Munsell, 1869).

APPENDIX A. SERMONS DELIVERED BEFORE WOMEN'S CHARITABLE SOCIETIES

Timothy Alden, Jr., *A Discourse, delivered Before the Members of the Portsmouth Female Asylum* (Portsmouth, 1804).

Thomas Baldwin, *A Discourse delivered before the members of the Boston Female Asylum,* September 26, 1806 (Boston, 1806).

Thomas Barnard, *A Sermon Preached Before The Salem Female Charitable Society* (Salem, 1803).

William Bentley, *Discourse delivered . . . Salem Female Charitable Society* (Salem, 1807).

Lucius Bolles, *Discourse delivered before the members of the Salem Female Charitable Society, September 27, 1810* (Salem, 1810).

Daniel Dana, *A Discourse delivered May 22, 1804, before the members of the Female Charitable Society of Newburyport* (Newburyport, 1804).

Theodore Dehon (Trinity Church, Newport), *A Discourse delivered in Providence, September 6, 1804 Before the Female Charitable Society for the Relief of Indigent Widows and Children* (Providence, 1804).

Joseph Eckley, *A Discourse delivered before the members of the Boston Female Asylum,* September 24, 1802 (Boston, 1802).

William Emerson, *A Discourse, delivered before the members of the Boston Female Asylum* (Boston, 1805).

Abel Flint, *A Charity Sermon, delivered in the North Presbyterian Meeting House in Hartford, . . . by desire of The Female Beneficent Society* (Hartford, 1810).

John S. J. Gardiner (Trinity Church, Boston), *A Sermon, delivered at Trinity Church, September 22nd, 1809, Before The Members of the Boston Female Asylum* (Boston, 1809).

John Lathrop, *A Discourse ... Boston Female Asylum* (Boston, 1804).

Jedidiah Morse, *A Sermon, Preached in Brattle-Street Church, Boston, September 25, 1807, Before the Managers of the Boston Female Asylum* (Charlestown, 1807).

Eliphalet Nott, *Discourse delivered in the Presbyterian Church in Albany Before the Ladies Society for the relief of distressed Women and Children* (Albany, 1804).

Samuel Stillman, *Discourse delivered before the members of the Boston Female Asylum* (Boston, 1801).

Nathan Strong, *The Character of a Virtuous and Good Woman* (Hartford, 1809).

Moses Stuart, *A Sermon, delivered by request of the Female Charitable Society in Salem* (Andover, 1815).

INDEX